AMERICANS IN BRITISH
LITERATURE, 1770–1832

For Sulipsa

Americans in British Literature, 1770–1832

A Breed Apart

CHRISTOPHER FLYNN
St. Edward's University, USA

ASHGATE

Published by
Ashgate Publishing Limited
Gower House
Croft Road
Aldershot
Hampshire GU11 3HR
England

Ashgate Publishing Company
Suite 420
101 Cherry Street
Burlington, VT 05401-4405
USA

Ashgate website: http://www.ashgate.com

British Library Cataloguing in Publication Data
Flynn, Christopher
Americans in British literature, 1770–1832 : a breed apart
   1. English literature – 18th century – History and criticism 2. English literature – 19th century – History and criticism 3. English literature – American influences 4. National characteristics, American, in literature 5. Travel in literature 6. United States – Description and travel
   I. Title
   820.9'352913

Library of Congress Cataloging-in-Publication Data
Flynn, Christopher, 1964–
   Americans in British literature, 1770–1832 : a breed apart / by Christopher Flynn.
     p. cm.
   Includes index.
   ISBN 978-0-7546-6047-7 (alk. paper)
   1. English literature—18th century—History and criticism. 2. English literature—19th century—History and criticism. 3. English literature—American influences. 4. National characteristics, American, in literature. 5. Travel in literature. 6. United States—Description and travel—History. I. Title.

PR129.U5F56 2008
820.9'35291309033—dc22

2007038066

ISBN: 978-0-7546-6047-7

Printed and bound in Great Britain by TJ International Ltd, Padstow, Cornwall.

Contents

Acknowledgements

Many people and institutions contributed to the writing of this book. Thanks to Anne Mellor for her support and teaching from the beginning. Fred Burwick, Helen Deutsch, and Stephen Behrendt also contributed significantly to the thinking, writing, and revising that went into this undertaking. Colleagues at St. Edward's University, at the University of Nebraska at Omaha, and at UCLA helped in many ways, especially David Peterson, George Klawitter, Catherine Rainwater, Alan Altimont, Barbara Filippidis, Joan Latchaw, Charles Johanningsmeier, Norman Jones, Michelle Levy, Martin Griffin, and Chris Loar. My colleagues at a National Endowment for the Humanities Seminar on Romantic Fiction were especially generous with their reading and fellowship. Special thanks go to Anne Frey, Miriam Wallace, Julie Shaffer, Daniel Schierenbeck, Samantha Webb, and Daniella Mallinick.

St. Edward's University has generously supported this project with two Presidential Excellence Grants. The University of Nebraska at Omaha also provided funding for research, as did The Huntington Library, the William Andrews Clark Memorial Library, UCLA, and the National Endowment for the Humanities. I would also like to thank the staffs at The British Library, The Huntington Library, the William Andrews Clark Memorial Library, UCLA Special Collections, University of Nebraska's Love Library, and the Harry Ransom Center at the University of Texas.

Special thanks go to my parents, my brothers, to Pádraig, Siobhán, to everyone in California, Ireland, and Panamá, and to Sulipsa.

Introduction

America and the Question of Time

Scottish cleric and historian William Robertson set out to do for the British Empire what his contemporary Edward Gibbon did for Rome, but with a happier direction and ending. Robertson's sweeping *History of America* (1777) begins with the beginning—the Mediterranean world at the historical moment that late eighteenth-century Europeans considered the dawn of civilization.[1] It places the Americas, and North America particularly, at the end of a telos crowning Britain as history's ultimate victor. While Gibbon explained how Rome declined and fell, Robertson was laying out a rise and apotheosis of the British Empire—with all the religious implications the latter term carries. But American independence ruined Robertson's design as much as, for the time at least, it ruined Britain's. He ended up publishing his *History* unfinished. By 1777 it was clear to him that rather than representing the ultimate achievement of British and European civilization, America was in the process of leaving the empire and Robertson's world behind.

Robertson discusses Mediterranean exploration and maritime activity, the rise of Roman power and its effect on trade, and the increasing circulation of people and goods, first to Rome, and later to Constantinople. He continues with the decline of Roman power and rise of "[b]arbarous nations [which] rushed in from several quarters with irresistible impetuosity," wrecking "the arts, sciences, inventions, and discoveries of the Romans."[2] The barbarian incursion put Europe into "a second infancy," which it outgrew only with the aid of an event he terms "the most extraordinary, perhaps, in the history of mankind"—the Holy Crusades.[3] Robertson establishes a threefold march of human advancement, written as physical progress across the globe, and more specifically, European, Christian progress. Explorers, merchants, travelers and thinkers encouraged Christianity's extension, expanded trade and profit, and widened knowledge, all for the good of humanity according to Robertson's narrative and so many others of his time. Pope Innocent IV's order to Kayuk Khan, Genghis Khan's grandson, "to embrace the Christian faith, and to desist from desolating the earth by his arms" in the thirteenth century, along with the Crusades and the exploration of regions in the East and West unknown to Europeans in the medieval period, all helped open much of the world to European influence.[4] In this massive expansion of European power, the discovery and settlement of the

---

1 William Robertson, *The History of the Discovery and Settlement of America* (New York, 1855).

2 Ibid., p. 27.

3 Ibid., pp. 27, 29.

4 Ibid., p. 30.

Americas looms largest, marking modern history's beginning, which Robertson wrote as a philosophical expansion of civilization in all its manifestations.

The war between Britain and its American colonists challenged and ultimately contradicted the meaning of the historical sweep informing Robertson's narrative. British control of North America was crucial to his design, which cast the New World as the final place in a spatial teleology of Christianity and culture. "As I had written between two and three hundred pages of *excellent* History of the British Colonies in North America," Robertson wrote in 1784, "I long flattered myself that the war might terminate so favourable for G. Britain that I might go on with my work."[5] Note here the treatment of America as a British text as much as a place, a figuration crucial to later writers' treatments of the former colonists. "But alas," Robertson continues, "America is now lost to the Empire and to me, and what would have been a good introduction to the settlement of British Colonies, will suit very ill the establishment of Independent States." As Robertson notes, the loss was Britain's as well as his, epistemological as well as physical. The American Revolution made English writers come to terms with the loss of what had seemed the next stage of their history.

While Robertson found it impossible to rethink what America meant to Britain, his *History* participates notably in a discourse that over time would provide the answer for authors with vastly differing aims as well as for Britain's reading public. Since Spanish exploration of the Americas, European writers had developed a view of their native peoples as examples of humanity in an earlier stage of development. Seventeenth-century English thinkers, most notably Hobbes and Locke, contributed significantly to this discourse. As Locke wrote in his *Second Treatise*, "in the beginning, all the World was *America*."[6] Locke meant that the Native American peoples' modes of subsistence represented history's earliest stage. As such, human development could be discussed in spatial terms as well as temporal ones. Robertson, Adam Ferguson, Adam Smith, and others believed that America's discovery enabled a "philosophical history" that could not have been written before. America exhibited humanity from its barbarous, hunter-gatherer beginnings, through the modern state the colonists represented, with their advanced participation in farming and commerce, all existing at once.

This historical sweep presented problems for writers who followed Robertson. Over time they recast the roles the various actors played on the savage-civilized continuum, with the former English colonists losing pride of place. But this recasting—which eventually turned Anglo-Americans into semi-savage hybrids—ran into the fact that the citizens of the new United States were not clearly "other" the way Native Americans were. They spoke English, practiced Christianity and lived in a developed, commercial society. While the discourse existed for rewriting the Anglo-American as an inferior "other," thereby refiguring Americans from the embodiment of the future to an example of the past, this "other" was not easy to

---

5   Robertson to [Sir Robert Murray Keith?], 8 March 1784, British Library Add. MS 35350, fol. 70ᵛ. Quoted in David Armitage, "The New World and British Historical Thought: From Richard Hakluyt to William Robertson," in *America in European Consciousness, 1493–1750,* ed. Karen Ordahl Kupperman (Chapel Hill, 1995), pp. 52–75.

6   John Locke, *Two Treatises of Government*, ed. Peter Laslett (Cambridge, 1988), p. 301.

manipulate, even—or perhaps especially—discursively. It could be argued that the United States is the most thoroughly post-colonial nation, in that it has escaped the colonial condition so completely that it has become the colonizer. An "other" that not only could answer, but contest representations made by those who sought to constitute it as inferior, presented a persistent problem to English writers from the 1770s into the early Victorian period. But eventually a discourse took shape that reconfigured the difference in space between England and the United States as a difference in time, constituting an Other that was neither civil nor savage, neither at the forefront of history nor completely outside of it.

Throughout this study I examine several ways English writers manipulated the spatial separation of North America from England, treating it as a temporal gap that created cultural, and, eventually, evolutionary distance. In English writings Americans went from being participants on history's frontier in works like Robertson's in the 1770s, to being objects of amateur cultural anthropology in travel works like Frances Trollope's widely read *Domestic Manners of the Americans* (1832). By the Victorian period, British writings almost always depicted Americans as a separate breed— ill-housed, ill-mannered, badly spoken, under the sway of dangerous religious enthusiasms, vain, shallow, whiskey-soaked, and constantly given to spitting on the carpet.

Johannes Fabian argues in *Time and the Other* that modern anthropologists create the objects of their discourse through their acts of writing that follow field work and the information gathering at its center. This constitution of the Other, Fabian writes, may begin as a synchronic exercise, with the anthropologist and the people under study occupying the same time during their encounter. But the observer's field notes become the anthropologist's narrative, introducing a diachronic structure that generates subjects and objects. This distance always, Fabian argues, constitutes the Other as someone who occupies an earlier, often primal time, irreconcilable with the time of the anthropologist. Creating the Other for Fabian, then, following Foucault, is an epistemological and epistemic event.

Fabian mainly concerns himself with ascertaining "whether and how a body of knowledge is validated or invalidated by the use of temporal categorizations."[7] This book's purpose is one Fabian dismisses on his way to this task, which seems to me ultimately unanswerable in its attempts to arrive at a judgment concerning what makes knowledge authentic. In writings by one people concerning another, or an Other, authentic knowledge is always knowledge *for*. For this study, it is knowledge by English writers about Americans *for* English readers rather than a stable epistemology translatable to other readers of English, most conspicuously in this case, the Americans. My primary interest is in identifying what Fabian calls a "grammar of Time," and exploring how English authors used it to explain the Americans.[8] Fabian rejects the relevance of such a project because it can, he insists, only show *how* time is used in constituting the Other, and because the results "from

---

7   Johannes Fabian, *Time and the Other: How Anthropology Makes its Object* (New York, 1983), p. 25.

8   Ibid., p. 25.

such analyses would ultimately pertain to questions of style and literary form."[9]
While one can see why an anthropologist would dismiss how we know things in
favor of trying to establish the authenticity of knowledge—though many, Clifford
Geertz in particular, concern themselves as much with the former as the latter—
literary studies can, and probably should, focus on method and style, the ways texts
communicate as much as their "truth." Throughout this work, then, I am not so much
concerned with the accuracy of English representations of the emerging American
Other so much as with exploring how English writers explained their subject. My
topic is the style and literary construction of an Other that had long been considered
part of the collective national self.

Some might object that I use Fabian's argument anachronistically. He argues,
after all, that the creation of the Other through space rewritten as time is mainly the
legacy of Victorian anthropology, and still pervasive in the methods of contemporary
professional anthropologists. But it is crucial to point out that the English writers
who invented the American Other were travelers whose accounts served as amateur
ethnographies, not professionals concerned with creating "official" knowledge. And
as Fabian points out, Victorian and later anthropologists, by denying their Others
coevalness "accomplished a major feat of scientific conservatism by saving an older
paradigm," the one employed by Linnæus and eighteenth-century natural history.[10]
Accounts about America from the end of the American Revolution through the
1830s extended the eighteenth-century project of describing the New World's natural
wonders and the peoples these wonders helped shape. These texts apply the terms
defined by such eighteenth-century cultural and racial theorists as Johann Friedrich
Blumenbach to people who had very recently been considered English. While I do
not wish to suggest that the writers I discuss anticipated Victorian anthropological
practices, it seems clear that rather than "saving an older paradigm," the Victorian
anthropologists Fabian critiques continued a tradition that amateur ethnography
had kept very much alive. Travel writers addressing an increasingly literate middle-
class audience preserved the eighteenth-century tradition of classification. The
difference between the work of the writers examined here and that of the Victorian
anthropologists Fabian has in mind is one of intent. The writers this study discusses
practiced anthropology without defining it as such, constituting the American Other
for a popular English audience with intentions more nationalistic than scientific. An
independent America was unwelcome, but undeniable. An equal race—or even a
superior one in many Enlightenment versions—a race of English-speaking people,
politically and culturally distinct from the English, was intolerable.

English accounts of Americans and the temporal gap between their two nations
can be placed into at least four categories. The first appears most clearly in works
by late eighteenth-century writers seeking ways to rewrite a connection between
England and her former colonies. Several sentimental epistolary novels of the 1780s
and 1790s attempt this by treating the political relationship as an emotional one that
could survive technical dissolution. These attempts all fall apart as the separation

---

9   Ibid., p. 25.
10 Ibid., p. 16.

between the two nations becomes insurmountable. In these works the traumatic recognition of spatial distance appears as temporal irreconcilability.

The second of these categories moves from the sentimental to the utopian. I examine several works from the 1790s that attempt to place various visions of utopia in North America. Projected English utopias in America in the 1790s, such as Samuel Taylor Coleridge's and Robert Southey's Pantisocracy on the banks of the Susquehanna in Pennsylvania, and imagined ones like Mary Wollstonecraft's, which developed from a desire to move to the Illinois territory with her American lover Gilbert Imlay, tended to displace European political issues onto American soil. Most of these utopian plans were responses to the violent turn the French Revolution had taken. Events in France had offered English liberals and radicals an opportunity to imagine a fresh beginning for European history, retaining all the cultural advances of the past without the repressive politics of the present. The Terror and Napoleon's rise destroyed this dream. But the interior of the United States seemed an alternative space for staging this new history. Joseph Priestley was in exile in Philadelphia, and his sons, along with another emigrant, Joseph Cooper, had purchased several hundred acres they intended to sell to disaffected English radicals seeking an American refuge from domestic repression. Stories of abundant land and sublime landscapes, circulated by land speculators and competitors Cooper and Imlay and repeated in newspapers, books, and letters, reached a large audience. Americans are conspicuously absent from these accounts, as I show in my discussions of Coleridge's sonnets, Imlay's utopian novel, *The Emigrants* (1793), and Blake's *America: A Prophecy* (1793).

My third category focuses on English writers who saw America as a place where history could be escaped altogether. Late eighteenth-century writers such as Tobias Smollett, in *The Expedition of Humphry Clinker* (1771), and Charlotte Lennox, in *Euphemia* (1790), depicted an America where savagery and civility blended, resulting in people who seemed simultaneously to represent widely disparate epochs. Using America as a setting that combined times like this questioned the historicity of the western hemisphere. Wordsworth and Byron would later enter this discourse in deliberate and explicit turns away from the present history of the 1810s. They sought escapes from the Napoleonic Wars that they conceived of as escapes from history altogether.

The final version of American time I examine is the anthropological time I have discussed above. Frances Trollope's *Domestic Manners of the Americans* (1832) represented Americans as coarse, imperfectly civil, primitive in their customs and religions, and in every way inferior to the English, despite their possession of a developed commercial society. Trollope, Basil Hall, William Cobbett, and others who came to America after 1815 suggest that despite the economic factors that should make the United States an advanced nation, its people are less civil, and in most respects less temporally advanced, than the English.

While I separate these four ways of looking at time into distinct chapters, they all existed throughout the period this work covers. I would argue that the sentimental connection late eighteenth-century novels attempted to make between England and the former colonists was more prevalent earlier than later, and that the anthropological view presented by Trollope in 1832 had become by that time the predominant way of imagining Americans for English writers. I have ordered the chapters to emphasize this chronological shift. But just as there were those who saw Americans as a semi-barbaric people before the American Revolution, others were still traveling to America in the 1810s and 1820s to form utopian communities. They included people like Morris Birkbeck and George Flower, who founded Albion, Indiana, in 1818, and Frances Wright, who Trollope accompanied to Nashoba, Tennessee, in 1828. Americans were an epistemological problem for the English throughout the eighteenth and nineteenth centuries. It would be wrong to suggest that any single interpretation satisfied England's writers and readers. But the images of the frontier and frontiersman exerted as powerful a hold on the imagination of the English as they did on the Americans. The interpretation of the effect of the newness and wildness of American soil on the Americans attracted writers of both countries. Both American and English writers by the early decades of the nineteenth century constructed Americans as a breed apart. Whether they represented this new breed as progress forward or a slide backwards towards barbarism was an entirely different matter.

At least four persistent opinions about what "American" means seem relevant to the study at hand. First, the patriotic, nativist strain—seen in people who buy and fly American flags, who use the term "American dream" without a trace of irony, who believe the United States is unambiguously a land of freedom and a guarantor of freedom everywhere else, and who get lumps in their throats when they hear the Star-Spangled Banner—has always asserted itself aggressively, and often inspired some of the most spirited denunciations of the Americans in the works I examine here.

Secondly, what passes for the political left in the United States—in my daily experience, people who teach in universities, but I suspect there are others—presents "America" as a highly contested and contestable idea in ways that stem from American and English writing dating back at least to the years of the American Revolution. Marginalized others—those for whom the American dream has never existed, victims of racial prejudice, gender discrimination, genocide—perceive "American" very differently, of course. Some of these perceptions made it into print in the period I study here. Most did not. Finally, those on the outside looking in—this study's main focus—often represent the people of the United States as "ugly Americans," capitalists, imperialists, anti-intellectuals, among other things. All of these ways of seeing America and Americans have their roots in the years preceding American independence. Hopefully a study that looks at those roots will help us to think about why we see the United States the way we do—how much of our seeing stems from ways of thinking that are centuries old and how much of it results from more recent developments.

My method generally belongs to what most people term New Historicism, but rather than focusing on the anecdote, I tend to focus on Fernand Braudel's middle version of historical time, what he terms a bit dismissively "the mirage and reality of the cyclical rise and fall of prices," or, in this case, manners and perceptions.[11] I have chosen this approach as opposed to the focus on a single year or highly localized series of events that marks several major recent works of New Historicism, such as James Chandler's *England in 1819* or John Barrell's *Imagining the King's Death: Figurative Treason, Fantasies of Regicide, 1793–1796*, both of which have,

---

11 Fernand Braudel, *On History*, trans. Sarah Matthews (Chicago, 1980), p. 25.

nevertheless, heavily influenced this book.[12] I have chosen this method because American identity for the English was a developing cultural process best identifiable over time, rather than a case study which can be limited to an event, or related series of events, like Peterloo (Chandler), or the Treason Trials (Barrell). I do, however, try to focus on the importance of cases and casuistry. So, while I do not focus on a single year, I consider individual works important to my project here. As Chandler puts it: "The emergence of this distinction—between writings as marking and making history—is a crucial part of what *defines* the new concept of culture and what now, as then, underwrites historicist interpretation."[13] One thing this work is not is anthropology. It uses concepts borrowed from anthropology's self critiques, such as Fabian's, but it does so in order to examine the discursive field that re-imagined Americans for England, not to offer a "correct" or even corrective version of that field's subject.

---

12 James Chandler, *England in 1819: The Politics of Literary Culture and the Case of Romantic Historicism* (Chicago, 1998) ; John Barrell, *Imagining the King's Death: Figurative Treason, Fantasies of Regicide, 1793–1796* (Oxford, 2000).

13 *England in 1819*, p. xvi.

Chapter One

English Novels on the American Revolution

More than a thousand of Charles Dickens's readers stood on the docks in New York in 1841 waiting for the shipment of the London periodical *Master Humphrey's Clock*, which contained the latest installment of *The Old Curiosity Shop*. These readers feared, quite literally, for the life of the heroine with an intensity and to an extent often recalled in discussions of the connections between writers, readers, and texts. When the ship neared the dock one called out to those on board, "Is Little Nell dead?"[1] Like readers in England, Americans were thoroughly engaged in Dickens's maudlin tale, and tearfully sympathized with Little Nell as if she were one of their own children. Sadly, Little Nell had perished back in England, and nations mourned. Later Oscar Wilde would declare that no one could read of the death of Little Nell without laughing, a verdict our age would likely agree with, but in 1841 the joke was not yet apparent.

This well-known anecdote exemplifies many of the aspects of transatlantic literary sympathy this chapter discusses. First, it highlights a fellow feeling between English and American readers, centered on questions of loss and innocence. Second, it suggests that the material means by which texts were transmitted prior to the laying of the first transatlantic cables in 1851 both heightened that feeling and blocked its communication. The emotions of people on one side of the Atlantic have always already happened for those whose access to them comes through acts of reading, at least six weeks earlier during the 1770s, and still usually three or more weeks by the 1830s. Finally, as Elizabeth Brennan suggests in her introduction to the Oxford World's Classics paperback version of *The Old Curiosity Shop*, this incident quite possibly never happened. As far as we can tell, it is an anecdote without an event, a discursive history and nothing more.[2] The relevance of this—and of beginning this chapter with a story that may not have happened—is that at least since the era of the American Revolution, the difference between America and Britain has always been one of time—time manifesting itself in writing as irreconcilable lacunae that sympathy seeks to fill, but in the process only exacerbates. The result of this

---

1 David Cody, "Dickens's Popularity," *The Victorian Web: Literature, History, & Culture in the Age of Victoria* (http:// 65.107.211.206/dickens/dickensbio4.html), includes the anecdote without a reference.

2 Elizabeth Brennan, "Introduction," *The Old Curiosity Shop* (Oxford, 1998), p. xxii. As Brennan points out, "no verifiable evidence" exists for the anecdote. "(P)age proofs were sent to Lea and Blanchard of Philadelphia" before "the publication of each number of *Master Humphrey's Clock* in London."

temporal gap takes a human relationship—or the textual version of one—that seems synchronic in unemotional times, and unmasks it as a diachronic fiction, a twice-told tale of a specifically transatlantic type. Writing the Anglo-American relationship as diachronic is the overarching activity that controls the fictions that aim to show connection but instead demonstrate the impossibility of imagining this "nation" as existing in a single time. Also, just as distance became time for Dickens's sympathetic American readers, apocryphal or real, time has now distanced those who would discover whether this anecdote is an example of fictional Anglo-American sympathy, or actual Anglo-American sympathy focused on fiction. For this reason, British fiction of the 1780s and 1790s—fiction that focuses on the common and recent connections, history, and experiences of Americans and the English—is the best place to look for the English understanding of America as another country that is also another time.

The possibility that this anecdote is a fiction presents a major difficulty for a study such as mine. Where, in the twenty-first century, does eighteenth- and nineteenth-century culture exist? In texts? In anecdotes later rendered as text? In relationships between texts and rumors of texts? If crowds in New York waited for news of Little Nell, the story of their readerly sympathy may have been transmitted orally for a time, or through sources now lost, only to resurface in many accounts based on no apparent evidence. On one level, the anecdote's importance lies as much in its plausibility as its verifiability. Collective reading experiences inspired sympathy, and *The Old Curiosity Shop* was a major hit with the American public, which surely awaited news of Little Nell's fate with as much concern as English audiences did. The anecdote is no doubt true, if not verifiable, up to that point. Shipping news was in every paper, and ships from England took at least two weeks to reach New York in 1841. This meant Dickens's audience in New York was aware of the existence of knowledge—published, textual knowledge—that it had no access to for several weeks, turning a gap in time and communication into an epistemological gap as well. New Yorkers knew that English readers had already been mourning Little Nell's death or celebrating her recovery for several weeks by the time it knew what to feel, which in this case extends that epistemological gap into the realm of sympathy. The point is that while New York readers may not have waited at South Street for the ship carrying *Master Humphrey's Clock*, relatives and friends awaiting the news of a death or birth of someone back in Britain certainly did, on a daily basis, and this certainty makes what is likely an apocryphal anecdote plausible, and to a great extent, true.

The concern New Yorkers may or may not have shown for Little Nell, while probably the most famous instance of transatlantic sympathy involving a writer and readers and complicated by slow transatlantic communication, was hardly the first. This form of sympathy and a similar hindrance to its immediate communication was crucial in introducing the idea of American identity to the English. The coincidence of the widespread taste for sentimental literature with the American Revolution spawned a host of novels in which the Atlantic, more than any human character, serves as antagonist, a narrative feature which violently creates two sets of English-speaking peoples by dismembering those meant to represent the possibility of unity. News of military events and lists of the wounded and dead faced the same dilemma.

Readers—whether real friends and relatives seeking news from Lexington and Concord, Saratoga, or Bunker Hill, or characters in epistolary novels waiting for news of loved ones enmeshed in the drama of war—suffered sympathetically from American events that seemed to be happening not just in a far away place, but in an irreconcilable time. This temporal rupture made itself felt in a way that challenged the epistemological soundness of the dominant metaphors of Anglo-American union.

The English public, if one judges by the number of editions of popular novels set during the war, or the proliferation of polemical poems, pamphlets, periodical essays, cartoons, prints, and other cultural productions, was hungry not just for news from America, but for explanations of what the Revolution meant. Did political separation suddenly create a new people across the Atlantic, imperfectly termed "American"? Before the Revolution "American" almost always refers to Native Americans, and almost never to the colonists. Afterwards the former colonists are almost always Americans, and Native Americans more consistently become "Indians" and "savages"—names they had already borne in European and Euro-American texts for centuries. Did this change in name signal a shift in ontological content? Or were a common language, culture, and history enough to maintain the wholeness of the English-speaking people across the Atlantic despite political separation?

English and American explanations of the Anglo-American relationship relied heavily on two complementary but ultimately irreconcilable metaphors: the empire as a family, and the body politic. American pamphleteers, novelists, cartoonists, and other participants in the Revolutionary-era public sphere fairly consistently presented the relationship as a familial one, as Jay Fliegelman has convincingly demonstrated.[3] English representations of the quarrel with America eventually tended to mix the two metaphors, reluctantly recognizing that families could separate, but that bodies were sounder containers for conceptions demanding organically or symbiotically structured relationships of parts to the whole. This recognition led to depictions that relied on an organicism that could not survive the violence time perpetrated on representation.

Globalization complicated many of the tropes through which authors established a sense of the nation as an identifiable entity. Was there ever such thing as an Anglo-American nation? If so, was this nation homologous to the English, or British nations? I argue here that the ancient rhetorical model of the nation as a body eventually provided English writers with a seemingly sound vessel in which to place the notion of an Anglo-American polity. I set up this argument with a brief discussion of the metaphor of the body politic's place in western European discourse, and identification of other metaphors that found their way into representations of the relationship between England and its colonies during and immediately after the American Revolution. The metaphor of the Anglo-American empire as a family whose children are capable of growth and independence dominated American political discourse, as Fliegelman has shown.

I will draw some conclusions about why the body politic metaphor tended to crowd out family politics in English writings of the same period. While English

---

3   Jay Fliegelman, *Prodigals and Pilgrims: The American Revolution against Patriarchal Authority, 1750–1800* (Cambridge, 1982).

writers were just as capable of seeing their American cousins or subjects as children, they were inexorably drawn to a more organic figuration, as my analysis of a large number of texts and images from the period will demonstrate. To draw this point more explicitly, and to illustrate the compulsion to mix the metaphor in English discourse, I take as a case study Samuel Jackson Pratt's *Emma Corbett; or, the Miseries of the Civil War* (1780),[4] the first English novel about the American Revolution. Finally, the identification of Americans as a separate people emerges through an inability to reconcile temporal schemes. English representations of the American Revolution tend to use sympathy while attempting to create an affective union able to survive political separation. The problem with this attempt is that it must take place discursively, and the distance across the Atlantic defeats efforts to portray the communication of sympathy adequately. Whether one tries to imagine the Anglo-American nation as an entity formed by simultaneous reading experiences, or as teleologically oriented with an identical trajectory through time, one fails.

The Body Politic

Samuel Johnson uses the body politic metaphor in "Taxation No Tyranny" (1775), his pamphlet justifying England's stance against its American colonists, in a way typical of the times and struggle. "A colony is to the mother-country as a member to the body," Johnson writes—combining his metaphors as many writers of the period did—

> deriving its strength from the principal of vitality; receiving from the body, and communicating to it, all the benefits and evils of health and disease; liable in dangerous maladies to sharp applications, of which the body however must partake the pain; and exposed, if incurably tainted, to amputation, by which the body likewise will be mutilated.[5]

Johnson characteristically sees the body as England with America as an extremity. His essay tersely sums up the logical consequences for extremities that fail to understand their organic dependence. "The mother-country," he writes, always considers the colonies thus connected, as parts of itself." But while "the body may subsist, though less commodiously, without a limb … the limb must perish if it be parted from the body."[6]

The metaphor of the political entity as a corporeal body has served writers of various leanings in the Western intellectual tradition since at least the time of Plato's *Republic*. Developed further in the *Laws*, and more explicitly by Aristotle in his *Politics*, it became a common frame for discussing the *polis* throughout the Middle Ages. It was especially useful to seventeenth-century theorists of absolute monarchy

---

4   Samuel Jackson Pratt, *Emma Corbett, or the Miseries of Civil War* (3 vols, London, 1780). Further references will be cited parenthetically in text.

5   Samuel Johnson, "Taxation No Tyranny," *The Yale Edition of the Works of Samuel Johnson: Vol. X, Political Writings*, ed. Donald J. Greene (New Haven, 1977), p. 425.

6   Ibid., p. 425.

in England such as Sir Robert Filmer and Thomas Hobbes.[7] Others who sought to incorporate the king's body into that of the polity as a whole, most prominently Locke, found the metaphor almost as useful, and especially consonant with their Enlightenment views. As Antoine de Baecque puts it, "(t)he metaphor of the body offers to politicians and men of letters alike the illusion of an organic ordering of the human community, an illusion that thus gives them a scientific claim to observe it and organize it."[8]

By the time of the American Revolution, the metaphor was enough of a commonplace to slip into popular novels and poetry about the conflict. Sentimental novels took hold of the notion of a political body to define the relationship between the colonists and those home in England. While those works can hardly be understood to be making the sort of scientific claims de Baecque has in mind, they do engage in a sort of Kantian ordering of perception, in this case a political one, employing a corporeal metaphor in their intersecting acts of grasping together parts they wish to present as whole. Sympathetic illness, often death, and weakened and decaying bodies are the inevitable results of the choice of the body as the governing metaphor in the Anglo-American conflict of the 1770s and '80s.

Late eighteenth-century fictional formulations of the body politic metaphor owe much to the way they rely on notions of sentiment, and more particularly sympathy, as understood in the period. Johnson defined sympathy as "(f)ellow feeling; mutual sensibility; the quality of being affected by the affection of another." His definition of "sensibility" included both physical sensation and perception. To "sympathize," he wrote, was "to feel mutually."[9] The first edition of the *Encyclopaedia Britannica* (1771), the Scottish Enlightenment's most significant instance of corporate thought, defined sensibility and sympathy in even more explicitly corporeal terms. Sympathy "in medicine," it asserted, "denotes an indisposition befalling one part of the body, through the defect or disorder of another; whether it be from the affluence of some humour, or vapour sent from elsewhere, or from the want of the influence of some matter necessary to its action."[10]

This sensational and bodily concept of sympathy caused a significant shift in the way the "body politic" was presented, probably by the end of the seventeenth century, and certainly by the time England's hostilities with America began in the 1770s. While Hobbes and earlier writers had stressed the importance of the body of the king as a containing and representational vessel for that of the nation, Johnson

---

7   Plato, *The Republic*, trans. Benjamin Jowett (New York, 1972); *Laws*, trans. Thomas Pangle (Chicago, 1988); Aristotle, *Politics*, ed. H. Rackham (Cambridge, Mass., 1988); St. Augustine, *The City of God*, trans. Marcus Dods (New York, 1994); St. Thomas Aquinas, *On Law, Morality, and Politics*, ed. Richard J. Regan and William P. Baumgarth (Indianapolis, 1988); Christine de Pizan, *The Book of the Body Politic*, ed. Kate Kangdon Forhan (Cambridge, 1994); Hobbes, *Leviathan*, ed. Richard Tuck (Cambridge, 1996), and *De Corpore Politico*, ed. J.C.A. Gaskin (Oxford, 1994); Locke, *Two Treatises of Government*, ed. Peter Laslett (Cambridge, 1988), among others.

8   Antoine de Baecque, *The Body Politic: Corporeal Metaphor in Revolutionary France, 1770–1800* (Stanford, 1997), p. 6.

9   Samuel Johnson, *A Dictionary of the English Language* (2 vols, London, 1755).

10   *Enclyclopaedia Britannica* (3 vols, Edinburgh, 1771), vol. 3, p. 880.

tacitly accepts the unpersonified nation as the primary body. As Jay Fliegelman notes, England's replacement of an absolutist monarchy with a constitutional one in 1688 contributed to a change in the way the nation viewed the relationship between sovereign and people. While he stresses the change in familial relations this change encouraged, his point seems also applicable to a change in the conception of the nation as an organic structure.[11] Janet Todd has claimed that religious Dissenters, seeking to further the democratic nature of the political body, "were reinforced by the sentimental interest in the deprived," and by the tendency of "sentimental literature" to reinforce that movement.[12] While Hobbes had argued in *Leviathan* that the monarch "presented the body" of the people in his own person, a reading of political theorists and popularizers of the notion of the nation as an organism shows that by the late eighteenth century the king's body was considered "present" in the body politic, as were those of all of the other participants in the nation. Though this move towards a democratization of the conception of bodily sovereignty that Todd locates in the culture of religious dissent was highly significant for English history, it kept the terms of debate organic, and represents continuity as much as it does change in the English conception of sovereignty in the period.

Another key difference between Hobbes's version of the body politic and that represented by authors of late eighteenth-century sentimental novels, and to an extent, Johnson, is that Hobbes maintains awareness of his trope's reliance on metaphor. Just as he compares the state to a body, he likens the body to a machine as easily as he recognizes its organic quality. The metaphors are, for him, interchangeable. "For what is the *Heart*," Hobbes asks, "but a *Spring*; and the *Nerves*, but so many *Strings*; and the *Joynts*, but so many *Wheeles*, giving motion to the whole Body, such as was intended by the Artificer?"[13] By the late eighteenth century the literature of sensibility had significantly constricted attempts to move from one metaphor to another when discussing the nation. Johnson's declaration that colonies derived "strength from the principal of vitality" rather than from the monarch as metaphorical head of this Anglo-American body aligns him with the concepts of sympathy that many novelists would write into their revolutionary fictions. Just as Johnson no doubt hoped that the use of an organic metaphor would communicate an understanding that the "nation," which for him included the colonies, must live or die together, novelists of the 1780s and '90s dramatized the severance of the American part as a grievous wound to the whole.[14]

Johnson's role in this debate is significant, and bears directly on what I want to suggest is a specifically English view of the Anglo-American relationship that was at odds with the one the colonists held. Johnson's position as an authority— possibly *the* authority—on the very words that became the terms of debate, and his statement of George III's case in "Taxation No Tyranny," placed him in a leading

---

11 Fliegelman, *Prodigals and Pilgrims*, p. 13.

12 Janet Todd, *Sensibility: An Introduction* (London, 1986), p. 11.

13 Hobbes, *Leviathan*, p. 9.

14 Johnson's definition of "nation," in contrast with the *Encyclopaedia Britannica*'s, did not insist on territorial limits. For him, a nation was "A people distinguished from another people; generally by their language, original, or government." *Dictionary*.

role in extending sympathetic language to the political conflict. The author of *Emma Corbett; or the Miseries of Civil War*, Samuel Jackson Pratt, for one, evinced more complicated sympathies concerning the colonies than Johnson did, but his understanding of the argument was epistemologically identical. While Johnson sided unequivocally with the crown and Lord North's government, and Pratt clearly had sympathy for the American cause, both couch their discussions of the conflict in terms of symbiotically invested parties, and these terms control the understanding of the colonial relationship and its organicism. Severing a part means killing the whole for Pratt. While, as the quote above from "Taxation No Tyranny" makes it clear that England, as the whole, could survive amputation, Johnson does not deny the pain or "incommodity" that will result.

Several cartoons from the period depict England and its colonies in various corporeal configurations, often mutilated or violated. An anonymous cartoon printed in 1768, "The Colonies Reduced," depicts Britannia as a living but clearly exhausted torso. This cartoon was printed during the furor over taxation that preceded the Revolution. The remnant of empire leans against her globe, with her severed limbs lying on the ground around her. The limbs are labeled with the names of North American colonies, but even these have suffered a textual dismemberment. One leg is labeled "Virg-", another is "New Eng-," an arm is "Pensyl-," with the other being the only fully named limb, "New York." This cartoon shows the British Empire in terms similar to those Johnson would use seven years later in "Taxation No Tyranny," but the resulting distress is more acute. The British body survives, as Johnson would have it, "incommoded" by the loss of it limbs, but just barely.[15]

Another cartoon, also anonymous, depicts America as a partially disrobed young woman being force fed tea by Lord Bute while Lord Mansfield looks up her skirt. While in this case the body is violated without being dismembered, Britannia covers her eyes and weeps in the near background as the British Navy bombards Boston in the far distance, exhibiting her sympathetic involvement in the assault.[16] This sort of metonymic identification, where sympathetic Britons feel the attack on a feminized America, finds its way into much of the poetry and fiction of the period as well.

Thomas Day's poem, "The Desolation of America" (1777), likens America to "A tender virgin breathless with her fears."[17] The poet then

> see(s) swift bursting thro' the shade,
> The cruel soldier, and the reaking blade.
> And there the bloody cross of Britain waves ...
> ...
> See! where they rush, and with a savage joy,
> Unsheath the sword, impatient to destroy.
> Fierce as the tiger, bursting from the wood,
> With famish'd jaws, insatiable of blood! (ll. 29–31, 37–40)

---

15 Michael Wynn Jones, *The Cartoon History of the American Revolution* (New York, 1975), p. 53.

16 Ibid., p. 58.

17 Thomas Day, "The Desolation of America" (London, 1777), l. 3.

The description of an American woman follows. She attempts to flee the British army, but is caught, raped, and murdered by British soldiers (11. 41–155).

Many works of the period evoke this sexualized view of Britain as a masculine, rapacious figure. Charlotte Smith's *The Old Manor House* (1794) draws on images nearly identical to those in Day's poem. The novel's hero, Orlando, has gone to America to fight in 1777, knowing little about the struggle. He is horrified at seeing his fellow British soldiers mistreating American civilians. Smith writes of American "women and children exposed to the tempest of the night, or, what was infinitely more dreadful, to the brutality of the military."[18]

The anonymous *Tales of Truth* (1780), written by "A Lady, under the patronage of the Duchess of York" who signs herself "E.H.", tells the tale of Mrs. Marshall, an American woman whose house has been taken over by a troop of British soldiers. Her daughter, Antonia, escapes rape at their hands only through the intercession of Rodolpho, whom the novel styles a "man of feeling," as intent upon saving his honor as serving his government. The British have disrupted the domestic sphere through their violent means of occupying Mrs. Marshall's house. "A piano forte, a pair of globes, a range that had been filled with books, some of which were gone, others on the ground; the glasses broken, *all* told in strong characters that an informed mind inhabited the house, and that the savage hand of *power* had been there."[19] Her daughter's fainting has saved her from suffering the fate of the piano, globes, and books, but the imputation of sexual violence lingers over the scene.

Irruption of Body Politic Discourse

The Critical Review ran a brief critique of Samuel Jackson Pratt's *Emma Corbett; or the Miseries of Civil War*, in June 1780. The work's heroine, wrote the reviewer, "formed upon the models of Clarissa and Eloisa," was "in point of literary composition ... hardly inferior to either of those characters."[20] The novel was apparently fairly popular on both sides of the Atlantic for about twenty years. But despite this contemporary popularity, *Emma Corbett*, like so many sentimental novels of the late eighteenth century, has vanished from critical consciousness. It is time to address this neglect. *Emma Corbett* was the first English novel to focus on the American Revolution. That choice of subject matter, the fact that several novels in the decades following its first publication represented the Anglo-American community similarly, and its combination of the rhetoric of sympathy with metaphors of the body politic and familial authority, make it a significant document in the emergence of a new English discourse about America that dominated popular fiction well into the 1790s.[21]

Emma Corbett marks the irruption of the American Revolution into English novelistic representations. Along with *Louisa Wharton*, an anonymous tale also

---

18 Charlotte Smith, *The Old Manor House* (London, 1987), p. 345.

19 *Tales of Truth. By a Lady. Under the Patronage of the Duchess of York* (3 vols, London, 1800), vol. 2, p. 133.

20 *The Critical Review*, June 1780, pp. 460–62.

21 See Robert Heilman, *America in English Fiction 1760–1800* (Baton Rouge, 1937).

published in 1780, it marks the beginning of a thread in the relationship between the colonies and England of a discourse that imagined the Anglo-American community not as two elements of an empire, but as a single nation. Many works followed Pratt's novel—which ran to five English editions and at least four in the United States—both in taking the American Revolution as subject matter, and in the ways in which they intertwine the body politic metaphor with that of the sympathetic family. The anonymous *Liberal American* (1785), Susannah Willard's *Francis the Philanthropist* (1786), Robert Bage's *Mt. Henneth* (1788), the anonymous *School for Fathers* (1788), Helen Maria Williams's *Julia* (1790), Eliza Parsons's *Voluntary Exile* (1795) and George Walker's *Cinthelia* (1797), are just a few texts that sought to create an Anglo-American nation bound by metaphors designed to survive the political dissolution between the two communities formalized by the Treaty of Paris in 1783.[22]

One could see these novels as representative of a discursive rupture in Foucauldian terms, where a new discourse disrupts and replaces an entrenched one. Pierre Bourdieu's related concept of an interruption in a cultural field where representational fields co-exist, to some extent at least, and the question admits divergent cultural locations that challenge the centrality of epistemological determination that characterizes Foucault's view, also provides a way of approaching these works.[23] Either approach helps us see how these sentimental texts mark two significant rhetorical shifts. Prior to 1775, the term "American" almost always refers to Native Americans. After the news of the battle of Lexington and Concord in April of that year reached England, this term almost always refers to the colonists, as an extensive reading of political pamphlets shows. The point I wish to stress here is that the group of popular novels ushered in by Pratt's text both built on the increasing semantic invention of an English-speaking American people and, paradoxically, subsumed Americanness within Englishness in a way which inevitably led to fictions of mutilation and dismemberment. The second shift contradicts the first: by becoming "Americans" it would seem the former colonists had gained cultural independence, but the new English version of Americanness was submerged in an Anglo-American nation animated by bodily sympathy.

The anonymous *School for Fathers; or, the Victim of a Curse* (1788) shows no sympathy for the colonists' side—they are referred to as "the deluded and rebellious Americans"; however, it portrays the war as an attack on the family structure just as persistently as *Emma Corbett* does.[24] It contains a long episode detailing the

---

22 Anon., *The Liberal American: A Novel, In a Series of Letters, By a Lady* (London, 1785); Susannah Willard, *Francis the Philanthropist: An Unfashionable Tale* (London, 1786); Robert Bage, *Mt. Henneth: a Novel, in a Series of Letters* (London, 1788 [1782]); Anon., *School for Fathers; or, the Victim of a Curse* (London, 1788); Helen Maria Williams, *Julia; A Novel, Interspersed with Some Poetical Pieces* (Dublin, 1790); Eliza Parsons, *The Voluntary Exile* (London, 1795); George Walker, *Cinthelia; or, a Woman of Ten Thousand* (Oxford, 1797).

23 Michel Foucault, *The Archaeology of Knowledge & the Discourse on Language* (New York, 1972); Pierre Bourdieu, *The Field of Cultural Production: Essays on Art and Literature*, ed. Randal Johnson and Lawrence Kritzman (New York, 1994).

24 *The School for Fathers; or, the Victim of a Curse*, vol. 1, p. 98. Further references cited parenthetically.

dissolution of an English family living in the colonies at the outbreak of unrest over Parliamentary policies in the years before the Revolution. Pleydel, an English civil servant, refuses to turn information over to the colonists or to join their side, and is imprisoned in Boston. "Ye seek to dismember yourselves from your mother country," he tells the rebellious Americans. "(A)narchy, with all its consequent evils, will sooner or later overtake you" (II:5). But this curse rebounds on its author. Pleydel's wife, Matilda, and their six children are forced to flee, destitute, to Pleydel's aunt's house in Albany. Three of their children die during the journey. Once Pleydel manages his escape and joins the remainder of his family, he and Matilda decide to flee to New York—occupied by the British in the early part of the war—and get on a ship to England. Another of their children dies from fever before they can leave Albany. An American privateer sinks their ship on the voyage home. Matilda narrowly prevents herself from another separation from her husband. But though they manage to save themselves in a lifeboat, as it is thrown upon the shore, "one of the dear little children was dashed to pieces before the eyes of his distracted parents, who were unable to afford him the least succour" (II:33). Just as in *Emma Corbett*, the war between America and England plays out as a war on kinship, with the English family the greatest sufferer. That family is flesh and blood, and "dashed to pieces" unmercifully.

Mt. Henneth (1788) is the work of a midlands paper miller, Robert Bage, who began his literary career when he was past fifty. Bage went on to publish six novels—beginning with *Mt. Henneth*, which went through three editions, and was popular enough thirty-five years later to be selected by Walter Scott for inclusion in *Ballantyne's Novelist's Library* (1824)—and ending with perhaps his best-known work, *Hermsprong* (1796). All are on political and social topics, and Bage is generally considered a "Jacobin" novelist, along with Elizabeth Inchbald, William Godwin, and Thomas Holcroft. His membership in the Derby Philosophical Society brought him into contact with Joseph Priestley, Erasmus Darwin, and Josiah Wedgwood.[25]

Mt. Henneth is an epistolary novel about two brothers, John and Henry Cheslyn. Henry's fortune, which had been invested in an American trading house, was lost when the war broke out. The human aspect of the American war is introduced through the character of a virtuous woman—Miss Melton—in danger of being violated, and in need of rescuing. Henry meets Miss Melton accidentally when a friend of his demands they visit a brother. He falls in love first with her dignity, then with her beauty. After several failed attempts, he rescues her from prostitution. She had been captured at sea when her ship was sunk by a British ship. The captain, frustrated by his loss of the plunder of her ship, had taken her as his rightful prize and sold her to a bawd in London.

Mt. Henneth depicts a contest between America, as represented by the virtuous, but helpless woman, and a commercial England, which sees everything and everyone as a commodity, and the rightful property of the nation. The British ship captain originally sent Miss Melton to his home, where "the captain was guilty of some indiscretions, which excited tumults in the bosom of his gentle spouse" (72). The

25 Jerry C. Beasley, "Robert Bage." *Dictionary of Literary Biography.* Vol. 39. *British Novelists, 1660–1800.* Ed. Martin C. Battestin. (Detroit, 1985), pp. 18–23.

captain's attempt to make Miss Melton part of his family has come into conflict with a monogamous England, which has no patience for this attempt at multi-national polygamy, and she's brought to the brothel.

Once in the care of the bawd, Mrs. P—, Miss Melton refuses to behave as a prostitute. "Mrs. P— is a well-bred woman," a friend of Henry's sarcastically tells him before his initial meeting with her.

(She) informed Miss Melton of her situation with all the politeness imaginable. Miss Melton was not so polite: on the contrary, she asserted her claim to independency and freedom, (for she is an American) with great spirit and force of language; not without mingling certain inuendoes, by no means agreeable to the elegant ears of Mrs. P—. The captain swore she was his property by the laws of war: he had a better title from the lady's poverty and want of friends (73).

The novel is, in part, a polemic against this view of America and Americans as English commodities, and Bage constantly uses Miss Melton's situation to make this argument. It also serves to show the difficulty of considering America and England as part of the same nation. In *Mt. Henneth*, as with most novels or poems that portray America as female, the tension associated with considering America part of an Anglo-American nation during or after a war that changed the political equation is more pronounced than in the other two metaphors with which I am concerned here.

Mt. Henneth also touches on the concept of the nation as a corporeally identifiable entity. Miss Melton's abduction, and the understanding among the characters responsible for her being held captive in a London brothel that her body is English property, introduces the concept of the colonies as legitimate whores for the enrichment of the nation. The novel opens with a brief account of Henry Cheslyn having lost his fortune through investment in American trade that the advent of war in 1775 destroyed (14). His honorable resignation to his financial loss is contrasted with the behavior of the sea captain who captured Miss Melton on the Atlantic. This captain considers her body a proper substitution for the material goods that sank when her ship went down. The bawd who ends up with possession of Miss Melton considers her body entirely in terms of trade. "I can make two hundred of her the first month, and, before she is blown upon, sell her to some gouty lord for another," she tells Henry Cheslyn, who's attempting to buy her freedom. "A very profitable commerce, Mrs. P—," he responds. "Lord, gentlemen," she says, "so it ought. Consider our risques" (79). Henry's attempts to argue Mrs. P— out of viewing Miss Melton's body as her possession, and instead into treating her as a debtor whom he can relieve, are rebuffed. "No, she said; Miss Melton had been the property of Captain Suthall; he took her prisoner upon the sea; he gave her into my custody …" (96). Whether America is treated as part of England's body, or as a body possessed by the English, and thus incorporated into the general body, it is not seen as something that can be related to England in a less organic way.

These metaphors all faced a problem that seems obvious in retrospect, but that, for many reasons, their authors attempted to evade. They all rely on connectedness— organic connectedness in the case of the body, and physical proximity in the cases of the family or lovers. These novels go out of their way to get English characters into contact with Americans, usually in the colonies but occasionally—as in the case of *Mt. Henneth*—in England. They strive, through epistolarity, to place the writer and reader in an emotional communion of readership that in many novels constructed under the same principles can present the illusion of the collapse of time and space.

Charlotte Lennox's *Euphemia* (1790) provides marked examples of the failures of such an attempt once the Atlantic comes between correspondents. *Euphemia* is told mostly through the correspondence of two young ladies, Euphemia Neville and Maria Harley. The first two volumes of this four-volume novel take place in England during the 1740s, and time is measured in minutes and hours. The collapse of time and space that epistolarity strives toward are achieved in this section. Maria is able to write to Euphemia about retiring "to my own apartment, to have the pleasure of conversing with you, my dear friend; for when I am writing to you … I fancy you are present, and I am talking to you."[26] Euphemia and Maria are able to share information by the next post, and advice before taking action. Their letters regularly reinforce a view of correspondence as conversation. Maria tells Euphemia she is writing "under the shade of a spreading oak, well furnished with pens, ink, and paper," and that she has "given orders to my maid not to find me till within half an hour of dinner … all the hours, till then, I will devote to you" (II:3). This gives the reader the sense of a closer communion between correspondents than between people physically present, such as Maria's maid, who is out of sight and not permitted to "find" her until "half an hour" until dinner; Euphemia, in the meantime, will get "all the hours" until that time.

This presentation of a correspondence as a conversation, with its constant references to "moments," "minutes," and "hours," turns into two narratives that never meet once Euphemia goes to America with her husband, who has accepted a commission in the British Army in Albany. The few months' duration of the first two volumes turn into more than twelve years of separation. A dramatic shift in narrative signals the long separation. Lennox moves from relatively brief letters which keep Maria and Euphemia fairly current concerning the happenings in each others' lives, to a promise from Euphemia to "begin a kind of journal from the day I leave England, and continue … as long as I am able to hold a pen" (II:172). The absence of reciprocity involved in the change in genres from letters to journal becomes immediately apparent. From this point, the novel becomes almost exclusively an adventure story entirely taking place in New York. Euphemia writes about traveling up the Hudson River by sloop, of meeting with Indians, the birth of her two children, the loss of one for years to Indians and his recovery, and the historical changes brought about by the Seven Years' War. Maria's role changes from correspondent to imagined reader.

Louisa Wharton (1780), a tale told in letters about a virtuous, wealthy English woman engaged to a soldier sent to America to fight, demonstrates how much more difficult communicating across the ocean was than sending letters to distant parts of England could be. Louisa's lover, Captain Francis Truman, sails for America,

---

26 Charlotte Lennox, *Euphemia* (4 vols, London, 1992), vol. 2, p. 80. Further references cited parenthetically.

and she does not hear from him for three months. When she does, it's by a hastily written letter, rushed by the uncertain and inadequate means of transmitting letters. He quickly writes to her because "(t)he packet was getting ready to sail, as soon as we came into harbour, therefore I was obliged to write, with the utmost expedition, both to you and my father."[27] Louisa understands the inadequacy of his letter, but soon circumstances make even this slight sort of correspondence difficult.

Louisa's father has made the family fortune as a merchant in Philadelphia. He sails for America to guard his investment at about the same time as Captain Truman. When Louisa receives Truman's letter she is "in hopes" that she will soon hear from him. But finally she hears from her brother in a way that highlights both the importance of the letter as connection between America and England, and its failure to keep up with the narrative of daily life. She describes the scene to her correspondent:

> My mother held out a letter to me, having just broke the seal but was unable to read the contents; I observed the wax, it was black, I trembled, desired the young gentleman to be seated, I looked at the bottom for the signature, and found it was my brother's; I hesitated, turned pale, and trembled, yet determined to know the worst, and read as follows. (28)

The letter informs her, as expected, of her father's death. While the outward form of the letter and her brother's signature communicate a great deal, the letter fails in that it informs her that while she was "in hopes" of hearing of his safe arrival, he had been buried for at least six weeks.

Louisa's body takes full part in the need to communicate and the failure to do so in a healthy way. Before finding out about her father's death, or the eventual safe return of Captain Truman and her brother to England, she imagines that "the leaden death invades my Truman's heart, my brother bleeds, my father, –oh! my dear Fidelia, the idea is too horrible to support" (25). Throughout the tale Louisa's body registers the emotions of the multiple separations she must endure. She and Captain Truman attempt to remain connected through a highly charged, embodied sympathetic tie. Louisa gives Truman a miniature, which he repeatedly kisses, both when she gives it to him and, according to his letters, while he's in America. She takes a ring from him which she puts on a chain around her neck "and let it fall into my bosom" (9).

The death of Louisa's father impoverishes her and her family, making receiving mail even more difficult. Captain Truman's father, Sir James, has no interest in having his son marry a woman without a fortune, and Louisa's only means of hearing from her lover had been through her father's packets of letters from America. She laments that she is "now cut off from the means of hearing or of sending to him, if he writes, his letter will be kept from me" (43). Her brother had already complained that "all intercourse but that of chance is stopped between the two countries," and that he knows "not when you will hear of me again" (29). She soon reads in the newspapers that Truman is dead, and the next day that he is alive, which further emphasizes the difficulty (59). The failures of communication persist until Truman and Louisa's

---

27 *Louisa Wharton. A Story Founded on Facts* (London, 1780?), p. 21. Further references cited parenthetically.

brother walk through her door at the end of the tale, testifying through their bodily presence to their safety, something none of their letters or other written accounts have been able to do.

In these novels, time, as we have seen, insistently foregrounds spatial distance and breaks apart metaphorical communities. The simple but persistent difficulty of communicating anything while it is still relevant places America and England in a doubled temporal structure that, before the laying of the first transatlantic cable in the middle of the nineteenth century, could not be collapsed or elided. As Euphemia writes to Maria: "When I reflect upon some passages you have related, I cannot help smiling at the blunder which distance produces. At the very moment when I had reason to fear that fortune was preparing some obstacles to your happiness, that happiness was already secured" (III:96). Space, in passages like this, almost imperceptibly becomes time, as seen in the move from the blunders "distance produces" to the unfixability of those "very moments" that give epistolarity the conversational illusion Maria Harley regularly refers to in *Euphemia*. Space was always obvious, but the attempt at epistolary communication foregrounds the temporal separation between these two communities. The letter as a piece of writing is also symbolic of a social contract. It has not fulfilled its purpose until it is read, is not complete as a written document alone, but requires an audience. The fact that the letters in these novels are not read until the events they discuss are already fixed in another time enforces the separation that their writers strive to defeat.

English and American Sympathy

The important difference between the American and English, or Anglo-American figurations of the polity as a sympathetically animated organism is that English writers overwhelmingly presented their transatlantic nation as an entity that had long existed and that war was tearing apart. American fiction of the same period generally adheres to "the notion that a democratic community can be forged through the power of sympathy."[28] To put it simply, Americans, as Fliegelman has convincingly argued, viewed the Anglo-American community in familial terms. English writers like Pratt viewed it through a mixed metaphor that incorporated elements of familial connection with corporeal identification. George Washington's cameos in *Emma Corbett*, Helen Maria Williams's *Julia*, the anonymous *School for Fathers* and others provide the contrast of a sentimental hero as a "citizen (fighting) for his country," as Wollstonecraft put it, with the representatives of the affective Anglo-American nation, who wallow in a debilitating version of sympathy, controlling and defeating in its organicism.[29] One is a story of endings, the other of beginnings that, in the 1780s and 1790s, at least, threatened unmanageable entanglements rather than separation. While American authors constructed a new paradigm, their English counterparts sought to explain the losses of the recent past with the fractured one

---

28 Lennox, *Euphemia*, p. 11.

29 Mary Wollstonecraft, *Vindication of the Rights of Men* (London, 1790), p. 143.

which they had inherited, and which would soon resurface to explain Englishness with greater success in Burke's *Reflections on the Revolution in France* (1790).[30]

The American writing that found its way into the British marketplace in the 1770s and 1780s was still overwhelmingly political and polemical, and persistently represented the quarrel in familial terms. The mixed metaphor that controls works such as the novels discussed above, on the other hand, produces an unnatural epistemology. One might imagine the mother country with its children's limbs growing out of and being amputated from its own body, though one would probably rather not. The damage to Pleydel's family in *School for Fathers* is a perfect example of this mixed metaphor and of how it works in the fiction of the period. His children die one by one, often violently, as with the one who is dashed upon the rocks as his parents watch. The attack on the body and the family is simultaneous. In the novel of sensibility, the pain of such scenes is written to involve the readers as well, in this case, readers who are also members in the same mix of body and family that the Anglo-American community becomes in the period's writings. For these readers the field of representation is both endlessly refracted and persistently mutilated with layers of previous sympathetic affect. In the end, it is as impossible to imagine an Anglo-American nation united by sympathy as it is to stop the course of the Revolution. I turn now to Pratt's *Emma Corbett*, a text I wish to take as representative of this novelistic discourse of the mixed family-body metaphor, to demonstrate how the novelistic text, when focused on the Revolution, becomes a fraught medium, unable to narrate a connected story.

The Case of *Emma Corbett*

Emma Corbett is the story of a young woman in love with a British soldier setting off for America to battle the colonists. Their sentimental attachment runs deep. The novel's initial conflict arises when it becomes clear that Charles Corbett, Emma's father, sympathizes with the American cause, both politically and in the most extravagant bodily sense, as I shall demonstrate more fully below. The Corbett family and its battles over authority and sympathy's proper outlet become metaphorical figurations of the conflict between America and England. Pratt uses the body's organicism and the symbiotically dependent families to figure an Anglo-American nation just as it falls apart. This representation of the nation as a body, or a sympathetically bound family of bodies, is in line with late eighteenth-century concepts of both sympathy and the nation.

Since few readers are familiar with *Emma Corbett*'s plot, I will present a fairly extensive summary combined with an exegesis showing how the discourses of sympathy and the body-family metaphor overdetermine the way the text and its characters represent the Anglo-American relationship. But first, a few words about its author. Pratt was briefly a curate, then an actor under the stage name Courtney Melmoth in Dublin and London from 1773–74. He reportedly turned to writing after

---

30 Edmund Burke, *Reflections on the Revolution in France*, ed. J.G.A. Pocock. (Indianapolis, 1987).

receiving bad reviews for his theatrical work. He authored, edited and translated more than forty works of fiction, poetry, commentary on philosophy and religion, and criticism between 1774 and his death in 1814. To know him was to hate him, judging from comments in the letters of Sarah Siddons, Anna Seward—who called him "a wretch, convicted in twenty instances of assassination upon the fame of those to whom he owes no common obligations"—and Byron.[31] But despite Pratt's apparent inability to inspire sympathy in his own acquaintances, his works in the 1770s and 1780s show a dedication to the cult of sensibility then so popular. He even authored a work entitled *Sympathy: A Sketch of the Social Passion* (1781), a poetic essay in the tradition of Pope and Thomson in rhymed couplets that ran to sixty-six quarto pages and sold for sixpence a copy. At least five editions were printed in 1781–82.[32]

Emma Corbett is unabashedly sentimental at first, and quickly becomes drenched in sensibility. While Jerome McGann has argued that British writing evolved from a primitive sensibility into a more refined sentimentalism by the end of the eighteenth century, the cultural productions that arose out of the American Revolution challenge this progressive view of emotional rhetoric.[33] Civil conflict engenders situations— on the battlefield, at sea, between family members and lovers unable to transmit important news in a timely fashion—where the reflection requisite for sentiment is absent and an overflow of sensibility involves bodies, sometimes against their inclinations. In this respect, sensibility becomes a complex calculus, as Julie Ellis argues, not a primitive form of sociability.[34] The period covered by the novels about the American Revolution that I have mentioned and the relationship they explore are deeply invested in sensibility in an attempt to forge a geo-political entity despite geographical separation, a highly sophisticated endeavor.

A conflict between Charles Corbett and his daughter Emma sets *Emma Corbett*'s plot in motion. The latter loves the dashing, "sentimental" Henry Hammond—who will become controlled by sensibility before long—and before the novel proceeds too far she accepts his marriage proposal despite her father's vehement disapproval. These lovers have parallels in Emma's brother Edward and Henry's sister Louisa, who are secretly married. Charles Corbett also opposes Edward's and Louisa's union, though his reasons are vague. To keep the matter all in one family with the requisite obstinate patriarch in charge of all four improperly inclined children, Henry and Louisa are penniless orphans whom Charles Corbett has raised alongside his own children.

But despite *Emma Corbett*'s apparent similarities to so many sentimental productions with its theme of paternal resistance to the marital inclination of grown children, Charles Corbett is no gouty old James Harlowe seeking to increase the family fortunes through profitable alliances.[35] Corbett's chief objection to Henry

---

31 April London, "Samuel Jackson Pratt." *Dictionary of Literary Biography*, vol. 39. pp. 356–63; 356–7.

32 S.J. Pratt, *Sympathy: A Sketch of the Social Passion* (London, 1781, fifth edition).

33 Jerome McGann, *The Poetics of Sensibility: A Revolution in Literary Style* (Oxford, 1996), pp. 7–8.

34 Julie Ellison, *Cato's Tears and the Making of Anglo-American Emotion* (Chicago, 1999), p. 6.

35 Samuel Richardson, *Clarissa: Or, the History of a Young Lady*, ed. Angus Ross (New York, 1985).

Hammond is his decision to join the British forces sailing for the colonies in order to reduce America to subjection. Corbett has land in the colonies and believes his son Edward has died defending it from the British. Partly because of this, and partly for political reasons, Corbett's sympathy for the colonists has inspired a paternal affection greater than the one he feels for his own daughter. He addresses America apostrophically in a letter to a friend:

> Oh, thou hapless land! thou art precious to me beyond the breath which I am now drawing!—beyond every hope that I can form on this side Heaven!—beyond my daughter—yes, even beyond Emma, because thou art equally the object of my love, and more of my *pity!* The rapacious HENRY is gone to plunge another poignard in thy bosom!—the bosom of my country—the tomb of Emma's brother, and the vault of every generous affection. Nature herself lies bleeding on thy shore, and *there* the inhuman mother has plunged the dagger (with her own barbarous hand) into the bowels of her child!— (I:160–62).

Corbett's representation of the conflict relies on an intertwining of familial and corporeal metaphor. Many events have activated his sanguinary view, beginning with the (mistaken) report of his son Edward's death. "The blow which killed a son," Corbett writes, "had well nigh killed a father also" (I:6). He struggles to keep up a healthy appearance, "(b)ut the wound is not healed; it is still bleeding at my heart. To men's eyes it seems well. I have tied about it a political bandage, yet I secretly detest every principle which *begun*, and every motive which *continues*, this *assassination of America*" (I:6). Edward's death, the resulting debilitation of his father, and the association of an embodied America in their sufferings are all typical of the way Pratt works to maintain his controlling metaphor. The individual characters and the Corbett family are synecdoches for America *and* for the conflict. America is a political space, an elemental one—the "grave" in which Charles Corbett imagines his son—and a suffering child whose wounds are wounds on its parent.

Henry views the situation quite differently. His disagreement is both political, and more importantly for the purposes of this argument, representational. Corbett finds Henry's feelings against the "rebellious" Americans physically unsettling. He tells him by letter that his plans to join the British Army are "shocking to my nature. Whom I thought tender, him I find bloody" (I:7). But Henry will not battle on Corbett's chosen epistemological battlefield. A general sense of "duty" to his king binds him to Britain and its cause. "It is sufficient to a soldier that he believes his quarrel to be just," he argues. "You arraign my humanity. Wherefore? ... May we not consider a public contest in different points of view, and yet be friends?" (I:10–11). But for Corbett, this is not only a *public* contest, but one that concerns his family and his bodily constitution. Henry uses the language of honor in refusing Corbett's attempts to sway him to the American cause through his attachment to Emma. "Change sides! No, Sir; if these are to be the terms, take back the hand you *permitted* me to win, and possess, undivided, her fortune and your own. You have not looked accurately at my soul ... I am not ... so *sensual*, to gratify my passion at the expence of the holy faith and the solemn services which I have sworn to my country" (I:12).

The extreme sympathy for America that negates Charles Corbett's long-seated affection and fatherly concern for Henry brings his physical connection to the colonies to an unhealthy pitch. While he wears his "political bandage," his sympathies debilitate him throughout the novel until he is almost too weak to feed himself. His is clearly a case of what Claudia Johnson has called "emotions … saturated in turbulent and disfiguring excess."[36]

Emma's demonstration of the debilitating affects of sympathy takes the form of a heightened susceptibility to representations of war and its effects. Unlike her father, she is somewhat neutral in the conflict. She invests her sentiments and sympathy in Henry and because of this she tacitly accepts his cause. But she is too much her father's daughter to see the separation Henry's departure for America necessitates in terms of "duty" and "honor". Reflecting on the mixed emotions of feeling secure in his love for her, yet fearing for his safety, she allows her sensibility full play. "What feeling of the soul did not alternately assert its dominion?" she writes Henry as he prepares for his voyage to America; "I was disturbed, quieted, agonized, and made supremely happy" (I:30). Henry counsels against giving way to her feelings, but in terms that show he is not immune from sympathy's power, which will draw all of the novel's characters in before long. "Alas! what is to be done with this bleeding tenderness of your's (sic)?" he asks. "For Heaven's sake, temper your sensibility with a little discretion, my beloved Emma. Your elegant and affecting pages penetrate me to the soul. The tears of anguish mingle with those of admiration as I read them. Yet let me implore you to strengthen *your* mind a little, lest you wholly debilitate *mine*" (I:50). This admission of sensibility and sympathy in the midst of counseling against giving way too much to it soon yields to an exchange where emotional and bodily restraint soon disappear in a mutual "plight of feeling," in Julia Stern's phrase.[37]

Henry attempts to reassure Emma by invoking the materials of representation themselves. "The wide world of sentiment and sensation still opens upon us," he writes to her. "By aid of this little friendly instrument"—the pen—"we may range through those paths which ocean seems to separate" (I:51–2). Henry's invocation of distance and sympathy as reconcilable forces through the means of correspondence touches on the activating principle of Anglo-American sympathy. This is not necessarily a sympathy *for* America. In Henry's case it is far from that. But rather it manifests itself as an ability to feel sympathetically despite physical distance, and specifically to feel across the Atlantic despite threats that war will diminish not just sentiment, but the physical means of communicating it. "However remote" they may be from each other, Henry writes, Emma "should still learn to think it a superior blessing, that, in some part of animated nature, there still exists the counterpart of nature, there still exists the counterpart of Emma … who must ever remain true to every touch of joy, and every trembling of woe" (I:52). Correspondence, then, can convey even *physical* manifestations of sympathy, the "touch of joy" and "trembling of woe." It has already brought forth "tears of anguish mingle(d) with those of admiration," demonstrating representation's actions on the body, and its ability to mingle seemingly contradictory emotions in a single bodily fluid.

---

36 Claudia Johnson, *Equivocal Beings: Politics, Gender, and Sentimentality in the 1790s* (Chicago, 1995), p. 1.

37 Julia Stern, *The Plight of Feeling: Sympathy and Dissent in the Early American Novel* (Chicago: University of Chicago Press, 1997).

Sending and receiving letters across an ocean and the vicissitudes of weather and shipping creates a temporal gap of six weeks in the best of times, in addition to the geographical one of thousands of miles. War only exacerbates this. Emma rarely hears from Henry after he leaves for America. She never receives news in direct response to urgent pleas she sends. While her sympathy remains firmly with Henry, she displaces her sympathetic responses onto two representations of war and dismemberment that shape her understanding of the American conflict. The first occurs when she receives a torn collection of papers entitled "A Military Fragment" written at an uncertain time in the past by the father of her cousin Caroline. This distant relative was a soldier who came across two brothers serving as orderlies at a field hospital at an undisclosed location. The second comes when Emma views a painting of a battle and draws out its bloody meanings through an examination of various details. I will return to these two aspects of the text later to show how acts of narration set up a refracted understanding of war's effect on the Anglo-American nation. Emma's readings become moments of ekphrasis, with war the subject and sympathy the controlling aesthetic through which it   becomes understood. By absorbing these violent accounts, Emma suffers and, presumably, the late eighteenth-century reader did as well.

Emma's ekphrastic breakdowns drive her on a secret trip to America to find Henry. She realizes that as long as her sympathy remains temporally and spatially distanced it cannot bring about any healing. Julie Ellison, in a discussion of Adam Smith's *Theory of Moral Sentiments* where Smith argues that one does not need to have sympathy "for those 'out of the sphere of our activity,' 'those at the greatest distance' from us, people who might as well inhabit 'the world in the moon,'" asks a number of questions relevant to the Anglo-American national body Pratt conjures up in *Emma Corbett*: "How fast should our sympathies outrun our agency? Will liberal guilt proliferate under expanded representational conditions? Does our changing of our role in a global system of interdependence increase the legitimate range of duty? Are the Age of Sensibility and the Age of Mechanical Reproduction the same thing?"[38] Space keeps sympathy from creating community, but not from operating and debilitating those who feel it. The reproduction of Pratt's text spreads his sympathetic message to a body of readers on both sides of the Atlantic, making his argument for Anglo-American sympathy plausible.

Emma, unlike Pratt and his readers, has to rely on ships, pen, ink, and paper rather than on presses and bookshops to send and receive her sympathetic narrative. This fails much more often than it succeeds as long as she remains in England. To put it briefly, she discovers that Anglo-American sympathy leads only to pain and illness. Her distress over her father's refusal to make peace with Henry affects her deeply. Corbett can take sides, although he reacts bitterly to the fact of having to do so. Emma is connected to both men and feels obliged to reconcile the two. She challenges the language of amputation that runs through much of the book by characterizing the war as "civil pestilence," which she hopes will not rage between her father and herself "in the form of a *family-war*" (II:201). A pestilence, while rampant in this case, at least leaves an outside possibility of a cure. A "*family-war,*"

---

38 Ellison, *Cato's Tears*, p. 11–12.

she feels, "would violate the gentle law of nature, and tear down those conciliating ties which fasten *kindred* in one vast chain of connexion, ample as earth, and beautiful as heaven" (II:201). But Charles Corbett derides his daughter's feelings and forces her to flee his house and seek Henry across the ocean. He argues that his affection for America is deeper and better founded than her love for Henry.

Once in America she disguises herself as an Indian boy and comes across Henry's wounded, nearly dead body, in the forests near Washington's army. She finds "the body yet warm, the pulse slowly moving, and the heart languidly beating with life." An Indian allied to the Americans has shot Henry with an arrow. She extracts the arrow, "and suck(s) the wound—she had heard of the Indians using shafts whose points were envenomed: and rightly concluding *this* to be one of them, applied to it her lovely lips without hesitation" (III:113–14). Love and the immediate presence of her object of sympathy, it seems, turn Emma into something of a superwoman. But in attempting to take the wounds of others onto herself, she brings down the entire sympathetic structure. Henry heals, but the poison from the arrow slowly works its way into Emma's system until her death is a foregone conclusion. Henry reacts by contracting a fever brought on by excessive worrying, and dies. Emma, pregnant with their child, lingers long enough to get back to England and give birth, after which she dies as well. It seems that Henry's earlier emphasis on duty and honor was effective as long as England and America were seen as political entities whose metaphorical connections remained on a rhetorical level. But once the conflict between the two becomes embodied, first in his own blood through the poisoned arrow that brings him down, then in Emma's system through a transfusion of the same poison, and finally in both as their sympathetic dependence on one another deepens, affective responses trump intellectual ones.

By the time of Emma's death, other sympathetic deaths, interwoven with hers, have reduced the Anglo-American Corbett family to the impotent, enervated Charles Corbett and his orphaned grandchildren. Corbett comes closest to representing liberal English sentiment towards the colonies. His emotional excesses place him almost in the position of one of Mary Wollstonecraft's "equivocal beings." He is both "unmanned" and "unsexed" by his susceptibility to affect.[39] George Washington makes a brief appearance in *Emma Corbett*, and by contrast shows how one can be both "manly" and sentimental. He displays "the graceful dignity of a tear" at hearing the story of Emma's separation from Henry while both are captives of the Continental Army, and sets them free (III:69). But then, rather than anguishing over the disruptions between the colonies and England, he proceeds to prosecute the war.

The English characters, or those who might be considered Anglo-American, like Emma's brother Edward, are less able to separate affect from politics. Edward, initially thought dead, is discovered alive in America, but soon dies in his sister's presence after moving undecidedly between family concerns and military duties and, in the process, exposing himself to the enemy. Louisa, home in England, gives birth to a child that resulted from her secret marriage to Edward, but she dies when she hears the news of her husband's death. The only character to survive with any degree of

---

39 Mary Wollstonecraft, *Vindication of the Rights of Woman*, ed. Carol Poston (New York, 1988), p. 138.

health is Sir Robert Raymond. An apolitical friend of the family, Sir Robert contracts a respectful passion for Emma and follows her to America, where he helps her find Henry. He eventually helps her home where she dies almost immediately in childbirth and he becomes the guardian of the orphans Emma, Henry, Louisa, and Edward have left behind. Significantly, Sir Robert is the only character who expresses complete neutrality in the political conflict, and who has no family tie to any of the Corbetts. The sympathetic family as nation virtually dissolves in the end, with Sir Robert left to take care of Emma's feeble father and two children who will grow up without parents. Their orphaned status breaks the dependence of the novel on the mixed familial-corporeal metaphor, but at the cost of the imagined nation and its rightful leaders.

War Games and the Violence of Representation

The "Military Fragment" that brings on Emma's first breakdown figures the nation as a mutilated body. *The Critical Review*'s discussion of *Emma Corbett* focuses almost entirely on this section of the text. "As a specimen of the work," the reviewer writes, "we shall present our readers with an extract from a digression entitled, A Military Fragment."[40] The review's terms—"specimen," "extract," and "digression"—are significant to the argument I have been trying to make concerning both the representative nature of *Emma Corbett* and its representational mode. The text's main work is fragmentary and digressive. Through this rhetorical strategy Pratt communicates the dissolution of the controlling metaphor. While the "Military Fragment" is a digression both from the plot and from the focus on the American Revolution, it represents the attack on the bodies of the characters who represent the text, and on the text that offers the representation. *The Critical Review* shows a contemporary engagement with the notions of bodily transmitted sympathy and fragmentary narration's role in heightening this experience.

The fragment tells the story of brothers Julius and Nestor Carbine, who have been serially maimed throughout decades of common soldiering for England. Each wears his wounds as badges of honor that represent, cumulatively, the political progress of the nation in their lifetimes. Significantly, the meaning borne in their mutilated bodies attaches neither to generals nor monarch. The understanding that the anonymous soldier's body is metonymically the body of the English nation supports contemporary descriptions of the political unit as a sympathetically activated organism rather than a Hobbesian machine, or a set of bodies that make up the whole which the sovereign represents in his person. As such, it is significant that these brothers' mutilated bodies present relationships of kinship—both by blood and occupation—rather than representing kingship in a hierarchically structured nation. Pratt may have been attempting to parallel Julius and Nestor with the Indian warriors in *Oroonoko* who vie for the right to represent their tribe by mutilating themselves to determine who can endure more.[41] In any case, Caroline gives their story to Emma to reassure her that soldiers retain their ability to feel emotional attachments despite

---

40 *The Critical Review*, June 1780, p. 460.

41 Aphra Behn, *Oroonoko, or The Royal Slave: A True History*, ed. Joanna Lipking (New York, 1997), p. 50.

their brutal occupations. But Emma focuses on the maiming of these brothers, the death of Nestor's wife and the sympathy that makes these injuries and losses more acute rather than on a disembodied notion of sentiment that Caroline advocates.

Julius and Nestor have lost cheeks, legs, arms, and fingers in the nation's service. Most significantly, Nestor has lost his wife to a fever. She became ill nursing her husband on one of his furloughs and died of the illness war had initially inflicted upon him (II:67). This loss, described by Julius despite his brother's attempt to silence his narration, reduces Nestor to tears. In Julius's words, it "unsoldiers" him (II:67). Nestor has the consolation of several children whom he instructs in war games, training a new generation for mutilation just as he and his brother were trained as boys. "We slept in the same cradle, and were nursed up for the service," Nestor explains of their upbringing. "Our little arms—He flourished a stump which projected about four inches from the right shoulder—Our little arms—" he says, but is interrupted by a diversion in the narrative (II:40–41). In this fragment within the fragment—within an epistolary novel that often comes across as a patchwork of fragments—we see the epitome of the challenge the family metaphor gets from the corporeal metaphor. Nestor's useless stump of an upper arm is both an arm of national policy and an arm of war. By presenting it in a gesture that makes it a stand-in for a child's arm he implicates the ravages of war in both the dismemberment of his physical body and the destruction of familial bonds. These competing ways of figuring the nation contend throughout Pratt's novel and several others from the period in ways that make this particular mixed metaphor emblematic of the difficulty of expressing Anglo-America as a nation that could withstand conflict.

The "Military Fragment" communicates to Emma and the reader its failure as a representational space in several ways. Its content is its most obvious form of communicating dismemberment. These bodies in service of the nation, as mentioned, are almost too mutilated to represent men anymore. As its author, Caroline's father, remarks: "It is not without just cause that I called Nestor a *remnant*. Nature originally formed him in her fairest proportions. At the time I saw him he was a capital figure reduced" (II:41). The fragment depicts Nestor's loss of his wife in terms of debilitating sympathy that makes him unfit to serve the nation or his children in a consistent fashion anymore. As Julius tells the story of her death, Nestor seems to relive the feelings it caused. Instead of heeding his brother's commands to stop his story, Julius uses the death of his sister-in-law as an object lesson. "The brush of a bullet is nothing at all," he says. "(I)t may take off your head, or it may only take off your hat: either way, no great matter—but the cries of a woman, the piercing agonies of a wife, to come across one's thoughts in the last moments—no, Sir,—no, damn it—there is no bearing that—I will live and die a bachelor!" (II:66). The fragment's narrator concludes that the death of Nestor's wife was the death of him as well. She "lay dead before his eyes," he writes, "and there being but one bed of any size, the living and the dead lay together" (II:69). The ravages of sympathy here reduce all the brothers' bravado about their wounds to nothing, and make it clear that sympathetically incurred death reduces the nation, whether figured as a body or family, to commonality only in the grave.

Beyond the mutilated bodies and decimated family the fragment represents, a dramatic textual mutilation challenges the ability of even the most sympathetic story to make meaning. Foucault asserts that sympathy functioned as a form of resemblance in the sixteenth century, but fractioned with the Enlightenment.[42] One can see something like this fractioning on display in the fragment's persistence in creating narrative division. Asterisks and bracketed commentary make it clear that the fragment is defaced or torn in at least five places. Caroline's father has left the document ripped and spotted with the evidence of his emotional response to the events it recounts, as well as to his own act of recounting them. The soldier's tears on the defaced fragment link it to the corporeality of its writer, just as Emma's emotional reaction to the story it tells links it to her body. These rips often occur in places where sympathy overwhelms the reader, and through her, the text. One comes after Nestor's children finish a bitterly contested war game under the direction of their father and uncle, then patch up their differences and offer up "a general huzza" for "great George our King" (II:54). In this miniature version of civil conflict—directed by the mutilated, anonymous representatives of the nation, pitting brothers against each other—such an armistice can unite all under the national father. But the Revolution, which it metonymically gestures towards so insistently, cannot make narrative sense out of such an ending, and the document, like the story it bears, must fragment.

The fragment's most significant rip occurs at the point when it communicates the effect of war upon the organism as a whole as figured in Nestor's wife. At that point, the imagined editor of the collection of letters that make up the novel inserts a bracketed note: "(The fragment is here defaced, and illegible for some pages.)" (II:71). We are led to understand that the defacement is caused both by the anguish of shaking and convulsive hands, which have gripped the paper unconsciously and repeatedly, and the tears of Caroline's father, which have made the ink run until the feature of the textual body made up of pen marks has become illegible. But significantly, the text itself—the paper on which it is written, and the traces of ink that make the paper the bearer of a tale—remains to testify that some story once existed, and that its power to induce sympathy in its writer has effaced it, perhaps even as it was written. And even though the text is effaced, the knowledge that tears and turbulence have done the damage is enough to evoke sympathy in whomever attempts to read its mutilated remains. In a sense, then, bodies can survive excessive bouts of sympathetic response, but in doing so they become so altered that they fail to represent their original state.

The text's final defacement comes at the point when it most explicitly and complicatedly communicates sympathy's power to travel from one body to another. While leaving, Caroline's father and his child—whose name is never mentioned—notice a tear on Nestor's face, brought on by the tale of his wife's death. When one of his children attempts to wipe it off, Nestor says: "Leave it alone, my dear … IT IS YOUR MOTHER'S." Imperceptibly, the tear disappears from Nestor's face. In a moment Caroline's father notices it again, but now on his own daughter's face. "Good God, said I, how rapid an exchange!" In another moment, it finds its way to his own face. "I found the precious offering of sympathy had changed a *third* time its residence," the old soldier writes, "and was trembling on my own cheek. I

---

42 Michel Foucault, *The Order of Things: An Archaeology of the Human Sciences* (New York, 1994), pp. 23–5.

blessed it, and …" There, in mid-sentence, the fragment breaks off for the final time (II:73–5). The tear that Nestor's wife's memory has induced has traveled through texts and time, uniting speakers and listeners, writers and readers, texts and bodies in an almost endless flow of sympathy. While this presents a hope that the Anglo-American nation still maintains a circulating principle of vitality despite political and military conflict, this sympathy circulates destructively, eating at texts, bodies, and nations parasitically.

Caroline hopes this "precious offering of sympathy," from the dead wife of a humble soldier through a mangled text to Emma, will bring solace to her cousin. But instead of doing so, it induces a physical breakdown, showing that the effects of sympathy have been just as detrimental to her as to Nestor (II:77). This ekphrastically communicated sympathy leads to another. Emma goes to the country with her father to calm her nerves, but while there sees a battle scene in the library of Sir Robert Raymond's house. "See—see, into that wretch's quivering side, the ball has just entered!" she exclaims to Sir Robert at the beginning of a description that brings out all the gore in the painting.

> Here lies a head severed from the body.—There are the mangled reliques of an arm torn from the shoulder; and there the wounded horses are trampling upon their wounded masters! … '—Ah, EARTH, thou common parent—thou whose nourishing bosom furnishes to *all* the children of *content* that will *cultivate* thee, how art thou made the object of ambition, and the motive of sanguine altercation! (II:132–3)

She goes on to blame the Earth itself for tempting avarice by containing stores of gold.

But greed is a side issue here. The mixture of mangled bodies and unnaturally warring families is Emma's main concern. "(I)n yonder corner they are employed in removing the dying and the dead," she tells Sir Robert, transfixed by the painting:

> 'In that lacerated body there yet seems life. It is panting in the picture!—how the streams of—Ah, my God! the hoof of a horse seems ready to stamp upon his bosom—another sword is pointed at his throat.—Stop, stop barbarian—he is of thy *kind*—he is thy fellow-creature—perhaps he is closely, dearly, TENDERLY connected—restrain thy sacrilegious hand—kill not her whose existence is interwoven with his—kill not his helpless *children*—respect the tender state of unprotected infancy—respect the softening bonds of FAMILY—respect thy GOD' (II:134–5).

I have quoted at length to show the attempts—and failures—of the text to sustain connected narrative when controlled by the power of sympathy focused on civil conflict. The fact that letters both bear and inspire tears and that bodies "still pant" in paintings offers the hope that representation can bring about animation. But the halting nature of these representations testifies to their inevitable failures. Emma's narrative shows that this inability to communicate complete stories affects not only texts, but their makers, and the bodies of both. She responds to her own act of narration by fainting. A long illness follows, succeeded by a determination to get to America to see Henry. At this point in the novel sympathy has successively debilitated Emma and inspired her. But while inspiration restores health, it also threatens it by sending her into harm's way. Sympathy moves in and out of narratives and representations of those narratives, like the tear in Nestor's story, occasionally bringing the semblance of vigor, but more reliably serving as a carrier of something akin to disease.

Temporality and the Nation

Numerous inconsistencies in representing temporal alignment can be seen in the writings of those who wanted to argue America was a part of England. "Savages" in English writing were assignable to an earlier point on a shared evolutionary progression. But colonists could not easily be placed into a separate anthropological time. They were ostensibly treated as belonging to the same cultural moment. Still, the difficulty in communications across the Atlantic meant that a sick daughter in Pennsylvania might write a letter to the father of a dead one in England. And as we have seen, it is the time of reading in which the plot of America as related by blood or marriage, or organically integral to England, makes itself known in the English text and in the mind of the English reader. America thus emerges as belonging to a separate time in the succession of letters in an epistolary novel, but not a time that comes either before or after the time of the reader. The reader experiences the emotions of a first connection to events, and the agony of knowing that these new, unknown events have replaced the ones she is reading, almost palimpsestically. The events upon which plots rely—deaths, births, marriages, battles—are quick and sharp. But since their communication across the Atlantic is slow and uncertain, the reading of them is a triple trauma: the first akin to the event itself, a second that is empathetic, and a third that recognizes the reading party's powerlessness to avert or ameliorate the crisis or take part in the celebration. American events have always already happened in English texts.

"The author (as creator of the novelistic whole)," Bakhtin argues, "cannot be found at any one of the novel's language centers: he is to be found at the center of organization where all levels intersect."[43] While this explains how the author exists, and how meaning becomes manifest, Bakhtin was not talking about the novel as the document of national recuperation towards which these novels aspire. Also, the anonymously-published epistolary novels about America that I have been discussing introduce a challenge to the idea of authorship, since they contain multiple texts by multiple characters, without a single authorial presence arguing for their coherence in any "center of organization." Part of these works' aim is to create just such a "center of organization," but in this they rarely succeed. *Emma Corbett* is a text with multiple authors, and in that sense, one with multiple texts that strive unsuccessfully to build national narratives that include England and America. While there is always an assumed author, the combination of anonymous authorship and radical polyglossia is destabilizing, and possibly traumatic in works that consider who does or does not belong to the nation as a social, cultural and political entity. Helen Maria Williams largely solves this problem by treating the intertextual introduction of the American

---

43 Mikhail Bakhtin, *The Dialogic Imagination: Four Essays,* ed. Michael Holquist; trans. Caryl Emerson and Michael Holquist (Austin, 1981), pp. 48–9.

Revolution as a foreign, unincorporatable text in her novel *Julia* (1790), probably the most successful example of a novelistic positioning of Englishness and Americanness in terms of one another in the late eighteenth century. Williams avoids the higher emotional pitch Pratt registers by introducing Americans unknown to those reading their stories, as I show below in a discussion of sentiment in these novels.

Much modern criticism of the epistolary form optimistically seizes on the heteroglossia inherent to the form as a "narrative strategy." The term itself implies conscious intent. Some, like Nicola Watson, credit epistolarity with bringing about an "uncontainable formal extravagance" that "provided fertile material for novelists of all persuasions working in the wake of the (French) Revolution, and in the light of successive and competing interpretations of events in France and England alike."[44] Watson also claims that the language of sentiment "supplied what was undoubtedly a potentially radical politics of subjectivity, promulgating a notion of exquisite individual sensibility."[45] Elizabeth Cook discusses ways in which the epistolary novel

> is formally and thematically concerned with competing definitions of subjectivity: it puts into play the tension between the private individual, identified with a specifically gendered, classed body that necessarily commits it to specific forms of self-interest, and the public person, divested of self-interest, discursively constituted, and functionally disembodied.[46]

While such arguments about destabilizing subjectivity make it possible to recognize more important public roles for subjects marginalized along gender and class lines, they fail to take into account yearnings for national narratives in times of crisis. Epistolary fictions destabilize subjects, possibly in liberating ways, but they also destabilize nations and temporalities. They frustrate attempts to solve what Lukács describes as "the problem of the artistic mastery of history."[47]

The present's multiple temporalities become noticeably dissonant only when it becomes crucial that they not be so. In the 1780s temporal dissonance becomes one sign of an irreducible difference that had not been seen before, or at least not represented in literature until it was done so in a hopeless attempt to explain it out of existence. The persistence of this difference frustrates efforts to subdue or suppress other differences—those relating to cultural practices, religious beliefs, socioeconomic organization, national self-definition—and as such, it becomes the crucial point of rupture that prevents the re-imagining of the English and their colonists as part of the same community, or as participants in the same metaphor.

Popular fiction's main difficulty in representing the Revolution was related to its narrative conventions. Popular novelistic conventions in England at the end of the eighteenth century demanded teleologically oriented plots. But history, especially

---

44 Nicola Watson, *Revolution and the Form of the English Novel, 1790–1825: Intercepted Letters, Interrupted Seductions* (Oxford, 1994), p. 15.

45 Ibid., p. 25.

46 Elizabeth Heckendorn Cook, *Epistolary Bodies: Gender and Genre in the Eighteenth-Century Republic of Letters* (Stanford, CA, 1996), p. 8.

47 Georg Lukács, *The Historical Novel*, pref. Fredric Jameson; trans. Hannah and Stanley Mitchell (Lincoln, 1983), p. 22.

when recent or contemporary, while crying out for organization and direction in the form of a sequential, progressive, linear narrative, is incompatible with a telos. It is always still happening, and beginnings and endings are always arbitrary. For this reason, these novels, often political, always social, with ambitions towards presenting themselves as historical novels that explain events, as well as social and economic configurations, dynamics, and relations in the form of a plot, must fail one of the ultimate goals of emplotment, namely, conclusiveness.[48] Including news of America the way it would appear discursively in the lives of English readers meant reproducing temporal and textual ruptures, and placed the period's novels and other cultural productions in the position of having to admit to an inability to reconcile the two nations, and in the process, also to admit that there actually *were* two nations. Multiple plots figure persistently in these works. The American episodes, rather than serving as subplots, declare independence. If their beginnings are uncertain, their endings are definite, and independent of those of the novels as wholes. Henry, and Edward die in America in *Emma Corbett*. Captain F—, Sophia, and all their connections die in Williams's *Julia*. So does the title character in the anonymous *The Liberal American* (1785), which describes an Englishwoman's estrangement from everyone dear to her because of her forced emigration. These deaths are American deaths for the most part, not deaths belonging to the plots of the novels in which they occur. These novels' American episodes have endings that shape the time they relate, while English time keeps its isochronous succession flowing. The subplot becomes the plot with the ending, while the main plot aspires towards continuity.

While all epistolary novels present the temporal disjunction I have been discussing, at least four things about the relationship between England and America at this moment in history make representation of national trauma the issue, rather than simply literary devices for heightening dramatic tension. Distance, war, a desire for national identification, and radical polyglossia conspire to prevent epistolarity from being an enabling "narrative strategy." Instead, they make imagining the nation impossible as long as that nation is intent on spanning the Atlantic and maintaining temporal cohesion.

Time and Narrative

Time has been crucial to English relationships with ideas of North America for more than five hundred years. The earliest English writings about the continent's first inhabitants, published before any English settlers had arrived, mostly participate in denying these Others co-evalness with Europeans, in the way that Johannes Fabian has argued anthropological writing always does. Before colonization and the resulting establishment of a large English-speaking population, American time was written as primeval, and easily distinguishable from European time. During and immediately after the American Revolution a different sort of temporal disconnection emerges in English writing. Colonial Americans, while not represented as English,

---

48 See Paul Ricoeur, *Time and Narrative*, trans. Kathleen McLaughlin and David Pellauer (3 vols, Chicago, 1984), vol. 1, pp. 147–51.

were still assumed to be part of the same linguistic and cultural community, the same time-frame. But just when it was most important to suppress differences and gaps in this imagined community, temporality emerged as a discordant element, marring texts aimed at exploring consanguinity and familial ties. Neither Walter Benjamin's concept of empty homogenous time, with its emphasis on a continuous time filled by random events, ordered by clock or calendar, nor Frank Kermode's and Paul Ricoeur's notions of temporality manifesting itself through emplotted beginnings, middles, and endings, are able to address the aporia of time that crowds out metaphors of familial and bodily connection in late eighteenth-century English novels about America.[49]

The differences between concepts of temporality put forth by narrative theorists like Kermode and Ricoeur, and of a time that moved not from a beginning to an end, but sequentially and isochronically, as argued for by Benjamin and Benedict Anderson, are stark. But all depend on assumptions of co-temporal existence, and imply that the time of reading is what counts, both in the sense of being significant, and in the sense of marking time and events. The letter is a contract, which is only fulfilled once it has been read, unlike a diary or journal, which ostensibly exists as an individual's expression with no need of external validation. In that sense, the letter is the most social form of writing. Anderson's argument that the newspaper is also a socially binding form of textuality assumes that a nation, or a community, is bound by the extent of a publication's circulation. One is left to infer that a people experience a time; peoples do not. Anderson's idea of nations coming into being largely through simultaneous reading experiences places limitations on the geographical extent of imagined communities in an era of slow communication. His national formations depend upon "(t)he idea of a sociological organism moving calendrically through homogeneous, empty time." This motion "is a precise analogue of the idea of the nation, which also is conceived as a solid community moving steadily down (or up) history."[50] English readers didn't experience America as it "happened" in the late eighteenth century, but they still persisted in trying to imagine themselves as belonging to the same social body, the same national formation.

Several English novels from the last two decades of the eighteenth century show the frustrated efforts of characters to contribute—usually through letters—to an emplotted version of the Anglo-American community to which they believed they contemporaneously belonged. But the violence time does to these texts shows an irreconcilability between England and America that the mere use of the same language and invocation of the same cultural history cannot eliminate. It is precisely the notion of solidity and steadiness invoked by Anderson that these novels challenge and defeat. His idea that a member of a nation "has complete confidence" in the belief of the other inhabitants of his nation's "steady, anonymous, simultaneous activity" is

---

49 I am indebted to Stuart Sherman's discussion of time in eighteenth century texts in *Telling Time: Clocks, Diaries, and English Diurnal Form, 1660–1785* (Chicago, 1996) for many of the ideas that this section develops, including the distinctions between narrative time and empty homogeneous time.

50 Benedict Anderson, *Imagined Communities: Reflections on the Origin and Spread of Nationalism*, revised ed. (London, 1991), p. 26.

inapplicable to characters in novels where communication is frustrated by a gap of six weeks under the best circumstances, and in which there is a real uncertainty that letters traveling in either direction will *ever* reach their intended recipients (given the complications war adds to those of distance).[51] English novels about America in the late eighteenth century thus resist Bakhtinian chronotopes, those "time spaces" where "spatial and temporal indicators are fused into one carefully thought-out, concrete whole," no matter how hard their authors try to construct them.[52]

The America that English readers encountered in Pratt's *Emma Corbett*, the anonymous *The Liberal American* (1785), and Helen Maria Williams's *Julia* has much in common with England; all of these novels, written during the Revolution and in the decade following the Paris peace treaty that ended it, contain features that have often been put forth as evidence of cultural interdependence, such as manners, heritage, history and religion. But America often shows up as a separate text in these works. *Emma Corbett* and *The Liberal American* are epistolary novels, so everything is of course a separate text. But letters from America are especially separate. They come in packets enclosed in letters to friends of relatives, conveyed by ships that accidentally meet crossing the ocean, and are often second-, third-, or even fourth-hand accounts rather than direct communications. In *Julia* America shows up in a packet of letters from characters who take no part in the novel's main plot, and whose experiences introduce a world of violence and loss into what remains a safe, domestic scene.

The temporal dislocations shown in the crossing of letters across the Atlantic, the long delay of news of life and death, the fortunes of war, courtship, and marriage, all of which occasion serious misconceptions in the minds of several characters, communicate the sense that England and America are fundamentally separate societies. The novel's realistic form forces an intertextuality on communications between characters, highlighting the disconnectedness caused by America's physical separation from England. My intent is to identify a narrative about America that emerges through the multiple texts that constitute it. The task these novels try but fail to perform is the narration of a national configuration in which England and America both belong. The letters, journal entries, and other fragments are the texts put to work in the attempt to construct this narrative. The narrative that finally coalesces is a double one where England and America emerge as similar, yet incompatible, nations.

---

51 Ibid., p. 26. Throughout this section, as should be clear by my reliance on Anderson's concept of the imagined community, I will be using the terms "nation" and "national" to refer to a social and cultural construct with an unidentified form of Englishness at its center, not to the state. While this use of these terms is much less precise than some others, this is by choice. The "nation," as conceived by many late eighteenth century English writers, was a fluid concept. Some, such as an anonymous pamphleteer writing in 1778, were able to write that it was "a matter of total indifference whether the *English* under General Howe, or the *English* under General Washington prevail" ("Considerations on the Present State of Affair Between England and America." (London: J. Nourse et al, 1778). For such writers, "UNION is the INTEREST of ENGLAND," (4) and England is capacious enough to contain those on both sides of the Atlantic.

52 Bakhtin, *The Dialogic Imagination*, p. 84.

Williams's *Julia* is in many ways an anti-sentimental novel. As Anne Mellor has noted, Williams condemns "excessive sensibility" in this work that centers on the unlicensed passion of a man for his fiancée's—then wife's—best friend.[53] But as in *Emma Corbett*, the American Revolution enters this novel and brings chaos with it, all wrapped in the language of sentiment despite resistance to such language throughout the rest of the text. *Julia* functions for the most part as a social novel, focusing on the minor English gentry as a class, and the condition of young women with moderate fortunes and no maternal guidance in the late eighteenth century. Its main plot unfolds in undated, unhistorical time, but the first of its two volumes closes with a specifically dated, geographically located episode. *Julia* moves briefly and abruptly from being a social novel to an historical one. While lacking the consciousness of class struggle and economic conditions that Lukács argues separate the historical novel invented by Sir Walter Scott in the early nineteenth century from the realistic social novel that preceded it, *Julia* communicates, in its brief American episode, the sense of national trauma that arose from a specific set of historical events and conditions. These amount, to an extent, to what Lukács describes as an "understanding of history as a process, of history as the concrete precondition of the present," though that process was chaotic, and the present it conditioned must choose between accepting that chaos, or keeping it at a distance by not incorporating this intertextual interruption into the main plot.[54]

Missing in *Julia*'s ambitions towards historical novel status are, in Lukács's words, "the concrete possibilities for (people) to comprehend their own existence as something historically conditioned, for them to see in history something which deeply affects their daily lives and immediately concerns them."[55] Julia, unlike Emma, does not go to America to experience the ravages of war firsthand. The way the Revolution breaks violently into the novel with no apparent reason, and disappears just as inexplicably, prevents the characters with whom the main plot is concerned from connecting it to their lives in any meaningful way. An admirer of Julia, Mr. F—, shows up one day after his offer of marriage has been rejected, and tells her that his brother has recently died. He offers to share with Julia and her close friend Charlotte a packet of letters relating to the events that led to his death. In a novel that could, until that time, have taken place any time during the eighteenth century, any place in England, all of a sudden a date and place are announced. Mr. F—'s packet of letters is addressed "To G— F—, Esq., Long Island, August, 1776" (I:140).

Mr. F—'s name—or lack of one—is a perfect example of Williams's practice of effacing specificity throughout *Julia*. Several characters go by initials. Places are interchangeable, and the novel seems intent on teaching general lessons of conduct, not discussing specific situations or minute circumstances. Why, then, does a novel published in England in 1790 suddenly make clear that it is set in 1776? Why has the American Revolution gone unmentioned for most of the first volume if it represents the novel's historical context? *Julia*'s modern critics have ignored these questions.

---

53 Anne Mellor, *Romanticism & Gender* (London, 1993), p. 46.

54 Lukács, *The Historical Novel*.

55 Ibid., p. 24.

Williams has become important to feminist criticism of the Romantic period for her advocacy of rationalism over sentimentalism as the proper mode of female action and art, and her political interpellations, particularly in *Julia*, have been persuasively read as examples of female participation in the public discursive sphere. While her discussion of the American Revolution and its disastrous effects on familial attachments has been ignored in feminist criticism, a later episode entitled "The Bastille: A Prophecy," which also comes from nowhere and goes nowhere, has been discussed in connection to the public sphere debate.[56] But feminist criticism can be excused for ignoring the sudden appearance of dates and places in *Julia*, because the novel signals that these moments are incongruous with the rest of what it has to say. Ironically, these two specific historical moments in the novel come across as metaphors or allegories for what the novel's *really* about, while the rest of the text, undated and fairly traditionally plotted, reads like a document of cultural history. George Washington shows up briefly, but his presence as a character in a novel that has made no place for dates, places, or identifiable figures serves further to distance America from an England where time flows, rather than jerking along violently.[57]

One possible reason *Julia* does not incorporate its American episode into its plot is that America simply does not fit into English time. The insistence of the date that introduces the tragic story of Mr. F—'s brother, the woman he loves and her family already violates a sociological sense of time that depends upon accepted social conventions and relations between family and friends. It has not mattered what day or year it is up to this point because human history and national history have been kept apart. Dates, names, and places are all crutches for a storyline that does not make organic sense. War is anti-relational, anti-social, and unrelentingly historical. History wars on the social and the relational, which are *Julia*'s ideological concerns. Once dates and places begin to matter, people and relationships are threatened.

The threats are clear throughout *Julia*'s American episode. The story is introduced by Frances Lawrence, who has compiled a packet of letters between Captain F— and Sophia Herbert, his American lover. Lawrence frames the narrative with an accompanying letter. Through his action of compiling the packet that haltingly tells the violent story of how the Revolution has taken the lives of Captain F—, Sophia, her father and her brother, he achieves the status of author. But his authorship is exclusively related to America. In his plot, Captain F— is English, but significantly has nothing to do with England. The American plot's sentiment is directly at odds with Williams's determination to keep her English heroines rational. Both Sophia and her father fall victim as much to sentiment as to any outward force. Although Mr. Herbert dies in the war, it's only after his son has died and he joins the army in an irrational moment. Sophia's death comes in a fit of delirium after she hears of

---

56 Mellor, *Romanticism & Gender*, pp. 44–6; Watson, *Revolution and Form in the English Novel*, pp. 34–6.

57 Washington is a common participant in novels and other fictional works about the Revolution, so much so that it's hard to see how he had time to prosecute a war while giving aid to distressed English women on such a regular basis. For the most part he's treated sympathetically. One significant exception is Anna Seward's "Monody on the Death of Major André," about the execution of the British spy who was a longtime friend of hers.

Captain F—'s having fallen in battle (I:143–51). Part of what does not fit undated, unmarked English time, I would argue, is this forceful, fitful experience of a time that brings violence upon its participants through sentimental reactions to traumatic events. English time seems relatively free of events that qualify as historical. People talk, go on walks in the country, visit with each other, and occasionally attend functions. Everything moves in a stream of time whose moments lose individuality in the more important work of expressing thoughts and feelings rationally, and living carefully and safely. American time is made up of nothing *but* events, and all tend to the destruction of those foundations of the social world that *Julia* endorses. As Lawrence notes in the closing of his letter to Mr. F— concerning Sophia's fate, "(s)he is at rest, and this cruel war had made her happiness impossible" (I:152).

The sort of temporal disjunction this chapter focuses on has crucial consequences for the characters of *The Liberal American* (1785), an anonymous epistolary novel set half in England, half in New York, presumably right after the Revolution. Like *Emma Corbett*, *The Liberal American* is a sentimental novel dealing with the amorous ambitions of several young people. Sophia Aubrey, the novel's heroine, is an orphan dependent upon her aunt. She is brought to New York, where her aunt's new husband, Mr. Villars, has to go because of the loss of his fortune. He expects family connections in America to help him improve his financial standing. Sophia has no illusions about America and England being parts of the same nation. She laments the fact that she has to leave in a letter to her friend Louisa, and wonders "(w)hat can be more distressing to a feeling mind than to be removed from every dear connexion, and placed in a land of strangers!"[58] The Americans she meets aboard ship are crass and unfriendly. Those she meets in America, with a few exceptions, are uncultured and in some senses mingled with conceptions of savagery, a sign of the return of English representations of time to representations of anthropological difference after the war that Chapter Three examines. Will Honeycomb, who has eyes for Sophia, is an example of this pre-modern vision of Americanness. His unwelcome attentions put Sophia "into a horrid ill-humour. That such a being should imagine that his attentions can possibly be agreeable! I have been often inclined to shut my eyes to avoid the sight of his long visage … and he grins most horribly by way of shewing what pains he takes with his few remaining teeth" (II:7–8).[59] Commentaries like this that assign a rougher, anthropologically different physiognomy to Americans are common, here and elsewhere. Crèvecoeur's discussion of the almost savage condition and aspect of Americans in the western settlements in *Letters from an American Farmer* (1782), published just three years before *The Liberal American* and hugely popular in England, belongs to this discourse.

But Sophia's real temporal difficulties have to do with the time letters take crossing the Atlantic. Even though her trip was fairly swift—"After a voyage of six weeks we are safely arrived on the continent of America" (I:160) she tells Louisa— she is caught between her love for Sir Edward Hambden back in England, and a pressing need to marry to free herself from financial and physical dangers in New

---

58 *The Liberal American*, vol. 1, pp. 117–18. Further references cited parenthetically.

59 For a hilarious treatment of American boorishness, backwardness, and near toothlessness, see *The Adventures of Jonathan Corncob* (London, 1787).

York. She ends up marrying Mr. Elliot—the liberal American of the title—while a letter from Louisa telling her of Sir Edward's love and desire to marry her is in transit. A letter from Sophia, telling of her marriage, is in similar limbo at the same time. Sophia eventually returns to England with her husband, who, on his deathbed, gives his blessing to her re-marriage to Sir Edward. So while all ends as it should, the death of the representative American on English soil and in English time is necessary to bring about such a conclusion. In order for the English body politic to survive, it must be removed from America, and from the American body. American time, once again, is shown to be irreconcilable with English time. The gaps between the two disrupt lives and illustrate national differences, despite other efforts to perpetuate the sense of kinship between people who share a language and a culture.

A Failure to Communicate

As experiences of time traumatically affect the readers and writers one encounters in these novels and the public and private families they constitute, the succession of letters and, more importantly, the erratic quality of their communication, perform similar acts of violence upon the narratives they constitute. The text as an organism and, through it, the bodily and familial metaphors, suffer mutilation. On one level this violence is subtle. It consists in a departure from the practice of the eighteenth century's most popular epistolary novels—Samuel Richardson's *Clarissa* (1747–48) and Frances Burney's *Evelina* (1778)—that increases the heteroglossia already inherent in such works. While Clarissa largely controls the representation of her tragic end and martyrdom, and we read most of Evelina's progress and maturation in her own words, no single character's writing dominates these novels about America. In this sense, none of their many voices emerge with narrative authority. They are supplanted too rapidly. Time is still a significant issue in novels set entirely in England. Even with the speed of the penny post, with most letters taking just a day to reach most places in England, miscommunications occur. But these always affect individuals in novels like *Clarissa*, rather than nations. And the delay of a day or two, while often crucial in times of crisis, even fatal to individuals, is minor compared to the gap of three months which encourages the emergence of multiple narratives in transatlantic novels. The language of sentiment in *Emma Corbett*, *School for Fathers*, and elsewhere, reinforces attempts to connect America and England in an emotional discourse which moves fluidly from familial ties to lovers' wishes and national imaginings. This language makes no allowance for boundaries between types of relationships, but its pleas are consistently marred by a narrative which cannot enact its sentiments.[60]

---

60 See Barrell's *Imagining the King's Death: Figurative Treason, Fantasies of Regicide, 1793–1796* (Oxford, 2000) for an excellent discussion of the role of the language of sentiment in times of national crisis. While Barrell focuses on a later period, his argument that this language permeated political discussions and helped make George III, the "bourgeois" king, into a true national father figure in a sentimental age is true for the period of the American Revolution as well.

Sentiment's debilitating effects are both the cause and effect of the inability to communicate that *Emma Corbett* and other English novels about America from the time demonstrate. Rather than accepting that the three-month gap in communications makes an intimate, connected conversation impossible, characters agonize over this disconnection. Emotional consideration over their separations damages the health of many characters as a direct result. Through sentiment, temporal disconnection becomes crippling to the ability to maintain illusions about familial connection.

Sir Robert's politics are neutral in the American conflict because of the pain he sees the war bringing to all those around him and because of the distance from national affairs he felt during his years in India. Perhaps his years in the East have taught him not to consider his narrative as part of the larger English story. If so, this lesson fails him when he mistakes the national drama, in which he becomes an author or editor, for a family story. His desire seems to be to explain the war away, and in the novel he becomes the main conduit of news from Emma and Henry in America to Charles Corbett back in England. His work of writing, compiling packets of others' writings, and sending letters between the estranged parties is much like an attempt to narrate a plot that includes America and England. But Sir Robert can neither transmit a successive, journalistic account of American events, nor unify them with the English events about which he occasionally learns after they have become irrelevant to the situation of those dependent upon him in America.

The "military fragment," as has been mentioned, seriously interrupts the plot and focuses the reader's attention on the ravages of war it describes. The fragment's many rips make for a disconnected story. The inclusion of this episode is an attempt to use the violent events of war in general, and civil conflict in particular, as both an allegorical framework and a demonstration of the family's role within the nation. On the allegorical level, the two soldiers can be seen as competing representations of England, one with a family, or a collection of colonies, the other independent. Neither fares well, but the one who seeks to be both father and soldier fares much worse. On another level, the family is seen as an instrument of the nation, inextricably involved with its political and military fortunes, and only thriving in a time of peace.

Another crucial act of violence against the narrative is the pervasive practice of withholding news in the hope that events will bring about a clarity that will lead to a clear plot. Sir Robert goes to America after Emma, who has followed Henry, and is transformed—by sentiment—into the selfless friend of both. While Henry and Emma take turns flirting with death, Sir Robert writes letters to Emma's father, which he saves rather than mailing. He waits on death or miraculous recovery, finally sending large packets of letters filled with agonizing escapes and foreboding premonitions. These are often followed by more packets, which seek to clarify but only add further confusion. Charles Corbett waits, gorges on a packet, then waits some more, constantly misinformed, cognizant of the fact that he must be misinformed, but overwhelmed by his sentiment for Emma, Edward, and America. The unsteady flow of uncertain information takes its toll on his health, and he ends up near death by the time he learns that Emma and Edward are both dead. Time delays news, attaching temporality to textuality. The failure of the two to combine in any meaningful way— their failure to contribute to a healing narrative—are the direct cause of Charles Corbett's bodily dissolution, as well as of his family's near extinction.

Strategies of Containment

Williams's stance towards America is radically different from Pratt's. While Pratt, as we have seen, purposely works to induce "the tear of sensibility" in his readers, Williams is adamant that rational affection is the proper attitude of people towards those around them. Charles Corbett laments that "we are cruelly taught to make a sanguinary mark of distinction betwixt an Englishman and an American," and declares himself "the latter … I enter deeply, and pathetically into every wrong which America sustains" (II:189). Corbett is completely "unmanned" by his sensibility, and unable to act the role of the real father of Emma and Edward, the foster father of Henry and Louisa, and the metaphorical father of the nation. "The capacious ideology of sensibility," in Nicola Watson's words, "imagined a peculiarly disempowered individual, trapped within his own bodily sensations and unable to imagine or effect any social change whatsoever."[61] Corbett is precisely such an individual. Williams, by keeping her text of English country life segregated from her sensibility-laden American intertextual interruption, argues, through her characters' refusal to empathize in any open way, against allowing America into concepts of Englishness. Her characters resist identifying themselves with the emotions of the subplot and, by extension, with America as a component of the nation. But they can only do so because America remains an unincorporated text.

Bakhtin argues that while "(i)t is impossible to lay out the languages of the novel on a single plane, to stretch them out along a single line," that the various discourses within it are "a system of intersecting planes."[62] But as seen in *Julia*, sometimes these planes never intersect. One could argue that the presence of the packet of letters about the American Revolution in this novel is one such intersection. But the fact that none of the characters from the main plot have anything to do with the subplot, and the novel's refusal to allow Julia or the others even to discuss the packet after it has been read by all, signal a complete disavowal of everything it represents. The empire and the world beyond entered English texts long before the American Revolution, of course, and Williams is hardly trying to shut out that world. But in previous literature it was contained in things, as on Belinda's dressing table in "The Rape of the Lock," in characters who had to function in English time, or in locations that kept their distance, like Crusoe's island. The co-incidence that epistolarity and intertextuality made possible belong particularly to the American Revolution and English attempts to confine it to a plot that retained the identification between the imperial center and a periphery suddenly made central in importance by its threat to move beyond the containing powers of the national imagination. But Williams's efforts in *Julia* do more to show the impossibility, and maybe the undesirability, of trying to reconcile these two nations by displaying them as non-intersecting texts that present radically different types of temporality.

---

61 Watson, *Revolution and the Form of the English Novel*, p. 25.
62 Bakhtin, *The Dialogic Imagination*, p. 48.

Chapter Two

English Reforms in American Settings: Utopian Schemes and the Idea of America

European utopian thought during the Age of Revolutions drove much of the early history of New Harmony, Indiana.[1] The Industrial, American, and French Revolutions and the aftermath of the Reformation all influenced this experiment in communal living on the banks of the Wabash River. George Rapp, a Swabian dissenter who had fought with the Lutheran Church and local officials in his home town of Württemberg since the 1780s, sensed the approach of the Second Coming. In 1803 he set off for the wilderness in search of a place for his followers that would be safe from the wrath of God when judgment came down upon the decadent and ungodly in Europe. The wilderness, as it had been for three hundred years by that time, was North America.

Rapp and his community, at times numbering more than a thousand, flourished in the United States. They first settled in western Pennsylvania. After 1814 they built a settlement on the banks of the Wabash River in southwestern Indiana in a place they named New Harmony. Scottish traveler John Melish introduced Rapp and the Rappites to British readers with his popular account, *Travels in the United States of America in the years 1806, 7, 8, 9, 10 and 11* (1812).[2] Melish's description of the Rappites was reprinted in periodicals numerous times in the 1810s, and several utopian reformers and emigrants, including Robert Dale Owen, Morris Birkbeck, and George Flower, found inspiration in it for their own settlements. Owen would take over New Harmony itself in 1824, while Birkbeck and Flower founded the English Prairie on what would become the Illinois side of the Wabash in 1818.

Rapp, before settling in western Pennsylvania, scouted land in Kentucky, which he knew through Gilbert Imlay's popular and groundbreaking—literally and figuratively—work, *A Topographical Description of the Western Territory of North America* (1792). Imlay's book also influenced Samuel Taylor Coleridge and Robert Southey as they planned their model community, Pantisocracy. While causation is notoriously tricky, the role Imlay's book played in all of these plans points to influence, at the very least. While the millenarian hopes of Swabian exiles may be

---

1   For a good account of the Harmony Society and its experiments in New Harmony, Indiana, see Anne Taylor, *Visions of Harmony: A Study in Nineteenth-Century Millenarianism* (Oxford, 1987).

2   John Melish, *Travels in the United States of America in the years 1806, 7, 8, 9, 10 and 11* (Philadelphia, 1812; London, 1818).

quite distant from the land speculation of a Kentucky backwoodsman best known as the villain—or at least the rakish deadbeat dad—in Mary Wollstonecraft's personal life, they run in and out of the same set of published works which were the main source of information about America as a place for social and spiritual renewal in the late eighteenth and early nineteenth centuries. While the idea was similar to the one that sent seventeenth-century Puritans to New England, the texts had changed. The significance of this is that Europeans became reacquainted with America through a set of texts encouraging them to emigrate to start a new history, and these texts often ignored the fact that the United States already represented the culmination of an earlier version of the same project. Imlay and others tended to promote settlement by groups of Europeans away from American population centers. This encouraged a way of looking at the wilderness that catered to English needs after the American Revolution. The sense of temporal, and as a result, social and cultural irreconcilability of England and the new United States that Chapter One discusses, made it clear that America was no longer English space. But emigration schemes that encouraged settlement in remote areas preserved the notion of empty space, particularly for radicals who needed it. In doing so, they promoted the idea that a change of space could work as a change of time, from a decadent present to a somehow coexistent utopian future.

In many ways, the secular plan of the Pantisocrats of the 1790s was similar to that of the millennarian Rappites in the 1800s and 1810s, and to Owen's vaguely socialistic dreams in the 1820s. English utopias planted in America from the mid-1790s through the 1830s were about England, not America. The beginning of the French Revolution sparked utopian thoughts in the minds of many English radicals in a very different sense, with the place of perfection being an England transformed by the same revolutionary energy sweeping across France, turning the nation's attention away from the loss of America less than a decade earlier. But if the overthrow of monarchies and beginning of a worldwide revolution that would establish the rule of reason seemed imminent to English radicals in the latter half of 1789, the turn to violence in the 1792 September massacres, and fears that a tyranny from above might be replaced by a much bloodier one from below, inspired many to seek a way to escape Europe and begin utopia in what seemed a new place, at the beginning of a new, malleable history. Writers for centuries had located fictional utopias in America, beginning with Sir Thomas More. Several English writers did so as the 1790s progressed. As Lewis Mumford has written, "almost every utopia is an implicit criticism of the civilization that served as its background; likewise it is an attempt to uncover potentialities that the existing institutions either ignored or buried beneath an ancient crust of custom and habit."[3] The American utopias English radicals projected in the 1790s were all such attempts.

Repressive moves by the English government in response to fears that the pronouncements of the London Corresponding Society and the London Revolution Society were symptoms of a significant internal threat to the British constitution, possibly even a move toward domestic insurrection, made writers as diverse as Mary Wollstonecraft, William Blake, and Samuel Taylor Coleridge consider alternatives

---

3   Lewis Mumford, *The Story of Utopias* (New York, 1962), p. 2.

that seemed more in their control. Whether their solutions to society's ills were apocalyptic and millenarian, as in Blake's case, indolently utopian with poetic retreat foremost, as in Coleridge's, or rooted in political solutions to contemporary problems, as were Wollstonecraft's, all looked across the Atlantic to a space that seemed empty enough to foster plans at odds with English repression and French chaos. America, for these writers, was not so much a place as a theoretical space. But Americans, for Blake and Coleridge, at least, had a way of contaminating that space. Although all three writers looked to America, all either found fault with Americans, or failed to see them as anything but examples of what English people might become under more wholesome conditions.

Richard Gravil has rightly argued that for many radicals the problem with the American Revolution was its failure to spread to England.[4] For Blake especially, this problem was what made America, while potentially a model for radical change, ultimately a symbol of the failure of English thought. As I will argue, in *America: A Prophecy* (1793), he linked the ideology of the American Revolution to the political thought of John Locke, his personal demon of English rationalism. Coleridge's stance on Americans was contradictory. In the 1790s he seems to have dreamed of an America without Americans. In later years he would see Americans either as culturally tied to, and dependent upon, England—as they were politically before 1776—or as mongrelized subjects who had bastardized the English language. Wollstonecraft's positions on Americans and America are more sanguine, but no less Anglo-centric. When she looked to America, she did so in an attempt to work out contemporary English problems, not to identify or assess a different people. Simply put, Blake saw Americans as too English to be universal, and therefore too limited to participate in the apocalyptic renewal of the eternal man; Coleridge saw them as not English enough to participate in the genius of the only people to which he believed they could possibly belong; and Wollstonecraft failed to see them at all, despite—or perhaps because of—her relationship with Gilbert Imlay.

This chapter deals with a group of loosely connected writers who, for a brief time in the 1790s, held similar sentiments concerning political change. Wollstonecraft and Blake met in the early 1790s at bookseller Joseph Johnson's shop. Johnson's radical politics and publishing activities also attracted William Godwin, whom Coleridge knew fairly well during this period.[5] The web of radical writers connected either to Godwin, Johnson, or both, included Tom Paine, Joseph Priestley, and Richard Price, all of whom had written extensively about the American Revolution, and Joel Barlow, an American poet friendly with Wollstonecraft and active on the fringes of French revolutionary politics. Barlow's epic "Vision of Columbus" has long been recognized as an important source for Blake's *America: A Prophecy*. The inclusion in this radical web of such Americans as Barlow and Imlay, and of English writers familiar with the United States and its politics, gave its members better information regarding the former colonies than most writers in England possessed in the 1790s.

---

4   Richard Gravil, *Romantic Dialogues: Anglo-American Continuities 1776–1862* (New York, 2000), p. 21.

5   See Nicholas Roe's *Wordsworth and Coleridge: The Radical Years* (Oxford, 1988) for the best account of Coleridge's relations with Godwin during this period.

But while all looked naturally to America as an alternative to France, when they did so they tended to see themselves rather than a different people.

English radical writers in the 1790s wrote about Americans in order to write about themselves, in the process creating others they collapsed into versions of Englishness. Wollstonecraft's tendency was to see Americans as types of "Ancient Britons," free from the enervating luxuries of late eighteenth-century England. Blake saw the beginning and end as Albion, and Coleridge saw the English language as something divinely communicated, constituting those who spoke it as one people. As such, these writers and others used America as a palimpsest upon which they could rewrite the England they chose to imagine, one free from the confines of a European history that seemed to be collapsing in upon itself.

Blake's America: "Finite Revolutions"

Many critics, David Erdman most prominently, have argued that for William Blake, Britain's colonies in North America were the physical manifestation of the idea of freedom.[6] Coming of age as an optimistic radical during the American Revolution, Blake naturally considered that first modern struggle against monarchy as the dawn of a new era. So, while it is not surprising that when Blake turned to political epic writing in the 1790s he focused on contemporary events in France, it was perhaps inevitable that he would turn back to the earlier struggle in America as a way to think out his views about liberty and revolution. America was the space onto which he would map out his argument concerning the ideological shape he believed such conflicts needed to take if they were going to lead to an apocalypse that would build Jerusalem in England's green and pleasant land. But Blake's argument, while sympathetic to the colonists' fight, is less so to the ideology governing it. *America: A Prophecy* (1793), is Blake's first significant move against the intellectual tradition underlying the radicalism he believed in, yet struggled against.[7]

Independent North America was a convenient site for many European thinkers in the late eighteenth and early nineteenth centuries. It could be thought of as an empty space, where mankind was beginning anew in the midst of an Edenic plenty and an innocence that was, if not Edenic, at least free of the corruption of monarchical governments and increasing industrialization. As such, America was the perfect location onto which debates over ideas could be mapped. In the course of three years—1793 to 1795—Blake would write his prophecy on America, Joseph Priestley would emigrate to Pennsylvania with the idea of founding a semi-utopian society, and Coleridge and Southey would exchange rapturous letters over their Pantisocracy, a truly utopian society, especially since it remained at the level of an idea. America was an obvious place to turn for those confused about what they thought of the French Revolution and England's response to it. For Blake,

---

6   David Erdman, *Blake: Prophet Against Empire* (New York, 1977 [1954]).

7   Erdman himself, while generally of the opinion that Blake considered America the exemplum of political freedom, notes his dissatisfaction with the American Revolution in "*America*: New Expanses," in Erdman and John E. Grant (ed.), *Blake's Visionary Forms Dramatic* (Princeton 1970), pp. 92–114.

American independence three thousand miles away offered a way of thinking out ideas that the geographical and temporal proximity of events in France and at home complicated.

The namelessness of the "shadowy daughter of Urthona," who makes her entrance in the first line of the first plate of *America*, makes it clear that Blake is discussing an idea rather than a political realization of republicanism (A 1:1, 4).[8] Like a detached idea, she is "naked" and "silent," "For never from her iron tongue could voice or sound arise" (A 1:7–9). She is something like the "pure negativity" in Hegel's dialectic—a "Dark virgin" until brought into the material realm by Orc's rape of her. The "Preludium" signals the fact that America the continent will be treated as a battleground between Blake's visions of revolution and those of others.[9] While the others are not specifically mentioned, strategic omissions and a focus on failures by American philosophes Benjamin Franklin and Thomas Jefferson point in the direction of Locke and other Enlightenment political thinkers.

Looking at *America* as a contest for possession of the idea of liberty helps to clarify Blake's hostility to Locke's political thought. While writing his *French Revolution* (1791), or soon after, Blake reconsidered the implications of a political struggle whose idea of liberty was heavily based on Enlightenment Social Contract theory. His sense before working on these early prophecies that the American Revolution was the opening battle of a worldwide apocalyptic struggle to bring on the millennium leads him to this reassessment. In the end, he finds America's "warlike men" lacking because of their adherence to Locke's political philosophy, and turns toward the advocacy of a more radical form of revolution, organized more along class lines, and accepting a greater level of violence. Thus *America: A Prophecy* is a dialectical working out of the shape that revolutionary struggle should take, between the ideas of Locke as represented by the "warlike men" on one side, and the "rushing together" of the artisans, workers, and destitute on the other. Blake gives Locke a fair hearing in *America*, but finds him fatally flawed in that the American Revolution, rather than moving the world closer to a communion of man, separates off a "piece of eternity" without improving the rest.

Blake is almost always presented as an unqualified opponent of Locke's thought. But despite Blake's hostility to the philosopher's view of humanity, it seems possible he was willing to consider his political thought as a vehicle for transformation. It would not have been the only time Blake attempted—uneasily, to be sure—to justify ideas based on Lockean tenets. "In defending (Paine's) *Age of Reason* against the Bishop of Landaff," Wayne Glausser notes, "Blake finds himself aligned with a person who admired Locke and to some extent resembled him ... He admires

---

8   All citations to *America: A Prophecy* are from ed. D.W. Dörrbecker, *The Continental Prophecies* (Princeton, 1995), vol. 4 in *Blake's Illuminated Books*, gen. ed, David Bindman (Princeton, 1991–95).

9   James McCord has argued persuasively that Blake's view of this battleground *as* battleground was decidedly "unromantic" and that "revolution is part of a repetitive cycle of tyranny that includes reaction as well as revolt." "West of Atlantis: William Blake's Unromantic View of the American War," *The Centennial Review*, 30/3 (1986): 383–99.

Paine's decisiveness but can't quite decide about Paine."[10] Blake is driven to this ambivalence by the irreconcilability of his observations of the historical conditions of the late eighteenth century—and the only political approaches that seemed effective in reforming them—with his vision of a structure that obliterated—or at least incorporated—differences. His eventual move to the concept of "One Man," while not fully present in 1793, is not wholly absent either.

Blake's main quarrels with Locke in *America* are that the latter's philosophy calls for the recognition of separateness as an epistemological advance, which mentally binds the colonists to the notion that such separateness is a political ideal. By separateness I mean the division of sovereignty into branches of government that will keep each other in check much in the way that Blake's fallen Zoas keep one another from exercising their energies and realizing their possibilities. As such, the "warlike men" are under the sway of a Urizenic law. But Blake's prophecy does not negotiate its way out of this problem with American democracy by rejecting law completely. It substitutes Blake's own law in the form of a narrated move from historical time to visionary time. Andrew Lincoln clearly identifies the role law plays in Blake's history of empire: "(T)he bases of social unity are religion ... and law, both of which are ostensibly motivated by pity. It is Urizen's pity that urges him to liberate the bound Orc from what he sees as the torments of natural appetite—not by unbinding Orc's chains, but by educating him into an acceptance of law."[11] Blake's treatment of the French Revolution can be seen as an attempt to narrate history. His later prophecies are extended narrations of his vision. And while it would be too simple to say that *America* represents the narration of the movement from history to myth, it at least places historical events into a containing mythical structure that allows Blake to avoid endorsing what he had to consider flawed revolutionary ideologies.

In *Europe* (1794) he points to the failure of movements—and most likely has the American Revolution primarily in mind—that leave mankind only partially regenerated. He specifically ties this problem to "thought," and metaphorically to the American act of separation from Britain. "Thought chang'd the infinite to a serpent," he writes:

> ... then all the eternal forests were divided
> Into earths rolling in circles of space, that like an ocean rush'd
> And overwhelmed all except this finite wall of flesh.
> Then was the serpent temple form'd, image of infinite
> Shut up in finite revolutions, and man became an Angel;
> Heaven a mighty circle turning; God a tyrant crown'd (E 10:16–23).[12]

"Thought" in this context is the set of ideas that has been controlling revolutionary action, claiming to work towards the "infinite," but really separating the world "Into

---

10 Wayne Glausser, *Locke and Blake: A Conversation across the Eighteenth Century* (Tallahassee, 1998), p. 8.

11 Andrew Lincoln, "Blake and the 'Reasoning Historian'," in Steve Clark and David Worrall (eds), *Historicizing Blake* (London, 1994), p. 78.

12 *Europe: A Prophecy*, in *The Continental Prophecies*.

earths rolling in circles of space," formed by the containing ideological structures of "finite revolutions". Locke's argument that governments are legitimate only as far as they serve the people from whom they derive power has made America's "finite" revolution possible. Locke's law, even when used in a liberal cause, violates Blake's in the limits it places on the exercise of powers.

Blake's myth is, of course, no less controlled by law, which is immanent in the very form of narrative. As Hayden White has argued, "narrativity, whether of the fictional or the factual sort, presupposes the existence of a legal system against which or on behalf of which the typical agents of a narrative account militate ... (N)arrative in general ... has to do with the topics of law, legality, legitimacy, or, more generally, authority."[13] In Blake's vision, as Lincoln has observed, "a spirit of unity—which supplements law as an instrument of control ... has to be created by the prophet, who presents an image of human destiny in a collective form, a form that will persuade the individual that fulfillment is to be found within a unified community, through a love that transcends self-interest."[14] This narrative is the explicit rejection of Enlightenment efforts to divide and classify. *America* shows the incompatibility of Locke's law with Blake's. And while Nicholas Williams is correct in arguing that "Blake's loss of faith in the narrative of progress" leads him to move towards "discredit(ing) narrative altogether" by the end of the 1790s, in 1793 there was still hope that events in France would spread.[15]

Erdman's reading of the sixth plate of *America* as a rewriting of the "Declaration of Independence" represents the transformation of a Lockean statement of rights into a Blakean set of actions as if they were uncomplicatedly parallel to one another.[16] But Blake has difficulties with this throughout *America*. Note the passive, rational voice of the "Declaration":

> We hold these truths to be self-evident: that all men are created equal; that they are endowed by their creator with certain inalienable rights; that among these are life, liberty, & the pursuit of happiness: that to secure these rights, governments are instituted among men, deriving their just powers from the consent of the governed.[17]

Blake transforms Jefferson's set of rights, with which men "are endowed," into exhortations.

> Let the slave grinding at the mill run out into the field:
> ...
> Let the inchained soul shut up in darkness and in sighing,
> Whose face has never seen a smile in thirty weary years;
> Rise and look out, his chains are loose, his dungeon doors are open.
> And let his wife and children return from the opressors scourge (A 6:6–11)

---

13 Hayden White, *The Content of the Form: Narrative Discourse and Historical Representation* (Baltimore, 1987), p. 13.

14 Lincoln, "Blake and the 'Reasoning Historian,'" pp. 78–9.

15 Nicholas Williams, *Ideology and Utopia in the Poetry of William Blake* (Cambridge, 1998), p. 133.

16 Erdman, *Prophet Against Empire*, p. 25.

17 Thomas Jefferson, *Writings* (New York, 1984), p. 19.

The aggressiveness of Blake's approach to "life, liberty and the pursuit of happiness," sharply contrasts with the peaceful exercise of rights guaranteed by the social contract Jefferson invokes.[18]

This can be argued away as a difference in tone rather than philosophy, inevitable if one considers the distance between Blake's radical urban situation and Jefferson's aristocratic experience. But one can also see Blake's rewriting as a direct, active inversion of the "Declaration's" passive representation of the quarrel—as a political challenge to Social Contract theory, with its insistence on the necessity of relinquishing some rights to ensure others, couched in grammatical opposition. But the real failure of the Lockean model—the decision of America's Angels to break from England—goes beyond tone and grammar. Significantly, Blake's rewriting of the "Declaration" omits that document's central point: "that whenever any form of government becomes destructive of" life, liberty, and the pursuit of happiness, "it is the right of the people to alter or abolish it, & to institute new government, laying it's (sic) foundation on such principles, & organizing it's (sic) powers in such form, as to them shall seem most likely to effect their safety & happiness."[19] While the "safety" of the colonists may be secured by seceding from the collectivity, this can only come about through the rejection of Blake's overarching vision of revolution that ends in unification. The "safety" that the colonists were eager to secure is thus incompatible with the worldwide revolution Blake considered necessary.

Revolutionary approaches based on Enlightenment theories can only end oppression by endorsing disunification, or the bifurcation of corrupted Albion from the part of it that stands for the "idea" or "ideal" of liberty. The facts force Blake to recognize America's independence, and his republicanism forces him to applaud this. But his vision can represent the split between Albion and its children only as a further fall. Only through his own imagined system can Blake move towards his goal of One Man, and control the process of reforming or eliminating difference to the point of unification—absolute dominion of the subject over itself and—which for Blake is the same—over its physical surroundings, imaginative processes, and time itself.

Blake is moving towards a presentation of revolution as the prelude to an ordering of the world that includes all time simultaneously, and as such eliminates time as we know it. America, located in a theoretical space for Blake, seems to be the place where Albion can become the One Man of *Jerusalem*, able to repair his bifurcation and present a vision of energetic eternity. Blake's disappointment with America and its "finite revolution" rests in its inability to give him the model of this timeless world he would seek until the final plates of *Jerusalem* when he exhorts:

Awake! Awake Jerusalem! O lovely Emanation of Albion
Awake and overspread all Nations as in Ancient Time
For lo! the Night of Death is past and the Eternal Day
Appears upon our Hills ... (97:1–4).[20]

---

18 Jefferson, *Writings*, p. 25.
19 Ibid., p. 19.
20 *Jerusalem*, Morton D. Paley (ed.), vol. 1 in *Blake's Illuminated Books* (Princeton, 1991).

The passing of night and death into eternity, and the emanation of the regenerated geography of Jerusalem from Albion, are examples of Blake's desire for a worldwide revolution, yet his inability to see it taking place outside of England. He longs to see the fourfold manifestation of the One Man "going forward irresistible from Eternity to Eternity," conversing "in thunderous majesty," and "Creating Time," none of which can be seen in an America that has simply replicated England without a monarchy (J 98:27, 29, 31).

America is in this sense a test of Lockean theory and Painite praxis, both of which it finds faulty. In my reading, Blake is an Englishman—prophet or not—who anguishes over the loss of North America as a loss for the English of the "idea" of liberty. While he did not overvalue the American patriots themselves, they were fighting for changes with which he sympathized. America's falling away from English control is a defeat for his vision—as is the loss of England from American democracy. Nonetheless, Blake's point of view and stance remain English—and his move towards a more symbolic representation of history is the move he makes to control these events. It is also his way to remain a revolutionary and republican. He narrates his way out of the history his fellow radicals envisioned into a new, meta-historical order.

Blake begins *America: A Prophecy* by complicating the challenges his "warlike men" must overcome if they are to move towards his vision. While some critics have seen Orc's rape of the "shadowy daughter of Urthona" as "the mythical 'conquest and cultivation of a virgin land,'" or "as simply the 'ritual copulation' that 'reunites man and earth'"[21] it should be seen as a violent aggression against a hitherto ideologically empty space. Erdman's view of Orc in *America* is unambiguously positive. "(I)n *America*," he writes, "Blake sharply distinguishes the god of war, Urizen, and his Satanic Anger the Prince of Albion, from the Christ-like god, Orc, who is divine yet human and whose sword promotes peace."[22] But while his sword might banish the British army, his phallus introduces violence. Orc might be favorably distinguished from Urizen, and he functions as a key player in America's liberation, but he is also the embodiment of European political strife and revolutionary wrath. Its eruption on America's shore is directly related to Albion's Prince's chaining of the colonies—a necessary evil possibly, but not the act of a "Christ-like god." In *America*, Orc's specifically European version of revolutionary energy and violence are derived from the Promethean myth and Norse mythology. This historically located revolutionary energy has sown a polluted seed. The new, extra-sacred, millennial land is violated. And as the revolutionary energy that has enraged America is European, the ideology that the Angels who will rebel against Albion's Prince will follow will be European as well.

The voyage America's Thirteen Angels take to Atlantis is a voyage into the dialectical space between America and England, its shared brain or soul. It is in this setting, I would argue, that Blake makes clear his opposition to the controlling radical ideology of his time. This space—though used often by Blake, and incorporated effectively into his mythos—is also one contaminated by the writings and ideas of

---

21 Dörrbecker, "Introduction," *The Continental Prophecies*, p. 30.
22 Erdman, *Blake: Prophet Against Empire* (Princeton, 1954), p. 29.

others, who proffer opposing views of the political order. Several of the "warlike" men are not particularly warlike at all. As D.W. Dörrbecker has pointed out, Blake "does not represent" the leaders of the American Revolution "as heroes on the battlefield or even heroes fit for worship. They are made witnesses to the mystic struggle for liberty between Orc and the Guardian Prince but are not engaged in or even glorified for the bloodshed of war."[23] One thing that keeps them from being heroic, I would argue, is their error in seeking political transformation through Locke's prescriptions. Blake argues that the politics of secession are weak when, at the moment of America's greatest trouble, "The scribe of Pennsylvania"—Benjamin Franklin—"casts his pen upon the earth" and "The builder of Virginia"—Thomas Jefferson—"throws his hammer down in fear" (A 14:15–16). This abandonment of the revolutionary cause by America's foremost *philosophes* shows Blake's view of the hopelessness of the political ideology to which they subscribe. The American cause has to be rescued by Orc's revolutionary violence, which consists of a more Blakean direct engagement with the enemy.

Through the failure of the American patriots' ideology, and their necessary rescue by Orc as a representative of European revolutionary violence, Blake narrates the new symbolic order that would work its way into his future works. His new order is teleologically utopian—but not in the sense that it seeks a final exit from historicity. As Nicholas Williams argues, "(t)he problem of a utopia … as it is expressed in Blake, is not that of an escape from history, but instead the strategic problem of history's culmination, how to retain the particulars of history while bringing them to utopian perfection."[24] One of the particulars he must retain is the idea of liberty, as represented by the American Revolution. *America: A Prophecy* serves as a model for reform in that it clarifies the nature of radical political action in the late eighteenth century. Identifying the driving force behind revolutionary movements as bound to Enlightenment political philosophy helps Blake realize that not only must he create his own system, but that it cannot be governed in any way by the actions of fallen humanity, even at its best.

Transatlantic Authorship and *The Emigrants*

Gilbert Imlay poses the main difficulty to determining Wollstonecraft's views of America in the mid-1790s. Imlay, an adventurer from Kentucky who traveled in radical circles in London and Paris, was Wollstonecraft's lover, and apparently captivated many of the leading radicals in England in the 1790s. The author of *A Topographical Description of the Western Territory of North America* (1792), a work which inspired much Romantic-era writing about America, he promoted emigration to Kentucky, and helped inspire Coleridge's and Southey's plans to found a community in Pennsylvania on lands alongside the Susquehanna that rival adventurer and land speculator Thomas Cooper was trying to sell to disaffected English radicals. The *Topographical Description*, as Gravil notes, "has much wider ambitions than

---

23 Dörrbecker, "Introduction," *The Continental Prophecies*, p. 29.
24 Williams, *Ideology and Utopia in the Poetry of William Blake*, p. 31.

its short title suggests ... Its author presents himself as an emigré from a state of innocence to the realms of artifice, bringing messages of the patriarchal simplicity of the American wilds."[25]

One critic has argued that Imlay did not write *The Emigrants*, a novel usually attributed to him. Robert Hare, editor of a 1964 facsimile edition of the novel, claims that Mary Wollstonecraft was likely its sole author, while Amanda Gilroy and W.M. Verhoeven call Hare's arguments "weak, misinformed, and suggestive, and sometimes downright wrong or simply emotive" in a rather emotive passage in their introduction to a more recent edition of *The Emigrants*.[26] Despite Verhoeven's and Gilroy's arguments, it was *possible* for Wollstonecraft to have lent a hand in the authoring of the novel. The book was most likely begun after Wollstonecraft and Imlay met in November of 1792 (their affair began in the summer of 1793). It was published in September 1793, a few months after the two had become constant companions, and has the marks of a book quickly written. The very least that can be said is that *The Emigrants* is consonant with Wollstonecraft's political views.[27] Its composition during Imlay's and Wollstonecraft's affair—it appeared just two months before Mary became pregnant with Fanny Imlay, at least two months after the affair began—and its London publication by Joseph Johnson, Mary's publisher—gives at least a little credence to Hare's argument in favor of Wollstonecraft's authorship. But whether or not Wollstonecraft authored *The Emigrants*, or collaborated on it, it is a product of the radical circle in London in which both she and Imlay traveled. Its focus on working out English political and social problems in an American setting, published first in London by Johnson, justifies treating it as a transatlantically authored work.

The Emigrants can be read both as an encouragement to the disaffected English to consider new lives across the Atlantic, and as a critique of British institutions.[28] Marriage and divorce under British law are central topics in the novel. Gilbert Il—ray, an American gentleman who has befriended an English family recently arrived from London, introduces the topic in a letter to his friend Captain James Arl—ton, a man of education, manners, and an affinity for the wilderness. Il—ray explains how the emigrants—the T—n family—have come to America because their fortune has been dissipated by Mrs. T—n and her son, George. While the novel uses George as

---

25 Gravil, *Romantic Dialogues*, p. 38.

26 W.M. Verhoeven and Amanda Gilroy, eds, *The Emigrants* (New York, 1998), p. xliii.

27 Stuart Andrews, in *The Rediscovery of America* (New York, 1998) concurs with Hare on this point, with some reservations.

28 Amanda Gilroy, in "Espousing the Cause of Oppressed Women: Cultural Captivities in Gilbert Imlay's *The Emigrants*," in W.M. Verhoeven and Beth Dolan Kautz (ed.), *Revolutions & Watersheds: Transatlantic Dialogues 1775–1815* (Amsterdam-Atlanta, Ga., 1999), pp. 191–205, argues that "Imlay uses the issue of domestic politics to construct a utopian vision of American national character" (191). While this is possible, one might also argue that Wollstonecraft presents an idealized portrait of Americans while calling for English political, legal, and moral reform. Gilroy, in an essay that discusses the treatment of divorce laws in *The Emigrants*, admits that Imlay's "personal life shows no evidence of feminist ideals," and that "his real calling seems to have been for shady commercial adventures and actresses" (191). Wollstonecraft's life, of course, was dedicated to "feminist ideals," as are most of the admirable characters in *The Emigrants*.

an example of what is wrong with young Englishmen, the cause of his failures is ascribed to English institutions. "(W)here shall we look for the cause of this depravity but in our institutions?—institutions the more ungenerous and tyrannic because the oppressed are not represented" (34)[29] Il—ray lays most blame on marriage: "There is no reciprocality in the laws respecting matrimony ..." he writes. Unfaithful men go unpunished under the current system. But Il—ray laments that when

> a woman of honour and delicacy has been driven to seek for some mitigation of the sufferings of an afflicted bosom, in the friendship of an ingenuous heart, and when that friendship has led to more tender ties—ties with (sic) spring from the finest feelings, and which characterize the most humane and exalted souls, that she should be branded with contempt, and condemned to live in poverty, unnoticed, and unpitied (35).

Il—ray's complaint very clearly anticipates the central concern of the novel Wollstonecraft left unfinished at her death, *Maria: or, the Wrongs of Woman* (1798).

Three marriage traps figure prominently in *The Emigrants*. Caroline, the novel's heroine, discovers her long-lost uncle while crossing the Alleghenies in a symbolic move from the corrupt east—even Philadelphia, it seems, has succumbed to the enervating luxuries of Europe—to wholesome Pittsburgh. They begin a correspondence, most of which consists of Caroline's uncle, P—P— Esq.'s story of Lady B—'s suffering at the hands of her husband back in England. Lady B— is trapped in a marriage with a mercenary, drunken, debauched man who does not love her. Eventually, he obtains a parliamentary decree granting his divorce from her, and she ends up penniless and spurned by her own parents. P—P— is the unwitting and unintentional excuse for Lord B—'s divorce petition, and subsequently the losing defendant in a civil suit. Lady B—marries P—P— and lives in debtor's prison with him for ten years, giving birth to seven children, before they are able to emigrate to America at the outbreak of the Revolution, where she and all the children are killed by Indians acting under orders of the British Army.

A second woman trapped in marriage, Miss Lucy R—, is tricked by her husband into marriage. Il—ray describes Lucy R—'s husband, Mr. S—, as "a mere supercilious coxcomb, with all the pedantry of a classic, without the erudition; and with all the pomp and ostentation of a fine gentleman, he wants suavity of manners, and civility which consists in suffering other people to have part of the conversation" (74–5). Mr. S—'s main crime is an undefined wickedness. America, presented as a haven for those who deserve a second chance after falling prey to temptation in England, is no haven for the truly wicked. Mr. S—, "as he by degrees began to be known ... retired farther and farther from the stage of the great world, until he had reached the utmost limits where the polished arts are useless to the unprincipled" (263). His dishonesty is discovered, but before the novel can show whether divorce is more obtainable for women in America than in England, he drinks himself to death, dying "without pity or regard" (263).

The final example of a virtuous woman married to a bad man is Caroline's sister Eliza. Her husband, Mr. F—, lives a life of debauchery in London, running up debts

---

29 Parenthetical citations refer to W.M. Verhoeven and Amanda Gilroy (eds), *The Emigrants* (New York, 1998).

and refusing to help relieve the T—n family's neediness in America. Eliza's story is remarkably similar to Maria's in *The Wrongs of Woman*. Married to a man who does not love her, and who wastes their money on enervating pursuits, she eventually is asked to prostitute herself to maintain him (301). This brings an immediate call for her to leave England and live with Caroline and Uncle P— in America. Il—ray, who is in London when Eliza's troubles are discovered, writes that "certainly it was a cruel circumstance, that the pleasures of her life must be sacrificed, because she had been imposed upon by a man, who most likely the habits of life had rendered impotent" (302).

While the endings Wollstonecraft later sketched out for *Maria* make it appear probable that the title character's wrongs would go unredressed, *The Emigrants* offers hope that in America, and especially in its western settlements, where European manners and ideas have not yet penetrated, the oppressiveness of English institutions might be avoided. While Lady B— dies, it is significant that the text blames the English encouragement of Indian massacres during the Revolution for her fate rather than the Indians themselves, who throughout the novel are treated as noble figures. At one point Eliza sees three Indians while walking near Pittsburgh and faints with fear, only to be assured that they mean no harm. "Brother," they assure Arl—ton, who is with her, ready to sacrifice himself for her safety, "if we have been your worst foes in war, we will be your best friends in peace, and that they were going to Pittsburg for the purpose of burying the hatchet, that white people and Indians might live together like brothers" (56). Caroline later ends up being abducted by Indians and rescued by Arl—ton. But while her captivity strikes fear into the hearts of all who know her, Il—ray assures her uncle that her captors "treated her the whole time with the most distant respect, and scrupulous delicacy." He goes on to describe this form of captivity as desirable compared to marriage in England. "Indeed," Il—ray writes, "I have been told of instances, where women have been treated with such tenderness and attention by them, that they have from gratitude become their wives" (258).

Eliza and Lucy R— both end up free from their husbands, in love with more admirable men in a settlement Arl—ton builds on the banks of the Ohio in the Illinois territory, along Godwinian principles.[30] The institution of English marriage has been outrun by emigration, and a new government is proposed that will establish institutions based on reason. Il—ray's belief, straight from Godwin's *Political Justice*, in the "perfectability which he thinks society may arrive at in the progression of civilization," is put into practice in Arl—ton's new settlement. "(T)he western territory of this continent," he writes, is perfect for his plans, "as its infancy affords an opportunity to its citizens of establishing a system conformable to reason and humanity" (294).

While it is possible to see this as a vision of America as utopia, the evils it sets out to eradicate are all English. The first president of this new society is P—P—, the novel's most persistent critic of English institutions, and an English emigrant.

---

30 One of this society's central institutions is a place where all citizens will meet to discuss political matters, a clear invocation of Godwin's belief in the perfectability of society through rational debate.

America exists as a place of renewal for the English, rather than as a "New World" for a new people. Il—ray, one of the two representative Americans in the text, is more interested in critiquing English institutions, and, in a charged phrase, speaking for the "rights of man" in a universal sense, than he is with asserting any American uniqueness. "(W)henever the rights of man can be clearly ascertained," he writes to Arl—ton, "and equality established ... men will regain their pristine sincerity, and consequently, those base arts that have so often degraded the dignity of man will no longer be known" (282–3). A disquisition on the "rights of men" follows (283–4). Il—ray finishes by declaring

> that I prefer the unpolished wilds of America, with the honest affability and good humour of the people, to the refined address of the European world, who have substituted duplicity for candour, and cunning for wisdom. But I flatter myself, the period is hastening when its citizens will be regenerated, and when they must look back with shame at the sacrilege which has been committed (291).

America's role is to serve as a laboratory for European regeneration, a kind of moral and political rehab center. Throughout *The Emigrants*, the only institutions, manners, and customs referred to are European, and for the most part, English.

One of the causes of English matrimonial oppression is, according to *The Emigrants*, the dissipation and enervation of English and European society. The novel consistently portrays England as effeminate and weak in opposition to a masculine, virile America. Caroline's trip from Philadelphia to Pittsburgh brings her into contact with the wilderness beyond the east coast. Upon arriving in Pittsburgh, she is struck with the "impetuous" flow of the Allegheny River, the "fierceness of its aspect, and the wildness over its banks" (60). The novel celebrates the power of nature in America, but with some reservations. Western America marks "the line between civilization and barbarism" (61). While the emigrants choose this spot for outrunning the pace of a civilization addled by luxury and vice, Caroline's capture clearly demonstrates its dangers. Through this juxtaposition of danger and societal health, the novel argues that the work of renewal is fraught with dangers, but necessary. The goal is to recreate an English polity in its ancient purity, without giving up "the empire of reason and science" (61). Caroline's comparison of the area around Pittsburgh "with what must have been the state of Great Britain, and the manners of the Aborigines of that island, when it was first invaded by the more polished Romans," makes the project clear (62). Her brother George's reformation and flourishing at the novel's end reiterates this claim of America as still a new England, despite the outcome of the Revolution. "(H)aving no person to lounge with, he soon followed the example of those with whom he is living," and gained the "robust ... appearance of an Ancient Briton" (324), rather than a modern American.

The novel depicts emigration as necessary not only to the social and moral regeneration of England, but to its physical vitality. The young American men in *The Emigrants*, Il—ray and Arl—ton, constantly demonstrate their physical prowess, traveling the wilderness, rescuing Caroline from Indians, and building their new settlement. Arl—ton, far from being effeminate, spends his mornings "laying out his grounds, and planting the several fruits ... He not only attends to this business, but he does great part of it with his own hands, which gives him that exercise so necessary to invigorate the constitution" (313). George's transformation into an "Ancient Briton" is likewise described in terms almost entirely physical. As he works the land he "is every day marked with some new feature, distinguished by manly form" (323).

By contrast, the English men who remain in London sink into a degenerate effeminacy. Eliza's husband, Mr. F—, is the primary victim of this condition. "Effeminacy has triumphed" in England in general, Il—ray writes from London, "and while the sofa has been the pleasurable seat of the lover, the toilet has been the place where his manliness was displayed" (299). Il—ray goes on to argue that a society's strength depends on masculine health. "(T)he charms of fine women," he writes to Arl—ton, "can only be relished by men who have not been enervated by luxury and debauchery; and thus it has happened in every populous and wealthy city in the world, that the most lovely women have been neglected by men, whose impotence was as disgusting, as their caprices were unbounded" (300). This is all a prelude to explaining that Mrs. F—'s husband has become one of these impotent men: "The habits of his life had completely disqualified him for domestic pleasures," Il—ray writes. "(H)e was indulging himself in every extravagance" (301). After sinking to his lowest state, Mr. F— shoots himself in the head. He is described as falling "to those enervating passions, which first lead to the practice of folly, and prevent the exercise of that bravery necessary to combat the frowns of adversity ... he had the presumption to aim at the reputation of dying like a hero, when he had not spirit to live a man" (317).[31]

The men in America are not the only possessors of admirable virility. The landscape itself exhibits enormous potency. Caroline and Arl—ton marry and settle in the Illinois country on an expanse of land they name "Bellefont," after a fountain which "gushes from a rock," while the "flowery banks ... as if to return the load, spread their blooming sweets on every side" (312). This land, "adjoining to the rapids, which form a stupendous cataract," are located in a place where the river "shoots impetuous over its rocky bed," even more powerful than "nature," which, while seeming "to scorn its feeble power," cannot stop "the repercussive thunder" from proclaiming its "triumph ... (T)he ethereal hills on the adjacent shore give luster to the rising moisture, which creeping through the vistas of the groves, the country round, high illumined, in blushing charms its sweets diffuse, and nature shines effulgent to the joyous sight" (311). This sexualized landscape "yields bounteous plenty to all, and every being shares the golden stores that gild the variegated plains" (312). *The Emigrants* sets this picture of masculine health and fertility against the enervating environment of London, which "from its overgrown size has become the asylum of the licentious, and the den of the rapacious" (270).

The Emigrants thus depicts America as a place where the English—especially English women—can free themselves from oppressive institutions and corrupting habits. America as a spot of physical geography is idealized for its power and unspoiled quality. The novel praises American men who, in its pages, become Wollstonecraftian feminists with Godwinian ideas concerning the improvement of

---

31 This section echoes Wollstonecraft's attack on "equivocal beings" in *Vindication of the Rights of Women* (London, 1793), p. 138.

society. English men, like George and Uncle P—P—, seem to find their Englishness revived in America rather than becoming Americans themselves. Wollstonecraft and Imlay see America with what Mary Louise Pratt has termed "Imperial Eyes." Just as Pratt describes Alexander von Humboldt's capacity to see Venezuela without seeing its indigenous inhabitants, Wollstonecraft sees America as empty, a space onto which a society founded on English principles can be built with no preexisting societal restraints. "Nineteenth-century Europeans," Pratt reminds us,

> *re*invented America as Nature in part because that is how sixteenth- and seventeenth-century Europeans had invented America for themselves in the first place, and for many of the same reasons … They, too, wrote America as a primal world of nature, an unclaimed and timeless space occupied by plants and creatures (some of them human), but not organized by societies and economies; a world whose only history was the one about to begin.[32]

Caroline's descriptions of America are very much like von Humboldt's, though her acts of seeing are less appropriative, and do not participate in an explicitly imperialistic project. Still, she and the other characters see their spot of America very much as "a world whose only history was the one about to begin," in their case, on the banks of the virile Ohio River.

Coleridge's American Dream

"(T)he character of gentleman," Coleridge wrote in Biographia Literaria (1817), "is frequent in England, rare in France, and found, where it is found, in age or the latest period of manhood; while in Germany the character is almost unknown. But the proper antipode of a gentleman is to be sought for among the Anglo-American democrats."[33] More than forty years after the signing of the Declaration of Independence, Coleridge was still in the habit of either characterizing Americans as dangerous levelers with a vulgar culture, or denying them any cultural independence at all. Coleridge's hyphenation of "Anglo-American" in the foregoing quote—a culturally imperial bit of punctuation, as in "Anglo-Irish," rather than an indication of a relationship between two independent nations, as in "Anglo-American trade"—accompanied by his dismissal of American manners, is just one example of the simultaneously dismissive and appropriative stance he had demonstrated towards the United States and its citizens beginning with his "Sonnets on Eminent Characters," which appeared in the London Morning Chronicle from late 1794 to early 1795. Its liminality relates to Coleridge's conception of the way the two societies were situated in regards to one another, with language the conduit through which culture flowed. Those sonnets, often clearly about America, but never mentioning Americans, set the dual course Coleridge would take throughout his writings. He saw opportunities for the growth of English culture in America, even among the "Anglo-Americans," as long as they

32 Mary Louise Pratt, *Imperial Eyes: Travel Writing and Transculturation* (London, 1992), p. 126.

33 S.T. Coleridge, *Biographia Literaria*, ed. James Engell and W. Jackson Bate, *The Collected Works of Samuel Taylor Coleridge* (2 vols, Princeton, 1983), vol. 2, p. 76.

recognized their incorporation into a version of Englishness that crossed political borders. But he rejected any assertion of cultural independence as a violation of the laws of nature as manifested through language.

"Coleridge's writings are commonly punctuated," David Simpson writes, with distinctions between England, France, and Germany. "The German mind" in Coleridge's discourse "is typified by genius, talent, and fancy … the English by genius, sense, and humor … the French by cleverness, talent, and wit."[34] Coleridge's writings almost invariably link the American mind to Englishness. Either an American manner is the "antipode" of an English one, or it has no independence at all. This habit of submerging America within a discourse of Englishness, or placing it within the margins of a culture whose main text both shuns it and keeps it from escaping, has been perpetuated by Coleridge's critics, Simpson included. He relegates the quote that begins this section—a remark from "Satyrane's Letters" (1817)—to a parenthetical aside. He seems unsure that it has much to do with Coleridge's more developed "punctuations" concerning France and Germany, but offers it as a bit of comic relief to deserving readers who have endured a discussion of the theoretical implications of Ramism and Methodism. In that sense, Simpson's treatment of America's place in Coleridge's lifelong, fragmentary discourse on nationalism is prototypically Coleridgean. Americans belong in parenthetic asides, in one-liners in the Table Talk, but rarely in that part of the discourse that announces itself as the subject under serious consideration.

Another tendency of Coleridge's modern critics is to treat his remarks on America uncritically. Carl Woodring refers to "Coleridge's philosophic hope for a time when 'Laws, Manners, Religion and Language'," rather than governments, will define nations, and notes that the poet "was to versify the hope as a way of declaring the national identity of England and the United States," without commenting on or questioning such an identification.[35] Coleridge's omission of Americans from poems that specifically refer to heroic actions for but not by the colonists in the American Revolution is part of a surprisingly consistent argument, manifested in fragments, offhanded remarks, and journalistic squibs over four decades, that culture is sovereign, and that a people which has its origins in another people can never be a separate nation. Woodring's remarks on Coleridge's hopes for America are consistent with this reading. But his argument implies that Coleridge viewed the United States and England as involved in a partnership. Closer examination shows that he granted no such equality. He imagined an America attached to England, possessing English history, culture, and language, and therefore as English as if no separation had ever occurred.

---

34 David Simpson, *Romanticism, Nationalism, and the Revolt Against Theory* (Chicago, 1993), p. 40.

35 Carl Woodring, *Politics in the Poetry of Coleridge* (Madison, 1961), p. 40. This imaginative erasure of national distinctions is especially difficult to accept as representing Coleridge's true ideas. In addition to England and the United States, he includes France in this community of customs in the MS fragment from 1810 that Woodring quotes, despite his oft-stated antipathy to most things French. See Kathleen Coburn (ed.), *Inquiring Spirit: A New Presentation of Coleridge from his Published and Unpublished Prose Writings* (London, 1951), p. 343.

Coleridge's ambivalence about Americans and American independence can be traced back to his "Sonnets on Eminent Characters" of 1794–95, taken in conjunction with a sonnet included in a letter to Robert Southey during the same period about their plans to emigrate to Pennsylvania, and another on the same subject probably written in 1794, but not published until 1826.[36] Many of these poems refer to the American Revolution, but none recognize Americans as having acted in it. These early, awkward productions marked the public beginning of Coleridge's attempts to reconcile a universal view of mankind with a nationalistic view of culture and language.[37] They subtly deny that England had really lost its colonies, or that such a loss was even possible. He performed this historical reconfiguration by elevating language over government as the constitutional basis of English culture, and detaching Americans as a people from the United States as a political formation. Coleridge, insisting that a people's true idiom is communicated through poetry, relates language to nature, and through nature to divinity, thus asserting control over an American people who, *speaking* English, to him would always *be* English.

America, Language, and Culture

While Coleridge's views on language and its relation to race and nationality are complex and often inconsistent, he generally agreed with Wilhelm von Humboldt that linguistic variation was a major indicator of national difference.[38] Von Humboldt argued that "(t)he fact that some nations of more fortunate talents and under more favorable circumstances possess more excellent languages than do others derives from the very nature of the matter."[39] His argument that "(l)anguage wells from a depth of human existence which prohibits regarding it generally as a labor and as a creation of peoples" is based on his conviction that "it is no product born of activity …(or) a labor of nations, but rather a gift fallen to them as a result of their innate destiny."[40] Coleridge, like von Humboldt, viewed this "gift" as unequally bestowed. The English had received it in its most generous form. The French were less fortunate. He referred to France as "the most light, unthinking, sensual and

---

36 This poem was first published in the *Co-operative Magazine and Monthly Herald* on 6 March 1826, according to E.H. Coleridge's note in the *Complete Poetical Works* (Oxford, 1912). It is impossible to guess why Coleridge wanted a poem printed on Pantisocracy at this late stage, if indeed he was responsible for its publication.

37 See Robinson for a discussion of Coleridge's anxiety concerning his use of the sonnet as a form, and his self-consciousness concerning the awkward political and gendered negotiations he conducts within them.

38 Coleridge was acquainted with von Humboldt, and it is reasonable to surmise that they discussed language when, according to Coleridge, von Humboldt was alerting him that he "was a specified object of Buonaparte's resentment during (his) residence in Italy in consequence of those essays in the Morning Post during the peace of Amiens," *Biographia Literaria*, vol. 1, p. 216. But while Coleridge's views, scattered throughout his writings, are generally in line with von Humboldt's, no direct link between them can be identified.

39 Wilhelm von Humboldt, *Linguistic Variability & Intellectual Development*, trans. George C. Buck and Frithjof A. Raven (Coral Gables, Fla., 1971), p. 5.

40 Ibid., p. 2.

profligate of the European nations, a nation, the very phrases of whose language are so composed, that they can scarcely speak without lying!"[41] This chauvinism is consonant with von Humboldt's views, but Coleridge's ideas are distinct in an important respect. Both saw language linked to nation through nature, but Coleridge attached nature to divinity and its instrument, the English national church.[42]

According to these views, an America speaking English is part of the same nation as England. But since America was undeniably politically independent, Coleridge often falls into a contradiction. At times he seems to see Americans as defined by their political organization rather than anything more broadly cultural, and in those instances he suggests that while America has use of the English language, this use is questionable. Americans are speaking a language not their own, and as such are misapplying it. Language, which has a divine source, also has a direct connection to the people who have evolved with it, and who have learned it through their connection to nature, and through nature, to divinity. As early as "The Foster-Mother's Tale," a fragment from *Osorio* (1797) which first appeared in *Lyrical Ballads* (1798), Coleridge tells of a wild boy who "never learnt a prayer" but mocked the notes of birds, "And whistled, as he were a bird himself."[43] This boy, while able to learn English, is unable to learn religion. Having thus appropriated English without submitting to Englishness—he is declared to have been "most unteachable"—he escapes from England to "that new world" where "'tis supposed / He lived and died among the savage men."[44] This boy is only able to live in a place where no language is present to hinder the connection of a "savage" to the natural world.

Coleridge later acknowledged America's belief in its cultural independence:

An American, by his boasting of the superiority of the Americans
generally, but more especially in their language, once provoked me
to tell him that 'on that head the least said the better,' as the Americans
presented the extraordinary anomaly of a *people without a language*.
That they had mistaken the English language for baggage (which is called
plunder in America), and had stolen it. [45]

---

41 Coleridge, *The Friend*, in *The Collected Works of Samuel Taylor Coleridge*, ed. Barbara E. Rooke, (2 vols, Princeton, 1969), vol. 1, p. 61.

42 While Coleridge was *generally* in line with von Humboldt's views, he moved, like Kant, between an Enlightenment cosmopolitanism and a Romantic nationalism. As Simpson has argued in *Romanticism, Nationalism, and the Revolt Against Theory*, "(t)his cosmopolitanism is what the Romantic preoccupation with localism and patriotism so often displaced. The transition can be traced even within Kant's *Anthropology* (Cambridge, 2006), where the social-historical determinations that we now know as 'culture' are seen to produce national characters that are as good as innate by virtue of their strength and endurance, reproduced for instance in language, and especially in words that cannot be efficiently translated into other languages" (42).

43 William Wordsworth and S.T. Coleridge, *Lyrical Ballads*. ed. R.L. Brett and A.R. Jones (Routledge, 1991), ll. 30–32.

44 Ibid., ll. 29, 80–81.

45 S.T. Coleridge, *Table Talk*, ed. Carl Woodring, in *The Collected Works of Samuel Taylor Coleridge* (3 vols., Princeton, 1990), vol. 2, p. 388.

Anxiety concerning the possibility of American linguistic independence is clear in this remark. While Coleridge argues elsewhere that America is bound to England by the language of Shakespeare and Milton, here he claims Americans have no language.[46] The claim that the Americans "had stolen" English denies the former colonists rights to their cultural heritage, perhaps because by the time he made this remark Webster's and Jefferson's English and generations of speech had altered the relation the language was supposed to cement. He was conscious of this, at least to a degree, as is evinced in the last few words in his above remark, which point to the difference between "baggage" and "plunder". While it would be difficult to argue that Coleridge considered "baggage" a word that placed its speaker closer to God than "plunder" placed Americans, he clearly recognized the growth of an American dialect. This remark also reads as a grudging admission that if Americans had "stolen English," they were likely to escape punishment for the crime.

But a people who speak a language it does not possess naturally, even if it evolves its own dialect, is linguistically colonized since "language possesses (a) semantic and grammatical structure, imposed upon the 'given' phonetic material by the creative genius of the people who speak it," as James McKusick has argued in his study of Coleridge's theory of language.[47] Americans speak English, but if it is a stolen language, do they possess it? Can they hope to understand this language if they are not the people who possess the "creative genius" and imagination to access its meanings? Coleridge clearly did not think so. Like von Humboldt, he saw language as a "gift" to nations that helped constitute national identity. Coleridge saw England's language as a living, imaginative facility with a clear national alignment. Without this facility, a people cannot hope to understand the language of true genius, poetry. "The 'untranslatableness' of poetic language," Coleridge believed, "is a result of its naturalness."[48]

Coleridge's many remarks on the scarcity of true poetic genius would seem to preclude any but a very few—Shakespeare, Milton and Wordsworth, and possibly Chaucer and Spenser—from understanding the divinity communicated through the imagination. As he writes in *Biographia Literaria* (1817), "(t)he best part of human language ... is formed by a voluntary appropriation of fixed symbols to internal acts, to processes and results of imagination, the greater part of which have no place in the consciousness of uneducated man."[49] But in the same passage, he argues that all is not lost for the uneducated of England if they show proper respect for the nation and the national church. Coleridge asserts that "in civilized society, by imitation and passive remembrance of what they hear from their religious instructors and other superiors, the most uneducated share in the harvest which they neither sowed nor reaped."[50] He is able to reconcile himself to the loss of physically possessing America by declaring the concept of poetry and the property of genius the most legitimate sources of authority. His arguments in *Biographia Literaria* and *On the*

46 See *Table Talk*, ed. Carl Woodring, *The Collected Works*, vol. 2, 574–5.
47 James C. McKusick, *Coleridge's Philosophy of Language* (New Haven, 1986), p. 43.
48 Ibid., p. 32.
49 Coleridge, *Biographia Literaria*, vol. 2, p. 54.
50 Ibid., vol. 2, p. 54.

Constitution of Church and State (1830) for the clerisy as a civilizing branch of the nation yield a consistent message that language is the true sovereign, or at least a legitimate communicator of sovereignty, based partially on tradition (as defined by language, church, and state) and partially on imagination.

"For Coleridge," Jerome Christensen argues in this connection, "the genius is that individual whose symbolic and symbolizing place in the nation" and "in the language" of the nation "is the ideal monarch of the ideal commonwealth.[51]" By concentrating the authority over national imagination in the clerisy—which Coleridge defined extremely broadly, including not just those engaged in religious functions, but also lay people dedicated to its teachings and others who spread the culture of the nation through art and poetry—and arguing for its necessary civilizing mission within the nation, Coleridge neatly dissolves questions of state authority. He places imperial affinity on a linguistic course determined by a commonality he sees in America's—or any other colony's—use of the same language. In order for the nation to be "permanent" and "progressive" he writes, the clerisy must "diffuse through the whole community, and to every native entitled to its laws and rights, that quantity and quality of knowledge which was indispensable" for civilization. Such an arrangement is calculated "to guard the treasures, of past civilization, and thus to bind the present with the past."[52]

One of Coleridge's particular complaints with the way English was used in America was its overt performativeness, a quality inconsistent in his interpretation with an organically integrated poetic language communicated naturally by men of genius, binding "the present with the past" over centuries. Like many in England during the early years of the French Revolution, Coleridge saw dangers in language's performative potential. Coleridge's distrust of performative language and its democratic applications was not a product of his growing conservatism. In *The Watchman* on 11 April 1796, while still a supporter of republican ideals, he issued possibly his first pronouncement on the misuse of English in America, and his belief that it was related to using language to create actions rather than to describe them. "It has ever been our opinion," he wrote, "that in England the people are better than the government; in America that the government is better than the people. The Americans are lovers of freedom because their ledgers furnish irrefragable arguments in favour of it; but the vital spirit and high internal feelings of liberty they appear not to possess."[53] These "ledgers" are undoubtedly the various written acts that founded the American state and established principles of governance, the Declaration of Independence and U.S. Constitution foremost. As writings in a "stolen" language, they communicate the letters of ideas, but not the spirit. The true ideas of a people can only come through a language that has evolved with them.

---

51 Jerome Christensen, *Coleridge's Blessed Machine of Language* (Ithaca, 1981), p. 140.

52 Coleridge, *On the Constitution of Church and State*, ed. John Barrell (London, 1972), p. 34.

53 S.T. Coleridge, *The Watchman*, ed. Lewis Patton, in *The Collected Works of Samuel Taylor Coleridge* (Princeton, 1970), p. 212.

They cannot be communicated through a language illegitimately appropriated and transferred to alien, and as such unnatural places and purposes.

But despite his critiques, Coleridge had hopes for the new United States. He believed its errors could be corrected if its people could be made to understand their connection to England's speech and thought, and to submit to the genius of English in a new imperial configuration based on the sovereignty of language. In 1811, with Britain and the United States moving towards war, he anxiously, even pleadingly, stressed what he saw as the natural connection of Britain to America in terms that accept American political sovereignty, but reify American cultural dependence. In *The Courier* he wrote:

> Britain is *her* mother country, the dear land of her forefathers! And if the same language, the same books, the same laws, the same ancestry, and … the same history, can constitute *country*; if that dear and lofty word mean aught beside the clod under our feet; the Britons still remain the countrymen of Americans! Will she not then have said to herself, had the councils of wisdom been heard, instead of a violent and premature disjunction, I, like an elder child, should have been gradually released from parental authority, unalienated from parental affection. America would have been Great Britain with full elbow-room![54]

He returned to the metaphors of the "clod" and "Great Britain with elbow-room" almost twenty years later in "Lines Written in Commonplace Book of Miss Barbour, Daughter of the Minister of the U.S.A. to England" (1829), and similarly argued for a commonality of interests arising from "(l)aws, manners, language, faith, ancestral blood" (l. 5).[55]

While it often seems when sifting through Coleridge's discourse that America is "the clod under our feet" in more ways than one, his repeated references, however imperially hyphenated, to Anglo-American cooperation, show an unwillingness to let the colonies go, as most English writers had by the end of his life. While Frances Trollope and others were savaging American manners and customs in the 1830s, earning a lot of money and readers and attempting to discourage emigration, Coleridge held to his view of America as a province, in its way, of the Empire. A "country circumstanced as ours is … should become the Mother of Empires," he argued in the early 1830s:

> A Father should say, 'There, John now is a fine strong fellow and an enterprising lad, he shall be a colonist.' But then some fool like Lord— gets up and tells us 'Oh no! America should be a warning.' Good Heavens, Sir! a warning, and of what? Are we to beware of having two (sets) of men bound to us by the ties of allegiance and of affinity; 2 (sets) of men in a distant part of the world speaking the language of Shakespeare and Milton?[56]

This view of colonists as cultural and religious leaders filling the antipodes with culture coincides with Coleridge's aims for himself in 1794–95, and for the clerisy in

---

54 S.T. Coleridge, *Essays on His Times*, ed. David V. Erdman, in *The Collected Works of Samuel Taylor Coleridge* (3 vols, Princeton, 1978), vol. 2, pp. 235–6.

55 Unless otherwise noted, all citations to Coleridge's poems refer to the *Complete Poetical Works*, ed. E.H. Coleridge (Oxford, 1912).

56 Coleridge, *Table Talk*, vol. 2, pp. 574–5.

later years. In the 1790s he discussed the prospects of Pantisocracy in less calculating terms, but in ones that already saw America very much as "Great Britain with full elbow-room."

The Sonnets on Pantisocracy

Coleridge's later views, with Pantisocracy decades behind him, are distinctly more nationalistic, but not inconsistent with his youthful enthusiasm. America was not a physical place so much as an idea, and as such infinitely flexible in Coleridge's discourse. In this sense, Pantisocracy was *never* a physical place. In order to turn this abstract idea into one in which a feasible, tangible community could be created, Coleridge had to reconcile the irreconcilable. While America existed as an ideal standard of liberty, and an unpopulated paradise with unlimited room for a community of the elect on Earth, this ideal was made possible by physical and political realities. War and the establishment of a mercantile nation complicated the continuation of this "idea" of a godly, vacant place on Earth, but never erased it. Coleridge set the terms for his ability to entertain this contradiction in several of his "Sonnets on Eminent Characters" and his two sonnets on Pantisocracy.

The attribution of "On the Prospect of Establishing a Pantisocracy in America" to Coleridge is questionable. The editor of the most recent collected Coleridge, J.C.C. Mays, conjectures that this poem, not published until 1826, might be the work of George Dyer, a Pantisocrat in Coleridge's and Southey's company during the mid-1790s. E.H. Coleridge, in his edition of Coleridge's works, also questions Coleridge's authorship of this sonnet. But since it remains unattributed otherwise, and it deals with Pantisocracy in terms akin with those of the sonnet Coleridge enclosed in a letter to Southey in early 1795 treating similar sentiments, I will, with reservations, treat it as a Coleridge poem here. If it is not, it at least comes from the same collaborative imaginative project, and deserves attention for that reason.[57]

"On the Prospect of Establishing a Pantisocracy in America" begins unconventionally with a rhymed couplet—

Whilst pale Anxiety, corrosive Care,
The Tear of Woe, the gloom of sad Despair (ll. 1–2)

—and follows with four quatrains rhymed abba, cdcd, effe, inverting the traditional English sonnet form. Since the rest of Coleridge's sonnets from this period are painstakingly conventional in their rhyme schemes, it is difficult to dismiss this opening rhyme as an experiment. Coleridge seems to be playing with English literary tradition by making the traditional closing couplet the beginning of this sonnet. The poem, which expresses a desperation concerning political oppression at home, followed by an imaginative hope of creating a new society "on Transatlantic shore," could be saying one of two things. Either the idea of America that Coleridge is promoting here begins with England's end; or this planned emigration is a quest

---

57 See *Poetical Works: Part 2. Poems (Variorum Text)*, ed. J.C.C. Mays, in *The Collected Works of Samuel Taylor Coleridge* (3 vols, Princeton, 2001).

for the perfect, Edenic origins of human society, achieved by going through the apocalyptic experiences of the 1790s that seemed ready to push society, in a literally revolutionary way, to an end that was also its beginning.[58]

The poem's content lends itself to either interpretation. Coleridge first depicts what seems a hopeless abyss, brought on by political repression. The poem continues:

> And deepen'd Anguish generous bosoms rend; --
> Whilst patriot souls their country's fate lament;
> Whilst mad with rage demoniac, foul intent,
>   Embattled legions Despots vainly send
> To arrest the immortal mind's expanding ray
>   Of everlasting Truth; -- ... (ll. 3–8)

Then, in the middle of the eighth line, the *volta face* signals a geographic turning away:

>   ... I other climes
> Where dawns, with hope serene, a brighter day
>   Than e'er saw Albion in her happiest times,
> With mental eye exulting now explore,
>   And soon with kindred minds shall haste to enjoy
>   (Free from the ills which here our peace destroy)
> Content and Bliss on Transatlantic shore (ll. 8–14).

This better world—imagined as coming after, and as a result of a struggle against tyranny in (but not against) England—would seem to support a reading of Pantisocratic longing as a wish for a progressive societal evolution. The idea of leaving the "corrosive Care" of life in a politically torn England, which has sunk into a possibly bottomless "sad Despair," implies that the ending of one country's hopes of liberty marks the quest for a new life in a new land. But the poem's content argues otherwise. The opening lines, though forming a rhymed couplet suggestive of resolution, don't mark an end to the sonnet's concern with English oppression. The "Anguish," "lament," "rage demoniac, foul intent," and "Embattled legions" that dominate the lines that follow make it clear that the opening couplet has only begun an exploration into the current state of society.

A reading of Pantisocracy as a search for an idealized origin of natural self-possession becomes clearer in lines 6–8:

> Embattled legions Despots vainly send
> To arrest the immortal mind's expanding ray
>   Of everlasting Truth ...

---

58 This idea is of course consistent with M.H. Abrams's view in *Natural Supernaturalism: Tradition and Revolution in Romantic Literature* (New York, 1971) of Romantic discussions of revolution and return. Also, see Richard Jackson's article, "The Romantic Metaphysics of Time," *Studies in Romanticism* 19 (1980); 19–30.

Here we get a sense that the poem moves more persistently towards an inward, transcendental idea than away from a political materiality. The fact that the "expanding ray / Of everlasting Truth" leads towards "dawns, with hope serene," strengthens the image's Edenic resonance. The progress of this poem, promising "Content and Bliss on Transatlantic shore," moves away from an unacceptable present reality to a temporally nonspecific idea that is pictured as simpler and disconnected, as only a regression back through time could be. Only by isolation in this place where "a brighter day / Than e'er saw Albion in her happiest times," can man be reconnected with the nature from which language and culture originally spring. The Americans, having neither language nor culture, are silently imagined out of the lands the poem seeks, which can be read as welcoming the arrival of a more elevated innocence, which has passed through the apocalypse of contemporary events.

Coleridge's sonnet titled simply "Pantisocracy" was included in a letter to Southey. It communicates more clearly this belief in America as a tangible, post-apocalyptic state.

> No more my Visionary Soul shall dwell
> On Joys that were! (ll. 1–2)

His visions of a revived Golden Age, or Eden—"Joys that were!"—he expects soon to realize, when:

> O'er the Ocean swell
> Sublime of Hope I seek the cottag'd Dell,
> Where Virtue calm with careless step may stray,
> And dancing to the moonlight Roundelay
> The Wizard Passions weave an holy Spell (ll. 4–8).

Coleridge here places heaven quite firmly on Earth, in the homeliness of a "cottag'd Dell." Yet he anticipates "Kubla Khan's" visions of godlike creation and mystical rites with his dancing "Wizard Passions" which "weave an holy Spell." Yet unlike "Kubla Khan," where we hear "woman wailing for her demon-lover," (l. 16), in this redeemed version of England, "Virtue" can dance calmly in the presence of "Wizard Passions." Rather than responding to Kubla's presumption to create a world of his own by "Weaving a circle round him thrice" (l. 51) with pious Christian fear, we see the weaving of a "holy Spell" that comes from the political and social renewal of utopian Pennsylvania contributing to "Tears of doubt-mingled Joy" which behold "the rising Sun, & feel it dart / New Rays of Pleasance trembling to the Heart" (ll. 10, 13–14). The eyes of the poet, opening in his utopian community, behold a regeneration of society, and are distinctly contrasted with those that wake "From Precipices of distemper'd Sleep, / On which the fierce-eyed Fiends their Revels keep" (ll. 9, 11–12).

"Kubla Khan" was only three years off when Pantisocracy was in Coleridge's sights. His ability to imagine utopia in terms so idyllic yet clearly anticipatory of those that would express religious and creative guilt owes as much to the possibilities the world seemed to present before Pantisocracy's collapse as it does to his future anxieties, and their attendant opium addiction and bouts of creative paralysis. Only by understanding what America meant to Coleridge, and the contradictions therein, are we able to read the gaps in the poems of 1794–95 and see their consistent westward gestures.

Coleridge's political, populated America is a product of a European quest for freedom. This is why the "Eminent Characters" his sonnets celebrate are mostly Europeans who either helped the cause of liberty against tyranny between 1775–83, read a millennial promise in the events of the 1790s, or, in most cases, were involved in both struggles. But America isn't mentioned in these sonnets, largely because in reconciling the contradiction of an idea of America with a less perfect reality, Coleridge wants to exalt the elect who fought for freedom without highlighting the mundane result of their fight. Of his elect he said in 1795:

> (W)e turn with pleasure to the contemplation of that small but glorious band, whom we may truly distinguish by the name of thinking and disinterested Patriots. These are the men who have encouraged the sympathetic till they have become irresistable(sic) habits, and made their duty a necessary part of their self interest, by the long continued cultivation of that moral taste which derives our most exquisite pleasures from the contemplation of possible perfection, and proportionate pain from the perception of existing *depravation*.[59]

In *Conciones ad Populum* (1795) he added: "The perfectness of future Men is indeed a benevolent tenet, and may operate on a few Visionaries, whose studious habits supply them with employment, and seclude them from temptation."[60] His own group of Pantisocrats can be seen as these "Visionaries" who sought to "seclude them(selves) from temptation." Through the "Sonnets on Eminent Characters," Coleridge added Pantisocracy to a search for freedom he identifies with America. Pantisocracy in practice was only possible within the confines of a place that could be seen as empty, natural, and ideal. In Coleridge's imagination, that place in 1794–95 was America, but complicatedly so, since the American Revolution had rejected just such an English cultural usurpation.

Case Study: Imlay, Cooper and the Selling of America

Gilbert Imlay published *A Topographical Description of the Western Territory of North America* in London in 1792.[61] Above I have argued that Mary Wollstonecraft may have influenced its ideas. Whether or not she did, it seems likely that the Joseph Johnson circle helped shape the book, either through discussion or through Imlay's anticipation of the political hopes and frustrations of the group and the larger radical population it represented. While this book poses as an informative account in an Enlightenment vein, describing the "Soil, Climate, Natural History, Population, Agriculture, Manners, and Customs" of this region, it is, above all, a polemical incitement to republican-minded emigrants in England. An anonymous preface to

---

59 *Lectures 1795 On Politics and Religion*, ed. Lewis Patton and Peter Mann, in *The Collected Works of Samuel Taylor Coleridge* (Princeton, 1971), p. 12.

60 Ibid., p. 44.

61 Gilbert Imlay, *A Topographical Description of the Western Territory of North America* (London, 1793). Further references cited parenthetically.

Imlay's book, possibly by Johnson, the work's first printer—and in any case, in the radical vein of the Johnson circle—asks readers to treat "(t)he occasional remarks, which he has interspersed, respecting the laws, religion, and customs of Europe," with "the greatest indulgence," since it comes from a simple, honest sensibility (iv). Europeans, the preface's author writes, due to the pernicious influence of servile courtiers, have "imperceptibly lost much of (their) energy and manliness," and some straightforward words from an American just might be the antidote.

So, in Imlay the radicals of 1790s England found a refreshing viewpoint and an appealing idea: leave corrupted Europe behind and begin a rational, just society in the wilds of America. Imlay offers a blend of practical advice and aesthetic assessment, a combination of Enlightenment observation and Romantic description, laced with republican ideas. In the first letter of the book—framed as a series of letters written in Kentucky to a friend in England, but undoubtedly written in London—Imlay deplores "the unnatural habits of the Europeans" and their "universally bad laws," along with "the pernicious system of blending religion with politics, which has been productive of universal depravity" (1).

While Imlay continues his criticisms of Europe throughout his book, it is important to note that they are the same complaints radical English writers had been making throughout the eighteenth century. He combines these with thanks that the Enlightenment—and though he does not explicitly say so, he clearly means the works of the French philosophes—occurred at the same time that American identity was taking shape. Combined with a supposedly empty territory, this modern philosophy has made America not just an ideal place for forward-thinking English people, but the physical embodiment of an ideal *time* in history:

> There are æras favourable to the rise of new governments; and though nature is governed by invariable laws, the fortune of men and states appear frequently under the dominion of chances: but happily for mankind, when the American empire was forming, philosophy pervaded the genius of Europe, and the radiance of her features moulded the minds of men into a more rational order. (2)

Set against the "inflated grandeur of visionary plans for dominion, which the remains of gothic tyranny produced" in Europe, America stands for everything the Enlightenment was meant to produce in Europe, while Europe, despite supplying the philosophy, wallows in a degraded, "gothic" past (2).

Imlay builds upon this implication of temporal disjunction to assert the familiar concept of America as a "young" or "new" nation. But his version of this commonplace sees a place for Old World ideas and culture in the New World. Specifically, one finds traces of William Godwin's theories of perfectability in Imlay's description of the progress of civilization in the United States. He argues that the U.S. Constitution's allowance for growth and change through amendment is a perfect example of how it "is thus in the progression of things that governments will arrive at perfection" (31–2). Later he suggests that this perfection is most likely to occur in the physical space of America because of its virgin state and the needs of its growing population. "In the advancement of civilization," he writes, "agriculture seems to have been in every country the primary object of mankind—Arts and sciences have followed, and, ultimately, they have been relevant to each other" (92). America is unique in the history of this process because it is virgin land in an enlightened age. Agriculture, arts, sciences, literature, and government advance there "hand in hand," laying ideal foundations for the perfect society. Nature and art combine symbiotically in America, where a "government which, from its simple construction, and the unity and efficiency of its action," grows amidst "a natural history" in perfect harmony with "the physical world!" (64).

Imlay's depictions of Kentucky as a series of aesthetic objects were clearly intended to appeal just as directly to late eighteenth-century English radical sensibilities as were his promises for human development. His descriptions of various landscapes draw from Burkean concepts of the sublime and beautiful, and in other places he evokes a Gilpinesque picturesque, which he develops more fully in *The Emigrants*. His description of limestone on the Ohio River, west of Wheeling, about 300 miles from Pittsburgh, is typical of his approach throughout the book:

> Every thing here assumes a dignity and splendour I have never seen in any other part of the world. You ascend a considerable distance from the shore of the Ohio, and when you would suppose you had arrived at the summit of a mountain, you find yourself upon an extensive level. (42)

The passage continues in a long section that is quoted almost verbatim in Frances Jacson's "Jacobin" novel, *Disobedience* (1797), which I will discuss below. The passage describes the flowers, "full and perfect," the way the sun shines through "the azure heavens," the birds—"sweet songsters of the forests"—concluding that all one finds "gives delight" (42–3).

Imlay's praises of the republican spirit of America—occasionally the government, but more often the feeling one has in nature apart from European depravity—and his use of Burkean and Gilpinesque vocabulary are both calculated to appeal to a specifically English audience. His suggestion that in this virgin landscape settlers will find the Godwinian perfection they can only find in theory at home in England is clearly aimed at the radical circle among which he traveled while in Europe. But while one might expect to find Americans themselves praised in a work by an American citizen, Imlay rarely mentions the presence of any kind of culture in the lands he describes. In fact, he goes out of his way to condemn Thomas Jefferson as a hypocrite for holding slaves and as something of a tyrant in government.

Coupled with the fact that Imlay's books were published first in London—*The Emigrants* was not published in the United States until 1964[62]—his books must be seen as transatlantic works designed for English audiences.[63] Like Coleridge, Imlay erases Americans from America, for the most part, only referring to them as general types who embody liberty—and might as well be English or anything else since the landscape is what makes people what they are in Kentucky—or as corrupt hypocrites,

62 John Seelye, "The Jacobin Mode in Early American Fiction: Gilbert Imlay's *The Emigrants*," *Early American Literature* 22 (1987): 204–12; p. 204.

63 Tilar Mazzeo also makes this point in "The Impossibility of Being Anglo-American: The Rhetoric of Emigration and Transatlanticism in British Romantic Culture, 1791–1833," *European Romantic Review* 16/1 (2005): 59–78; p. 63.

like Jefferson. In this way he gives his readers what they need, clearing a space for Godwinian ideals much the way that earlier utopias had rhetorically cleared space for Puritan ideals with the imaginative, and then literal, erasure of Native Americans from New England.

Thomas Cooper's *Some Information Respecting America* (1794), also published by Joseph Johnson with the idea of encouraging English radicals to emigrate to America, brings a much less emotional but still enthusiastic voice to describing the New World. Coleridge and Southey read Cooper (as well as Imlay) when planning their utopia. Pantisocracy has been thoroughly discussed in terms of its effect on Coleridge's politics and poetics and in the context of 1790s British radicalism.[64] An essay by James McKusick extends the discussion of Pantisocracy to "the larger context of British maritime exploration and the colonization of the New World," concluding that the plan "arises from an imaginary representation of America that assimilates it to the South Sea Islands, with their fabled luxuriance and remoteness from European politics."[65] McKusick's discussion of Southey's and Coleridge's appreciation of Edward Christian and the famed mutiny on the *Bounty*, and of Captain Cook's exploits in the South Seas, usefully complicates the poets' relationship to empire, presenting both as drawn to adventure and exoticism as well as radical politics. But it ignores other relevant work from 1794–95—particularly the "Sonnets on Eminent Characters"—thus overlooking the scheme's multiple sources. Coleridge was in correspondence with Joseph Priestley, whose sons, along with Thomas Cooper, had scouted the land for the project. He is known to have read Cooper's tract that encouraged emigration to America.[66] Coleridge's sonnets express a strong sympathy with Priestley. McKusick's claim that the South Seas were attractive because of their "remoteness from European politics" ignores the fact that Coleridge's American references are embedded in discussions of people engaged in those very politics, often on the side he supported. Also ignored is the consonance of Coleridge's view of the "English-only" character Pantisocracy should have with Cooper's beliefs.[67]

These beliefs essentially set Cooper's book on America apart from Imlay's *Topographical Description*. While Imlay discusses Americans as general examples of a universal humanity, and by doing so leaves the English reader to imagine a free

---

64 See Richard Holmes, *Coleridge: Early Visions* (New York, 1989); Nicholas Roe, *Wordsworth and Coleridge: The Radical Years* (Oxford, 1988).

65 James McKusick, " 'Wisely Forgetful': Coleridge and the Politics of Pantisocracy," in Tim Fulford and Peter Kitson (ed.), *Romanticism and Colonialism: Writing and Empire, 1780–1830* (Cambridge, 1998), pp. 107–28; p. 107.

66 Coleridge, "To Robert Southey," 21 October 1794, in *Letters of Samuel Taylor Coleridge*, ed. E.H. Coleridge (Boston and New York, 1895), vol. 1, p. 112.

67 Cooper considered the predominance of English settlers especially important, and asserted that the part of Pennsylvania he recommended would become more English as more emigrants settled there: "(A)lthough American manners and society approach nearer to English than to any other," he wrote, "they are not quite English; I have no doubt of the inclination of English emigrants bending that way; in fact, I do not know where they can do better, or where upon the whole they can pitch their tents so eligibly." *Some Information Respecting America* (London, 1794), pp. 74–5.

cultural field in many ways, Cooper goes one step further and offers practical advice for how to make spots of American geography into English cultural space. Cooper goes as far as possible to write an America that is as much like England as possible. He looks for a similar climate and topography, going state by state, rejecting most for various reasons. Slavery is a major—and rather ironic—objection. Later Cooper would become a slaveholding citizen of South Carolina, and an advocate for the rights of fellow slaveholders, but in 1794 he was an abolitionist.

Cooper's reasons for rejecting New England have more to do with soil than morality. He finds Rhode Island most like England in terms of climate and precipitation, but the soil there is not good enough. The fact that by the 1790s settlement had advanced to such a state that buying enough land to found an English colony was problematic also served to disqualify Rhode Island.[68] Cooper declared New Jersey too swampy, and New York good, but not perfect. Its proximity to the Indian frontier made it dangerous.[69]

Pennsylvania answers Cooper's purposes best. "I know of very few objections that can be made to the state of Pennsylvania," he writes:

> In point of climate, the difference between this part of the American continent and Great Britain is not only very supportable, but in my opinion much in favour of the former, even to British feelings, especially in the northern and northwestern parts of the state. The summers are somewhat warmer and the winters colder here than at London: but the general state of the air, is more dry, more pleasant, and I think more healthy.[70]

Cooper framed his book similarly to the way Imlay had framed his *Topographical Description*. Formatted as letters to a friend in England, it pretends to give objective information to those in England who find the political climate of the early 1790s uncomfortable and the idea of emigrating to America something to consider. But Cooper neglects to mention his financial interest in encouraging emigration. He had purchased several hundred acres of land in Pennsylvania, partly in conjunction with Joseph Priestley's sons. While Cooper does not seem to have been a large scale speculator, he had definite interests in encouraging enough emigration to make a profit.

Cooper's bias for the lands he was in the process of purchasing can be seen most clearly in the pains he takes to dissuade people from believing what Imlay had told them about Kentucky. Imlay, also a speculator with a specific interest in the landscape he extols, "has told the truth," Cooper writes: "but he has not told (and perhaps he was not aware of) the whole truth."[71] Cooper then warms to his topic, declaring Kentucky's climate too hot, its atmosphere too moist, its reliance on slave labor intolerable, and its situation at risk from Indian attack. He writes that much of the land in Kentucky, though rich, is too dry for agriculture, and the rest is too wet for building roads.[72] He follows these reports with a 10-page anonymous

---

68 Cooper, *Some Information Concerning America*, p. 9.
69 Ibid., pp. 9–10, 15.
70 Ibid., p. 16.
71 Ibid., p. 24.
72 Ibid., pp. 24–6.

report on the inconveniences and discomforts of Kentucky for settlers, and an eight-page advertisement from the state of Pennsylvania that describes improvements in communications, roads, and canals.[73]

Imlay and Cooper undoubtedly believed in their schemes. Cooper spent the rest of his life in America, and while his politics changed significantly and his distaste for southern states evaporated, his attachment to the country he promoted only strengthened. The important point to recognize about these two works is that they were probably the most significant books published in England during the 1790s concerning America and the Americans. As I have tried to show, America was held out as a place that could still be English, and Americans were a people who either fit a universal type, or could safely be avoided.

Imlay's description of America in terms that would have been familiar to anyone interested in aesthetic ideas in late eighteenth-century England had an influence in literature as well as emigration. While I have argued elsewhere that Imlay's work might have influenced not just Pantisocracy, but "Kubla Khan," his influence shows much more clearly in several novels from the period that use emigration as major plot elements.[74] The 1797 Jacobin novel *Disobedience* focuses on oppressed English children finding freedom in a republican form in America. Eliza Parson's *The Voluntary Exile* (1795) also presents a case of members of a younger, freedom-loving generation finding what they need by fleeing England for America. Several works by Robert Bage, especially *Hermsprong* (1796) and *The Fair Syrian* (1787), use America as well to make a contrast between a corrupted, luxurious England and a simple, republican America.

The authorship of *Disobedience* is in question. The English Short Title Catalogue lists Frances Jacson as its author, but the novel itself is anonymous. The Huntington Library's copy of the first edition has Alethea (Brereton) Lewis penciled in as author. The work is typical of the many novels that have come to be known as "Jacobin novels" published in the period. It makes use of a romantic plot—in this case a marriage plot—to show the iniquities brought about by a system of hereditary wealth in Europe. This system is addicted to a luxury that weakens judgments, and perpetuates itself through cynical maneuvering with marriageable children so corrupted elders can improve their financial and social standings. What comes across as practical in most of Jane Austen's work tends to read as cold and reprehensible in Jacobin novels.

Two lovers, Mary Seabright and William Challoner, suffer from the shallowness and prohibitions of their parents for three volumes of this four-volume novel. They decide in the fourth volume to emigrate to America. William's father, Humphry Challoner, forbids his knowledge-loving son to read after he spends four years living with a bookish uncle, a curate in Bristol. He is destined to run the family farm, not to think. Soon after returning to the farm, his father wants him to marry a neighboring wealthy farmer's daughter. But William is already in love with another and cannot bear the thought of a mercenary marriage.

---

73 Ibid., pp. 29–47.

74 Christopher Flynn, "Coleridge's American Dream: National Genius, Natural Language and the Sonnets of 1794–95," *European Romantic Review* 13/3 (2002): 411–25.

Mary's parents abandon her at birth. Her mother is Lady Caroline L— and her father is an English officer with no fortune. The impossibility of the match infuriates Lady Caroline's parents, who disown her. Lady Caroline dumps her daughter on faithful family servants—in this novel the poor are almost always the rich at heart, and the wealthy rarely find a way to feel compassion—and these servants, Eleanor and Richard, move to a cottage in Wales where they raise Mary as their own daughter. There, in the Vale of Llamamon, she meets William. But over the years Lady Caroline's officer has found his way to a knighthood and a fortune, and the couple has married. Now Sir James Seabright, he and Lady Caroline decide to reclaim their daughter to use as a way into yet a higher reach of society. They try forcing her to marry a nobleman, but she manages to escape, and, to the reader's delight, William manages to find her.

Mary and William escape from most of the institutions of European oppression throughout the first three volumes of the novel—parents, convents, commerce— before finally escaping together to Ireland, where they marry. A man they meet there, Mr. Eddows, suggests they emigrate to America, and they decide on following his advice immediately. "I know not why we should be averse from quitting a country where we cannot promise ourselves that we shall find one friend, while we can go to another which offers us as favourable a field for our industry, in company with a person who appears to warmly to take an interest in our concerns," Mary says.[75]

This new William and Mary travel with Eddows to America, and decide to move inland to Kentucky. The novel seems quite clearly, not only with the protagonists' names, to be drawing parallels between the "Glorious Revolution" and the kind of republicanism it wants to promote. The American Revolution, according to Mr. Eddows, while bringing freedom from England, has actually introduced "luxury, and a relaxing of morals into the great towns" on the eastern seaboard of the United States.[76] Inland they find "simplicity, frugality, order, industry, and virtue."[77] This idyll is very specifically tied to the one Imlay painted in *A Topographical Description*. Soon upon arriving in America, William and Mary hear great things about Kentucky, which

> began to be spoken of as a country that offered every advantage that a new settler could desire. Its partizans extolled it as the garden of the world. They boasted of its fruits, its flowers, its climate; of the variety of its quadrupeds; the beauty and excellence of its feathered tribe; of the excellence of its fish. They spoke of the order that was already established; of the security it had obtained from the inroads of the Indians; of the importance it had risen to; of its noble and navigable rivers; of the canals that were to connect them; of its trade, which, by means of the Mississippi and the Ohio, was to embrace the productions of the whole globe; of its surprising natural curiosities; and, above all, of its agricultural advantages, that pointed it out as a nursery and paradise for American farmers.[78]

---

75 *Disobedience* (London, 1797), vol. 4, pp. 62–3.

76 Ibid., IV:65.

77 Ibid., IV:65–6.

78 Ibid., vol. 4, pp. 79–80.

While *Disobedience*'s version of late eighteenth-century Kentucky sounds wonderful, the absence of actual Americans, as seen above in the works of Coleridge, Cooper, Imlay, and others, is striking. Here we get unmistakable evidence of American industry, agriculture, and commerce, but American social life, customs, manners, all are absent. In a novel almost entirely focused on social life in England, the lack of such in America stands out. William and Mary seem to have gone from being sociologists in an idealist vein in England to materialists arguing that happiness comes from navigable rivers and rich soil. Going from oppressive parents to canals and commerce is a significant category shift.

We finally get a group of Americans, and like William, Mary, their parents and Mr. Eddows, they are a mixed lot. Some are born and bred republicans, while others feel drawn to the luxury of the eastern cities. A group sentiment evolves. Begun with remarks on Native Americans, it suggests that the best aspects of the American character derive directly from either English origins or English teaching. The generous landscape of the New World, in other words, brings out the essential Englishness of the people who enjoy it. At one point, Mary views Kentucky's sublimity with wonder. She listens to people tell her of "subterranean lakes; of the precipices of white marble, the banks of the rivers covered with groves of red cedar … of the amazing quantities of salt springs which constantly emit water that yields the finest salt in inexhaustible quantities … In a word, to all that variety of beauty and wonder that the enchanted land of Kentucky exhibits to the astonished and enraptured eyes of an European." But all this natural beauty, despite its capacity to "astonish" European eyes, is narrated very much in European aesthetic terms. There is much more Burke and Gilpin here than James Fennimore Cooper. And, somehow, despite the virgin quality of these scenes, this abundance of beauty leads to the conviction that "this land had once been inhabited by people further advanced in the arts of civilized life than are any tribe of Indians yet known," and that the tribes of the area originally "were Welch."[79]

Disobedience did not originate this idea, of course. The legend of Madoc, the Welsh warrior who settled in America, was long known in England. Robert Southey would write his epic poem, *Madoc*, based on the myth, in 1807.[80] Combined with an aestheticizing of the American landscape in English terms, the novel finds a way of making all that's good about America—even and especially the unmistakably indigenous people and nature—of European origin. Mary furthers this work by constantly drawing the landscape around her. Over time, she turns a young American, Agatha Humberton, from a spoiled urbanite into a true lover of drawn landscapes. Agatha, who is being brought to Kentucky from New York by her parents, has a realistic sense of the hardships of frontier life. But this realism goes against the novel's message, and as such it must be erased. Mary slowly draws Agatha into drawing the world around her, and in this way teaches a pragmatic American to have a romantic English view of her surroundings as an aesthetic experience.

Agatha wonders at Mary's excitement as they travel the Cumberland Gap on their way to Kentucky: "I see your cheek flushed with the roses of health, and your

---

79 Ibid., vol. 4, pp. 91–2.
80 Robert Southey, *Madoc* (London, 1807).

eye sparkle with the scintillations of delight; yet you, like me, are doomed to be for ever buried in the horrid wilderness to which we are going; there to waste your health and strength in laborious exertions, that are to be alone rewarded by a scanty and precarious subsistence."[81] But before long Agatha becomes as much an aesthete as Mary, just by being taught how to view the natural world properly. And just as the wilderness only becomes a landscape when seen properly, the American only becomes a worthwhile creature once Anglicized.

The novel ends in America, but in an America that has been chosen to mimic the Wales where William and Mary met and fell in love. They build a house on land that reminds them exactly of Llamamon. Agatha and Eddows marry, and build a mansion within a mile of William and Mary. Agatha's parents, the Humbertons, also build a large house in the neighborhood. They have quickly become an English village, with these three families as the gentry, and several others as the laborers. All three houses are described in terms of their views and prospects, much like country homes in England. The sublime aspects of the voyage from New York to Kentucky have become tamed, as if emigration were a picturesque tour, and home is an English village.[82]

Eliza Parsons' *Voluntary Exile*, set during the American Revolution, presents several variations of the parent-child metaphor seen so often in works during the period. Like *Disobedience*, America serves as a place for moral regeneration after the luxuries and iniquities of England have done their damage. Henry Biddulph and Ned Osborne both end up joining the British Army to escape arranged marriages of social advancement at home in London. They become friends and see scenes of bloodshed and horror. Henry ends up in a battle, very near death:

> Mr. Biddulph received several desperate wounds, and fell among the slain, for, careless of life, he had fought with all the impetuosity of courage goaded by despair. The Americans having subdued their enemies, hastened to rejoin their General, leaving the ground covered with the dead and dying. Biddulph lay for some time unable to move; his left arm was wounded in a dreadful manner, besides other severe hurts in the different parts of his body. He was sensible of his situation, and saw no help near; he therefore resigned himself to an expected death with calmness, supported by hope of being reunited to the objects of his love.[83]

But three Americans come along and rescue him from the pile of corpses. They turn out to be Quakers, and Henry lives with them for a while. The time he spends with them helps change him, as does his active viewing of American sublimity. But as in *Disobedience*, Henry learns more from his own ways of seeing America than from anything the Americans teach him. He returns to England, renewed in spirit and body. Again, America serves a recuperative function in the Jacobin novel.

Imlay and Cooper set out to sell America to disaffected English radicals. But the America they sold had very little to do with Americans. As we have seen, in Cooper's case it avoided them as much as possible, and in Imlay's it generalized

---

81 *Disobedience*, vol. 4, pp. 107–8.

82 Ibid., vol. 4, p. 50.

83 Eliza Parsons, *The Voluntary Exile* (5 vols, London, 1795), vol 2, 110–11.

them to the point where they represented Godwinian principles more than anything else. Henry Biddulph's experience at the end of Parsons' novel is a typical version of the function America was supposed to serve the English during the 1790s:

> (He) bid adieu to the shores of America for ever, where Biddulph had witnessed so many melancholy scenes; but where he had likewise experienced hospitality and friendship, and where he had met with a confirmation of happiness, such as he never expected to enjoy when he left England a 'VOLUNTARY EXILE' from his native country, and to which he never expected a return. His voyage was infinitely shorter than when he took his departure for America, and his mind, what a revolution had that undergone from the deepest sorrow and heart-felt despair to exultation, happiness, and … supreme delight![84]

America, as with all the works in this chapter, has succeeded in purging what was bad about Englishness from Henry without exposing him to anything particular about Americanness along the way.

Conclusion

Time and utopia are perpetually at odds. While the word coined by Sir Thomas More in the early sixteenth century from the Greek *eu* and *topos* translates roughly into "good place," More made clear in a punning set of verses often omitted from English translations of *Utopia* that his ideal commonwealth might also be "*ou*topia," or, "no place." The various figurations of utopian societies almost always assume both meanings at once, as well as an atemporal state, which might best be termed "no time," historically speaking. The point of utopia, after all, is perfection, a stage of existence beyond or prior to history, where any change diminishes the quality of life. Since historical processes are inseparable from change, utopias are necessarily ahistorical.

The English utopias of the 1790s and the first three decades of the nineteenth century stand out for several reasons. First of all, utopia, while always a literary genre, for radicals in the 1790s and those in the following decades, had an actual physical space in which it might be built. The political repression that English politicians instituted as a response to the French Revolution and the Napoleonic wars highlighted the cracks in a system at the same time that several texts about America offered a laboratory for change. As Paul Ricoeur puts it, the "development of new, alternative perspectives defines utopia's most basic function. May we not say then that imagination itself—through its utopian function—has a *constitutive* role in helping us *rethink* the nature of our social life?"[85] If we apply Ricoeur's assessment of utopia's function in social life to the situation that English liberals and radicals found themselves in during the 1790s, we see that America served as an imaginary space against which to measure English realities. It did so in part because it exhibited a functioning democracy in a time when many of the democratic elements of English

---

84 Ibid., vol. 5, pp. 260–61.

85 Paul Ricoeur, *Lectures on Ideology and Utopia*, ed. George H. Taylor (New York, 1986), p. 16.

political life were being challenged, and in part despite the presence of such a government. "If every ideology tends finally to legitimate a system of authority," Ricoeur writes,

> does not every utopia, the moment of the other, attempt to come to grips with the program of power itself? ... Is it not because a credibility gap exists in all systems of legitimation, all authority, that a place for utopia exists too? In other words, is it not the function of utopia to expose the credibility gap wherein all systems of authority exceed ... both our confidence in them and our belief in their legitimacy?[86]

So, the utopias ostensibly set in America from the 1790s through the 1820s exposed the gap between the promises of the English constitution and the realities of existence before the Reform Bill of 1832 much more than they commented on the actual state of the new American republic.

Still, this use of America as an imaginative space helps us see how English conceptions of Americans developed during this period. The very fact that America served as the space for utopias based on unrealized European ideals meant that in important ways it remained invisible to the English, while in other ways it provided yet another contrast to the utopia it was supposed to house. If English radicals used these utopias as measures of English decay, they also tended to see them as gauges of the failure of Americans to live up to European theories of the perfect society. Karl Mannheim has argued that while utopias are literary works, they are more essentially located in the sociology of the group dynamic out of which they emerge.[87] The works this chapter has discussed clearly show a similar dynamic. The next two chapters will examine what the English wrote about Americans when political events in Europe gave them more leisure actually to see them.

---

86 Ibid., p. 17.
87 Karl Mannheim, *Ideology and Utopia: An Introduction to the Sociology of Knowledge*, trans. Louis Wirth and Edward Shils (New York, 1956), pp. 206–9.

Chapter Three

Savagery and Civility: States of Nature and the Quest for Natural Man

Positive views of "natural man" in America—either Indian or pioneer—stem from Rousseau's concept of the Noble Savage, according to a commonplace that countless writers assert, and have been asserting for many years. This assertion, while persistent, is simply incorrect. The idea that a significant number of late eighteenth-century Europeans considered savages noble is a myth.[1] Rousseau never used the phrase, and, despite all of the statements in the more than two centuries since the appearance of his *Discourse on Equality* (1755), which is generally cited as the source of the concept of the Noble Savage, he viewed savages as naïve rather than innocent, and certainly not noble, with that term's aristocratic connotations, or in the broader sense of "(h)aving high moral qualities."[2] The "state of nature" as understood in the Enlightenment had become the America of the North American Indians prior to contact with Europeans in most English texts by the late eighteenth century. This locating of the natural state appears in major works by John Locke and Thomas Hobbes and, to an extent, Rousseau. This chapter examines the emergence of "Americans" (and here I mean Americans of European descent) from a mixture of European culture and communion with the American state of nature conceptualized as a savage space.

I will briefly discuss competing versions of the state of nature and savagery that influenced a discourse geared towards identifying features that distinguished Americans from the English. Savagery, as conceived by late eighteenth-century European writers, is a broad set of ideas, or an unfixed, unstable category at best, referring loosely to the state of people outside of European understandings of civilization, and specifically to North American Indians in many cases. Civility is just as broad a concept, usually defined by what it is not rather than according to any positivistic characteristics. The philosophical and anthropological validity of such terms is dubious at best—and in any sense "savagery" is inapplicable to the Native

---

1   See Ter Ellingson, *The Myth of the Noble Savage* (Berkeley, 2001), for the source of the phrase "noble savage" in the writings of early seventeenth-century French traveler and ethnographer Marc Lescarbot. Ellingson's book does a thorough job of debunking this tenacious myth.

2   Jean Jacques Rousseau, "Discourse on the Origin and Foundations of Inequality Among Men," in *The Discourses and Other Early Political Writings*, ed. Victor Gourevitch (Cambridge, 1997); *Oxford English Dictionary*, definition 4.a.

American peoples the authors considered here discuss. The broadest distinction between savage and civil in writings of the time is between simple and complex, and North American societies were not only richly complex, but recognized as such in numerous works of the period. What is significant is that such a discourse existed, and that it shaped the discussion of what happened to Europeans in America, and how Euro-Americans developed. Throughout this chapter, then, when I refer to "savages" and "savagery" I am referring not to actual people, but to discursive constructions by English and other European writers of the period fraught with instability and uncertainty.[3]

Johannes Fabian's argument that, in the ethnographer's text, travels in space are equivalent to travels in time, underlies this chapter.[4] I argue that at least from the 1770s, Europeans in America were seen as being in danger of degenerating in a world where the mixture of savagery with civility threatened to rewrite their identity. In many instances Europeans were portrayed as transitional figures in the process of becoming semi-savage who must struggle to return to their former civilized state. The emergence of anthropology as a discrete discipline occurred in the latter half of the eighteenth century, and as it did the concept of savagery changed. It had been principally a philosophical idea. But the very material encounters of Europeans with the indigenous peoples of the Americas beginning at the end of the fifteenth century generated a discourse whose influential participants—Montesquieu, Bacon, Hobbes, Locke, Rousseau, Kant, and Herder—developed a new science of humanity, which recognized racial difference by the end of the eighteenth century, and grappled with the question of time's role in human progress. "Nature," John Zammito writes, "came increasingly to be conceived as temporalized (e.g. by Buffon), while human history presumed a measure of 'universality' if only to encompass the profound 'otherness' that its variety presented to the observer."[5] The phenomenon of Europeans, with their "universal" ontological status, traveling to the temporally prior, natural environment of the Americas, displaced them for many authors. Their participation in natural history challenged their universal status, and offered other Europeans subjects for anthropological speculation grounded in concrete experience.

Novelists and poets entered this debate, and in doing so often removed their subjects from the then common understanding of human history, with its political, cultural, and social biases. The instability of identity in novels such as Tobias Smollett's *The Expedition of Humphry Clinker* (1771), Charlotte Lennox's *Euphemia* (1790), the anonymous *School for Fathers* (1788) and *The Adventures of Jonathan Corncob* (1787), suggests that the social and physical environment of America can make savages of the civilized. Twenty years later, after decades of war with France,

---

3   The idea of savagery held at the time is too heterogeneous to define clearly, but it basically meant "not civilized." As Bernard Sheehan has written in *Savagism & Civility: Indians and Englishmen in Colonial Virginia* (Cambridge, 1980), "throughout the early years of exploration and settlement European thinking and feeling about the native people of America occurred within the limits of the customary division between civility and savagism. Until the nineteenth century few serious European thinkers transcended this limitation" (1).

4   See *Time and the Other: How Anthropology Makes its Object* (New York, 1983).

5   John H. Zammito, *Kant, Herder, and the Birth of Anthropology*. (Chicago, 2002), p. 228. For an account of anthropology's development out of philosophy, see pp. 221–53.

the tide had turned; civilization had become a tainted concept for some. Wordsworth, Byron, and others rewrote the dichotomy of savage vs. civil as an opposition between nature and culture, with nature offering the best possibility for the regeneration of mankind. Their subjects' imagined pre-cultural state, which exists outside of the historical framework of modern events, becomes a site of retreat that is subtly, but importantly different from the utopias discussed in the previous chapter. Rather than seeking to begin history anew, those who yearned, however ambivalently, for a degree of savagery, did so in an attempt to erase history altogether.

The State of Nature and Concepts of Savagery

"(I)n the beginning all the World was America," Locke writes in his *Second Treatise on Government*, setting up Indian cultures as examples of humanity at the youngest stage of the continuum of cultural evolution all peoples traveled.[6] Locke's state of nature is directly antithetical to the state of war. The former belongs to an order and begins a rational sequence, while the latter is a deviation that violates it. Civil society develops progressively from the state of nature, so the opposition of savage and civil can be seen as temporal rather than—or as well as—spatial. As Locke writes, "the Indians in America ... (are) still a pattern of the first Ages in Asia and Europe."[7] They were uncomplicated and less developed because they occupied a physical location where land was abundant, making a hunter/gatherer economy feasible. But while Locke places American Indians in a temporal state prior to that of Europe and Asia, it would be a mistake to see him as assigning them to an anthropological category based on essential difference. Race does not figure into his rationalist view of man— a universal category—whose progressive social development can be plotted along a temporally organized line.

Hobbes's *Leviathan* (1651) similarly considers the natural state a temporal designation. "WARRE," he writes, "consisteth not in Battell onely, or the act of fighting; but in a tract of time, wherein the Will to contend by Battell is sufficiently known: and therefore the notion of Time, is to be considered in the nature of Warre ... So the nature of Warre, consisteth not in actuall fighting; but in the known disposition thereto, during all the time there is no assurance to the contrary."[8] As with Locke, Hobbes's natural state is the first stage in the historical development of a society. The differences between Locke's peaceful state of nature, where people only take what they need and are governed by reason, and Hobbes's violent state, where the lack of a single authority, be it commonwealth or king, keeps all in a constant struggle for a survival which is inevitably "nasty, brutish and short," are well known and not to be dismissed. But the fact that both used the American Indian as the contemporary example of a developmental stage Europe had left behind long ago meant that writers who later sought to define Euro-American society did so within the context of a discourse that denied co-evalness to people in constant intercourse

---

6   John Locke, *Two Treatises on Government*, ed. Peter Laslett (Cambridge, 1988), p. 301.

7   Ibid., p. 339.

8   Thomas Hobbes, *Leviathan*, ed. Richard Tuck (Cambridge, 1996), pp. 88–9.

with its object. As American Indians and Europeans in America became part of the same cultural landscape, the latter entered the emerging concepts of savagery that saw people in such a state as the embodiment of a prior stage of cultural evolution. Just as importantly, this discourse assigned the physical space in which this new society was developing to a primeval time.

The common misconception concerning Rousseau's supposed authorship of the concept of Noble Savagery comes from his blaming inequality on private property and the development of civil society in his *Second Discourse* (1755). Rousseau, like Hobbes and Locke before him, places the state of nature prior to the development of government. But unlike either, he finds things to envy in this state. "There is," he wrote, "I sense, an age at which the individual human being would want to stop; You will look for the age at which you would wish your Species had stopped. Discontented with your present state, for reasons that herald even greater discontents for your unhappy Posterity, you might perhaps wish to be able to go backward."[9] But while Rousseau frequently calls attention to advantages found in this earlier state of "your Species," he is clear that there is neither nobility nor progress in the existence of "Savage man." The "savage"—who the American Indian typifies for Rousseau, just as for Hobbes and Locke—wanders "in the forests without industry, without speech, without settled abode, without war, and without tie, without any need of others of his kind and without any desire to harm them, perhaps even without ever recognizing any one of them individually, subject to few passions and self-sufficient," with "only the sentiments and the enlightenment suited to this state."[10] While a tortured soul might find some solace in contemplating such a state, a thinking person could hardly consider it a noble one. In it, a man's "intelligence made no more progress than his vanity. If by chance he made some discovery, he was all the less in a position to communicate it as he did not even recognize his Children." The consequences of the perpetuation of this state are depressing: "(T)here was neither education nor progress, generations multiplied uselessly; and as each one of them always started at the same point, Centuries went by in all the crudeness of the first ages, the species had already grown old, and man remained ever a child."[11]

So much for "noble savagery." This negative picture of the state of nature was reintroduced to English readers, specifically applied to Americans, at the end of the War of Independence. Crèvecoeur's *Letters from an American Farmer* (1782) probably makes the clearest distinction between an America modeled on European civility and one still dominated by a primal state of nature. Crèvecoeur, like many of his contemporaries, followed Locke, Hobbes and Rousseau in considering western North America as a prior stage of human development, despite its contemporaneous existence with the civilized (European) world. And while this world was still

---

9 Rousseau, "Discourse on the Origin and Foundations of Inequality Among Men," p. 133.

10 Ibid., p. 157.

11 Ibid., p. 157. It is important to note that Rousseau did not believe American Indians were in a complete state of nature. He believed the state of "true savagery" completely absent from the earth. See Ellingson, pp. 83–5.

emerging from savagery, its progress toward civility was inevitable. "(N)ear the great woods," Crèvecoeur writes,

> Men seem to be placed still farther beyond the reach of government, which in some measure leaves them to themselves. How can it pervade every corner, as they were driven there by misfortunes, necessity of beginnings, desire of acquiring large tracks of land, idleness, frequent want of economy, ancient debts; the reunion of such people does not afford a very pleasing spectacle. When discord, want of unity and friendship, when either drunkenness or idleness prevail in such remote districts, contention, inactivity, and wretchedness must ensue. There are not the same remedies to these evils as in a long-established community. The few magistrates they have are in general little better than the rest; they are often in a perfect state of war; that of man against man, sometimes decided by blows, sometimes by means of the law; that of man against every wild inhabitant of these venerable woods, of which they are come to dispossess them. There men appear to be no better than carnivorous animals of a superior rank, living on the flesh of wild animals when they can catch them, and when they are not able, they subsist on grain. He who would wish to see America in its proper light and have a true idea of its feeble beginnings and barbarous rudiments must visit our extended line of frontiers, where the last settlers dwell and where he may see the first labours of settlement, the mode of clearing the earth, in all their different appearances, where men are wholly left dependent on their native tempers and on the spur of uncertain industry, which often fails when not sanctified by the efficacy of a few moral rules.[12]

I have quoted at length from this passage from the chapter entitled "What is an American?" because it engages in many of the tropes that characterize late eighteenth-century writings about Americans. They are seen as simultaneously savage and civil, with fluid racial identities, and an uncertain participation in modern time. Like the Indians in virtually every ethnographic text or traveler's account of the period, they are drunken and indolent. The "no-time" of utopia becomes a mongrelized time, ultimately a temporal frame used to develop a discourse concerning a supposed diversity of races that obtained not just between Europeans and those they had always considered different (and inferior), but between Europeans and Americans. While racial categories at this time were extremely unstable, as my later discussion of racial theorist Johann Friedrich Blumenbach will hopefully show, writers of the time were beginning to use characteristics that would become known as markers of race to distinguish people in North America.[13] Crèvecoeur seems to have been divided between older concepts of race as a universal category, equivalent to "humanity," or "mankind," and emerging categories of racial distinction, and to have placed backwoods Euro-Americans in this confused discourse. These "barbarous"

---

12 J. Hector St. John de Crèvecoeur, *Letters from an American Farmer*, ed. Albert E. Stone (New York, 1981), p. 72.

13 The term race, as Nicholas Hudson has shown, referred to what we today would consider nations, or even more widely, ethnicities, in the early modern period, only taking on its modern meaning pertaining to skin color during the eighteenth century, and then only becoming specifically formulated in that way in the Victorian period. See Hudson, "From 'Nation' to 'Race': The Origin of Racial Classification in Eighteenth-Century Thought," *Eighteenth-Century Studies*, 29/3 (1996): 247–64.

people, he writes, "are a kind of forlorn hope, preceding by ten or twelve years the most respectable army of veterans which come after them."[14] The state of nature, with its temporal structure, is replicated here by the American move westward. But it is significant that rather than becoming civilized themselves, those in the western settlements make way for settlers who arrive already in a civil state. Thus, the steady progression that seems inevitable to Hobbes, Locke, and Rousseau, is subtly replaced by the succession of races, however undefined and untheorized at this time, which, while seemingly the same, are essentially different.

Thus Crèvecoeur keeps his semi-savage Americans separate from his civil ones. Other writers tended to be less certain that such a distinction was valid in the wilds of North America. Several texts of the period depict North America as a place where one can lose one's civility when exposed to savagery. As historian Bernard Sheehan has noted, "(t)he ignoble savage always loomed as an external threat to Europeans and as an internal danger because he represented primal urges that, although subdued, remained part of the human condition."[15] But while savagery is apparently contagious, and contributes to the development of a new race, civility is not. For while some European observers found much to admire in the native inhabitants of North America, almost all concurred in placing them within the discourse of savagery. But the discursive representations of racial difference, or human diversity, that separated the peoples of the world into savage and civil categories, while owing much to Hobbes, Locke, Rousseau, and others concerned with the development of civil society, were equally influenced by writers who sought to define human development in ethnographic or racial terms, including Linnaeus, Buffon, Albrecht von Haller, and, most significantly, Johann Friedrich Blumenbach.[16]

In *On the Natural Variety of Mankind* (1776), the monogenist Blumenbach argues that there are four varieties, or races. In 1781 he expanded the list to five. These were the Caucasian, Mongolian, Ethiopian, American, and Malay. Unsurprisingly, the white, European Blumenbach found the Caucasian "the most beautiful, and that to which the pre-eminence belongs."[17] He differs from Hobbes, Locke, and Rousseau, however, in asserting that the Caucasian is also the most "primitive" race. This is because Blumenbach is dealing with races not as developing from a simple to a complex state, but rather as they exist. He places their origins in chronological order, the earliest being the Caucasion. Races generated later include the Mongolian, American, Malay, and Ethiopian, each developing under different climactic conditions on different continents. The Malay and Ethiopian races are the latest, or the "extreme degenerations" of the human species.[18] Americans (Indians) and Mongolians are transitional, the former arising in time between the Caucasian

---

14 Crèvecoeur, *Letters from an American Farmer*, pp. 72–3.

15 Sheehan, *Savagism & Civility*, p. 2.

16 For a discussion of Blumenbach's influence on English writers at the end of the eighteenth century, see Anne Mellor's "*Frankenstein*, Racial Science, and the Yellow Peril," *Nineteenth-Century Contexts*, 23/1 (2001): 1–28.

17 Johann Friedrich Blumenbach, *The Anthropological Treatises of Johann Friedrich Blumenbach* (London, 1865), p. xi.

18 Ibid., p. xi.

and the Ethiopian, the latter between the Caucasian and the Malay. He argued that several factors contributed to racial variety, most importantly climate, "mode of life and bringing up," and "the conjunction of different species, and the hybrid animals thence produced."[19] Simply put, changing one's climate and way of life for an extended period of time was sufficient to change one's race. He writes that "(a)n Englishman who had spent only three years with the Virginians, became exactly like them in colour, and (Captain John) Smith, his countryman, could only recognize him by his language."[20] So while Blumenbach attempts to establish firm racial categories, climate's ability to alter the category individuals occupied, and his own revisions, which added a race, together with his insistence on "transitional" races, keeps instability an integral part of emergent schemas of human diversity. Several late eighteenth-century novels present cases of characters whose sojourns in America introduce such racial instability.

Unstable Racial Categories

The Expedition of Humphry Clinker (1771) was Tobias Smollett's last novel. It concerns the peregrinations of Matthew Bramble, his sister Tabitha, nephew Jeremy Melford, niece Lydia Melford, and their servants, some of whom they pick up on the road, including the title character, an earnest, devoted man given to bouts of Methodist enthusiasm who has fallen on hard times. They travel in search of a spot that will improve the health of Bramble, an irascible yet generous hypochondriac. The novel's main theme could be taken to be instability. Its epistolary form turns many of its episodes into twice-told tales, with details added to the same event in letters from different characters told in different styles, and with the significance of these episodes interpreted differently by their multiple narrators. The novel rambles stylistically, as well as geographically, with various characters indulging themselves in discursive tangents while traveling together through England and Scotland. National and regional differences are regular topics, with the Scots seen as an hospitable but coarse people in many ways, the Londoners as licentious and extravagant, and the crowd at Bath as vapid and indolent. The novel's concern with racial variety appears in the tale of Lieutenant Lismahago, a Scotsman met on the road, who had spent several years with the military in Canada and New York, where he was captured and adopted by Indians.

Lismahago initially is portrayed as a character of indiscernible extraction. Bramble and his family come across him while staying at an inn at Durham in northern England:

A tall meagure figure, answering, with his horse, the description of Don Quixote mounted on Rozinante, appeared in the twilight at the inn door ... He would have measured above six feet in height, had he stood upright; but he stooped very much; was very narrow in the shoulders, and very thick in the calves of his legs, which were cased in black spatterdashes—As for his thighs, they were long and slender, like those of a grasshopper;

19 Ibid., pp. 72–3.
20 Ibid., p. 111.

his face was, at least, half a yard in length, brown and shriveled, with projecting cheek-bones, little grey eyes of the greenish hue, a large hook-nose, a pointed chin, a mouth from ear to ear, very ill furnished with teeth, and a high, narrow fore-head, well furrowed with wrinkles.[21]

Lismahago's physiognomy comically mingles features of the stock Scotsman—his height, angularity, and gauntness—with less civilized traits. His semi-erect posture and grasshopper thighs introduce animalistic elements.

The text soon makes it clear that Lismahago's physiognomy, particularly that of his head, have come by their appearance through direct, violent contact with savagery in America. When fighting in the Seven Years' War, he was wounded at the British battle against the French in 1758 at Ticonderoga. "(A) party of Indians rifled him, scalped him, broke his scull with the blow of a tomahawk, and left him for dead on the field of battle; but that being afterwards found with signs of life, he had been cured in the French hospital, though the loss of substance could not be repaired; so that the scull was left naked in several places, and these he covered with patches" (183). The inability of the French doctors to repair the "substance" of Lismahago is significant. Perhaps English doctors would have been more able, since this substance is linked with English civility, while the French were allied with American Indians during the war. Lismahago's encounter with savagery has left him not simply deformed, but, with his partially scalped skull, has given him the likeness of a savage.

Lismahago's manners have also been shaped by his American experiences. When the travelers first encounter him, he falls off his horse in front of the inn at Durham when an attendant neglects to hold his stirrup. When "certain plebeians that were about the door" laugh, his response is violent (182). "He forthwith leaped up in a fury, and snatching one of his pistols, threatened to put the ostler to death" (183). An illustration Thomas Rowlandson provided for an 1809 edition of Smollett's works depicting this scene remarkably suggests that Lieutenant Lismahago has acquired aspects of an Indian physiognomy, along with the Scottish features I have mentioned.[22] He stands next to his horse with the wig and hat he had been wearing on the ground at his feet. His face is seen in profile, and with his bald head, prominent nose, thick, protruding eyebrows, and lean body and face, he is very much like late eighteenth-century prints that depict North American Indians. Three Englishmen who watch him from the door laugh at him behind his back, as the ostler who failed to hold his horse runs away to the left. The English figures at the door accentuate Lismahago's "Indian" features by appearing full of mutton and ale—one of them is seated on the stoop of the inn, a mug in his hand, and all three are plump, Falstaffian characters. Visible in the background to the left is a covered wagon of the type used on the North American frontier, a vehicle described in several travelers' accounts of the period. All place Lismahago within the representational discourse of savagery, on the border with civility, in the backwoods of America. The fact that the ostler

---

21 Tobias Smollett, *The Expedition of Humphry Clinker*, ed. Thomas Preston (Athens, 1990), pp. 182–3. Further references will be notated parenthetically.

22 Tobias Smollett, *The Miscellaneous Works*, vol. 5, ed. Robert Anderson (Edinburgh, 1809).

is running, terrified, in the direction of the covered wagon, may place him in the category of English settler, with Lismahago acting the part of the bloodthirsty savage. Finally, the scene is framed as a battlefield. Lismahago and the ostler are cast as savage and civil combatants, while the markedly English characters remain apart as if sealed off from the encounter. The inn itself is marked as belonging to an ancient British history, with no traces of ever having existed in a natural state, by the signpost that hangs high above Lismahago's head, with its emblem of knights in armor jousting.

Lismahago's violent temperament and further acquaintance cause Jeremy Melford to form the opinion

> that this Caledonian is a self-conceited pedant, aukward, rude, and disputacious—He has had the benefit of a school education, seems to have read a good number of books, his memory is tenacious, and he pretends to speak several different languages; but he is so addicted to wrangling, that he will cavil at the clearest truths, and, in the pride of argumentation, attempt to reconcile contradictions (185).

Lismahago speaks "in such an ungracious manner as would be extremely disgusting, if it was not marked by that characteristic oddity which never fails to attract the attention" (186).

These faults could be owing to Lismahago's long military service, and the fact that he was brought up as a lawyer. But combined with his physiognomy, they suggest just as strongly that he is something of a civil-savage hybrid. European descriptions of the supposed irrationality of Indians contain complaints similar to those Jery Melford makes about Lismahago. The Dominican Tomás Ortiz wrote in the sixteenth century that the people of the Caribbean were "stupid and silly," had "no respect for the truth, save when it is to their advantage" and were "incapable of learning ... When taught the mysteries of our religion, they say that these things may suit Castilians, but not them, and they do not wish to change their customs."[23] English explorers and settlers in North America reported that the native population was contentious, and refused, like Ortiz's Caribbeans, to see universal truths, instead arguing for their beliefs even after they had supposedly been disproven by rational argument.[24] By the time Smollett wrote *Humphry Clinker*, irrationality combined with an insistence on arguing, while certainly not considered exclusively savage traits, were a well-established part of the discourse on savagery.

Lismahago's origins, while entirely Scottish, place him in a category that can be seen as a liminal one between Britain and America. The travelers learn that he is the great-grandson of one of the "original covenanters" (187), who were either subscribers to the National Covenant signed in 1638, "which proclaimed loyalty to the crown and to the true religion but denounced the liturgical innovations being forced by Charles I on the Church of Scotland; or subscribers to the Solemn League and Covenant of September 1643, designed to impose Presbyterianism on England and Ireland, as

---

23 Quoted in Tzvetan Todorov, *The Conquest of America: The Question of the Other* (Norman, Oklahoma, 1999), pp. 150–51.

24 See Sheehan, *Savagism & Civility* and James Axtell, *The European and the Indian: Essays in the Ethnohistory of Colonial North America* (Oxford, 1981).

well as Scotland" (n. 400). This connects Lismahago to a class of dissenters who formed one of the largest groups to emigrate to North America, and who contributed to a "primitive" religious environment often remarked upon during the period, and constantly lamented by Matthew Bramble throughout *Humphry Clinker*.

If Lismahago had a predilection for the primitive because of his religious background when he went to America, his captivity and adoption by Indians certainly confirmed it. After recovering from his wound, he was captured by "a party of Miamis, who carried (him and a fellow officer) away in captivity. The intention of these Indians was to give one of them as an adopted son to a venerable sachem, who had lost his own in the course of the war, and to sacrifice the other according to the custom of the country" (188). Smollett's presentation of Lismahago's prospect of either becoming a savage or a sacrifice is most likely drawn from English accounts of North American Indian life in several works, most particularly Cadwallader Colden's *The History of the Five Indian Nations* (1727).[25] At this point the "savages" consider Lismahago and his fellow soldier enough like themselves to incorporate them into their society, or to treat as they would treat Indians captured in war, as Lismahago's explanation of their treatment makes clear (188).

It is possible that Lismahago, as a Scotsman, and his comrade Murphy, presumably an Irishman, are presented as more assimilable to savagery because in English eyes their Celticness already places them in a somewhat barbaric category.[26] Considering Smollett's Scottishness, the way *Humphry Clinker* trades on the notion of the Scots as closer to savagery may be ironic, but his lifelong efforts to write himself into the national center, and away from any association with the border between Highland and Lowland Scotland, where he was born and raised, included the marginalization of unassimilable Scots. Later in the novel when Matthew Bramble comments on Highland Scots in general he says they live in "savage nature," and that "(t)hey are undoubtedly a very distinct species from their fellow-subjects of the Lowlands ... and this difference is very discernible ... The Lowlanders are generally cool and circumspect, the Highlanders fiery and ferocious" (244, 245). Lismahago, the novel's most representative Scottish figure, is kept at a distance first by language and physiognomy, and ultimately by his inability and unwillingness to participate in the commerce of the British nation.[27] His opposition to the Union between Scotland and

25 Thomas Preston cites Colden as Smollett's source in his edition of *Humphry Clinker*, but Charlotte Sussman suggests several other possibilities. See "Lismahago's Captivity: Transculturation in *Humphry Clinker*," *English Literary History*, 61/3 (1994): 597–618.

26 For a discussion of the experience Europeans had of their own people being adopted by Indian tribes, see Axtell's *The European and the Indian*, pp. 272–315.

27 Lismahago's very particular name, Obadiah Lismahago, invokes a Presbyterian adherence to the Old Testament, and belongs linguistically to his Scottish location. It does more to make him a "type" than many of the initials that name other characters. As Peter Miles has argued, initials make characters "textually more realistic by the erasure rather than the 'revelation' of" names, by making them more particular. Lismahago, on the other hand, is simultaneously singular and representative, confusable with no historical individual, and as such, more of an historical type. See Miles, "Smollett, Rowlandson, and a Problem of Identity: Decoding Names, Bodies, and Gender in *Humphry Clinker*." *Eighteenth-Century Life* 20/1 (1996): 1–23.

England, and complaint that the commerce of England never circulates to its Scottish periphery, mark him as a figure unable to negotiate a transition from Scottishness to Britishness, much the way Highlanders are depicted as undeniably "other" when compared to Lowlanders. This, Smollett suggests through Matthew Bramble, might be for the best. As Janet Sorenson has argued, "if, as Lismahago suggests, the core/periphery relationship deprives the periphery of its own extensive circulation, Matthew believes that that lack might not be an altogether bad thing" (118).[28]

Whether or not Lismahago's Scottishness is of a more savage variety, one step removed from the British version of Celticness that the Welsh Bramble has acquired, his case with the Miamis looks bleak:

> Murphy, as being the younger and handsomer of the two, was designed to fill the place of the deceased, not only as the son of the sachem, but as the spouse of a beautiful squaw, to whom his predecessor had been betrothed; but in passing through the different whigwhams or village of the Miamis, poor Murphy was so mangled by the women and children, who have the privilege of torturing all prisoners in their passage, that, by the time they arrived at the place of the sachem's residence, he was rendered altogether unfit for the purposes of marriage: it was determined therefore, in the assembly of the warriors, that ensign Murphy should be brought to the stake, and that the lady should be given to lieutenant Lismahago, who had likewise received his share of torments, though they had not produced emasculation (188).

This sexual violence by women and children serves to set the "savage" further apart from notions of the Englishwoman, who by the 1770s had become almost entirely desexed in the English novel; moreover, parts of the human anatomy had become completely unmentionable in polite English discourse, not to mention untouchable, and certainly un-emasculatable.[29] Murphy's handsomeness appears to have been his undoing, with his penis the site of both a savage fascination and extraordinary violence. Lismahago's proximity to savagery, already established by his partial scalping and his participation in a religious tradition that evinces a primitive enthusiasm similar to that ascribed by ethnographers to the Indians, seems to have saved him from Murphy's fate.

But Murphy's bravery during his ordeal wins him admiration. "The Indians themselves allowed that Murphy died with great heroism," and this sets the scene for a rite that merges the Celticness of the captives with the savagery of the Miamis. Lismahago and the Indians sing Murphy's death song, the Drimmendoo, together. This song, "an old Irish folk song entitled 'Draoigheanán donn' or 'Drynaun dhun' (Dear Black Cow)," has a complicated history (188). Its name "has been applied to at least three melodies in Ireland and one in Scotland, and this lament for the

---

28 See Janet Sorenson's *The Grammar of Empire in Eighteenth-Century Writing* (Cambridge, 2000) for a thorough discussion of Smollett's fraught position as a Scot invested in the promotion of an authentic British literary and cultural identity.

29 As Ian Watt has noted in *The Rise of the Novel* (Berkeley, 1957), women in novels were not even able to mention certain parts of the anatomy. By the 1720s, he notes, "the taboo on biological references seems to have been fully established: Mandeville noted that 'among well-bred people it is counted highly criminal to mention before company anything in plain words that is relating to this Mystery of Succession ...,'" p. 163.

loss of a cow was adapted as a Jacobite song" (n. 400). Murphy, wailing as he's burned at the stake, and Lismahago, singing in mourning and perhaps relief, are joined in a song which is both Irish and Scottish, by savages, who seem to "speak" the music's language and to know its melody, as the conflation of Celticness and savagery continues.

A wedding feast quickly follows this death rite, where Lismahago is honored and Murphy—still somewhat alive—is feasted upon. "After the warriors and the matrons had made a hearty meal on the muscular flesh which they pared from the victim, and had applied a great variety of tortures, which he bore without flinching, an old lady, with a sharp knife, scooped out one of his eyes, and put a burning coal in the socket" (188). Lismahago, saved from this fate, must prepare to marry one who revels in the event:

> Lismahago's bride, the squaw Squinkinacoosta, distinguished herself on this occasion.— She shewed a great superiority of genius in the tortures which she contrived and executed with her own hands.—She vied with the stoutest warrior in eating the flesh of the sacrifice; and after all the other females were fuddled with dram-drinking, she was not so intoxicated but that she was able to play the game of the platter with the conjuring sachem, and afterwards go through the ceremony of her own wedding, which was consummated that same evening (188).

Lismahago, rather than being repulsed by this behavior, seems to take to it naturally. He moves effortlessly from mourning his comrade to feasting upon him, and has no trouble moving from civil captive to savage husband, drawing on his Celtic proximity to barbarism. Over the course of two years, during which he "lived very happily with this accomplished squaw," he becomes fully incorporated into the Miami culture (188–9).

Squinkinacoosta gives birth to a son, but at the end of this time, to Lismahago's "unspeakable grief, she had died of a fever, occasioned by eating too much raw bear" (189). And though Lismahago's place in this tribe might be seen as entirely dependent on his wife and child, he has become a Miami in every sense. "By this time," the text informs us, "Mr. Lismahago was elected sachem, acknowledged first warrior of the Badger tribe, and dignified with the name or epithet of Occacanastaogarora, which signifies nimble as a weasel" (189). But while Lismahago's identity has altered so radically that he seems entirely savage, his captors maintain the option of returning him to civility, and do. He is forced to give up his place as sachem "in consequence of being exchanged for the orator of the community, who had been taken prisoner by the Indians that were in alliance with the English" (189).

But Lismahago's movement from savage back to civil is not as complete as his initial identity shift. He still retains the physical marks of savagery, and knowledge of his experiences in America shapes others' interpretations of his manners. His years among the Miamis have changed him, and shown that savagery can be learned, or more disturbingly, that the movement from a civil to a savage identity is simple and even natural for Europeans in America. Charlotte Sussman sees this "transculturation" and the "dangerous consequences of inter-cultural contact" in economic terms.[30] In

---

30 Sussman, "Lismahago's Captivity," p. 598.

a persuasive essay, she argues that through a "chain of association" similar to the one I have laid out above, "Lismahago's marriage to Tabitha becomes as much an interracial union as his marriage to Squinkinacoosta—he represents the presence of creolized North America on English domestic soil."[31] But I wish to focus here on the racial and anthropological consequences. Rather than depicting Lismahago as "creolized," Smollett portrays him as "savage," with no sense that his savagery can be done away with by incorporation into Englishness.

Another troubling aspect of Lismahago's captivity is the fact that the Miamis entirely control his identity. He is both incorporated into their society and removed from it according to their whim. While a discourse that places Scottishness closer to savagery was well established by the time *Humphry Clinker* appeared in 1771, that distinction had a way of collapsing. Lismahago, in the end, is accepted into the Bramble family, suggesting that even proper Britons are closer to savagery than it had it first seemed. While Lismahago is introduced into the field of representation only to be marginalized, one of the characters who the "gentleman-tourist sorts out ... and assigns" to his "proper place," the late eighteenth-century Briton cannot escape the fact that the expansion of empire has broken down spatial and racial barriers that had seemed permanent.[32] Formerly untraversable divisions, as formulated by Enlightenment philosophers and philosophes, have become routes of communication that challenge civility's security as a category.

Charlotte Lennox's *Euphemia*

Savagery and civility come into contact in Charlotte Lennox's *Euphemia* (1790) in less violent, but equally fluid ways. Lennox, perhaps best known as the author of *The Female Quixote* (1752), wrote *Euphemia* in an attempt to take advantage of the late eighteenth-century vogue for epistolary works. The novel, told in a series of letters between Euphemia Neville and her friend Maria Harley, takes place in England and colonial New York between the 1740s and 1760s. Lennox was the daughter of a colonial governor of New York. She lived in Albany from 1738–40, so her descriptions of the people are probably more accurate than those of other novelists who wrote American episodes, but they must also be considered rather dated, affected by a sixty-year-old's memory of scenes not visited since adolescence.

Like Smollett, Lennox associates a predilection for savagery with the Scottish. But she also includes the Dutch who have lived in America for generations, and eventually, Euphemia's very English son, in this intercourse with native identities. Most of the novel's treatment of New York Dutch characters makes it clear that they belong to a category separate from the English soldiers among whom Euphemia lives—her husband is a captain in the English army—and one she finds disagreeable. They are often very much like the backwoods people Crèvecoeur discusses in "What is an American?" On a trip up the Hudson from New York to Albany, Euphemia's party

---

31 Ibid., p. 604.

32 Michael Rosenblum, "Smollett's *Humphry Clinker*," in John Richetti (ed.), *The Cambridge Companion to the Eighteenth-Century Novel* (Cambridge, 1996) pp. 175–97; p. 187.

learns from the captain of their sloop that "even in these wilds some inhabitants were to be found, who lived there secluded from all converse with their species, except, sometimes, a straggling Indian or two ... They subsisted, he said, upon the milk of their cows, some game, when they were able to catch it, and the spontaneous fruits of the earth."[33] Euphemia, writing to Maria back in England, makes her ethnographic interest and judgment clear. "Our curiosity was strongly excited by this account; we were impatient to see these persons, whose manners, we supposed must be as savage as their way of life" (III:9).

The English traveling party is not disappointed. The Dutch settlers are not dangerous, but they are fearful and inarticulate. They finally speak Dutch to the boat's skipper, but cannot converse with the English ladies, who consider the settlers' speech barely human. Euphemia describes a call heard through some trees as "coarse," and is surprised when she discovers it is the voice of a woman. This woman is calling to her cow "by name," which of itself is perhaps not strange. What is strange is the fact that when the woman sees the English visitors and screams in terror, "the cow, who, obedient to the call of its mistress, was hastening to her, no sooner saw us, than, as if struck with a panic likewise, it turned about, and trotted back into the woods" (III:13–14). The woman's conversation with her cow, and their sympathetic panic in the presence of civilized visitors, brings her into a communion with the beast incompatible with civility. Such linkages of humanity with animalism are a repeated feature of English and European discussions of savagery. While in almost all accounts savages were considered human—their conversion to Christianity could not be sought if their humanity was denied—the discourse of savagery unavoidably placed Indians on a continuum between animals and humans.[34]

Soon after this experience, the novel conflates savagery and Scottishness in a way that shows a progressive movement towards the blurring of identity the further one gets from the settled parts of America. One day Euphemia comes across a Mohawk in her kitchen. She writes Maria that she was extremely alarmed to see one of the savages by the fire,

> smoking his pipe very composedly ... He had a fierce and menacing look; his copper-coloured face was painted in round spots of red, yellow, and black; his hair strewed with some kind of powder of a deep red, which looked like blood streaming from different wounds in his head; his ears were stretched to an enormous length by the weight of the strange ornaments he wore in them, pieces of tin, glass, strings of shells, brass rings, and even slips of woollen cloth of several colours, which hung down to his shoulders (III:18–19).

This man's savage appearance naturally frightens Euphemia, but she soon makes associations that give her the courage to remain in the kitchen with him until her husband returns. She notes that "(h)is dress was a shirt made of Osnaburgh linen, a

---

33 Charlotte Lennox, *Euphemia* (4 vols, London, 1992), vol. 3, p. 9. Further references will be cited parenthetically.

34 As Sheehan puts it, "(n)o Englishman formally proposed that Indians be driven from the ranks of humanity, but most Englishmen who wrote about them used language that in effect relegated Indians to a mesozone between animals and men." *Savagism and Civility*, p. 107.

short petticoat of the same, in the manner of the Scotch highlanders, and, over all, a mantle of coarse flannel ... adorned with several narrow borders of scarlet list" (III:19–20). Whether this is treated as a case of a Mohawk becoming a Scotchman, or Scottishness being seen as compatible with savagery, it both soothes and frightens this Englishwoman. She is able to place him, and in doing so reduce her sense of danger. She can consider his savage attributes as capable of translation into a barbarism close to home, while not having to worry that she is in danger of the same conflation.

But this soon changes. Euphemia has a son, Edward, while at the fort in Albany. His American birth marks him—quite literally—with a sign of savagery. He "bears under his left breast the distinct mark of a bow and arrow, the arms born by one of these savages" (III:124–5). Edward is a charming boy, loved by all, but some of the things cited initially as virtues hint that his connection to his surroundings is closer than that of his parents. He has "health, beauty, sweetness of temper, and early reason," we are told. But he also has "a growing taste for the climate, and wild yet not unpleasing scenes around (him)" (III:128–9). He is, in short, in danger of being shaped by his climate and surroundings as much as his birth, a development consonant with Blumenbach's arguments concerning the effect environment has on race.

A tribe of Hurons captures Edward when he is about five years old. His parents believe he is dead. He spends several years as a Huron and adapts to his surroundings. An Indian woman adopts him upon his capture and he quickly changes allegiance from his loving English mother to this Indian. When he sees compassion in the Huron woman's face, he "held out his arms to her; which seemed to please her so much, that she put him tenderly to her bosom, and covered him with her mantle, where, tired with his wanderings, he soon fell asleep" (IV:212). His abduction and captivity have been rewritten into "wanderings," and his rest from his journey places him contentedly in the savage's care. We are told that "(t)he Indian women are extremely fond of their children, and take the utmost care of them while they are young. She who had adopted little Edward, shewed an affection for him equal to that she had felt for her own son, who died a few days before she accompanied her friends in this expedition" (IV:213). The rapidity with which Edward accepts the Hurons as his kin, and their equal speed in adopting him, show that the blurring of racial categories Smollett had shown with Scottish and Irish characters, and that Lennox earlier shows among the Dutch, can affect even the most English of children if they are born in a savage climate.

As in the case of Lieutenant Lismahago, making the movement back to civility is problematic. During the course of Edward's captivity Euphemia gives birth to a daughter, Maria, who is three when her brother returns to them after some time with French Catholic missionaries in Montreal. His appearance frightens her. When Maria sees Edward for the first time, she says: " 'I shall never love him' ... he is an Indian: I shall always be afraid of him.' " But a friend of Euphemia's assures the child that her brother is not as different as he seems. " 'He is no Indian,' said Mrs. Mountfort, 'he is only dressed like one; you will love him when you see him in his proper clothes' " (IV:205–6). But the text challenges Mrs. Mountfort's belief that savagery is as exchangeable with civility as if it were a suit of clothes. Eventually,

Edward must undergo a rite of passage to move from his Indian identity to an English one. Edward's bow and arrow birthmark is countered with another "mark" of Europeanness at a ceremony in New York. He receives a sword from the governor and has "an ensigns commission in the Guards bestowed on him" (IV:249). This civilized mark of war replaces his savage one in a rite that aligns Edward with the ancient Britons of his heritage. The governor's daughter presents him with the sword in a mock ceremony: "bending one knee to the ground before her, (he) kissed the sword; and adopting the language of ancient chivalry, begged leave to vow himself her knight" (IV:250). Thus Edward moves from savagery to civility only by being brought back to an earlier stage of English history that counteracts the metaphorical temporal regression his move into savagery had represented.

While changing clothing is not enough to translate one from a savage to a civilized Englishman in *Euphemia*, it does so with great success in the anonymous *School for Fathers* (1788). This maudlin epistolary work is generally sympathetic to Indians. One of the characters, Matilda Pleydel, is said to have been "charitably sustained by the humanity of these so improperly styled savages" while waiting for the outcome of her English husband's trial at the hands of the Americans during the early part of the American Revolution.[35] Matilda hears conflicting reports about her husband, when finally, while out walking, she comes across a group of Indians. Her husband is with them, disguised as an Indian himself (I:243). Pleydel's impersonation of an Indian is extremely convincing. Matilda fails to recognize him at first, and later has difficulty convincing his aunt that it is really he. "It was some time before Mrs. Wellers could be convinced that in reality it was her nephew whom she saw, so effactually had he personated the manners and figure of an Indian chief" (I:249). Pleydel had escaped from prison in South Carolina, where the colonists had brought him from Boston for trial. Soon after escaping with his keeper, who turns out to be a loyalist, he ends up in a skirmish with Indians. His friend dies, but he manages to kill the Indians. He strips "the dead Indians, he habited himself in their clothing, stained his skin with some berries with which the woods abound, dropped a hasty tear over the fate of his faithful companion Clemson, and set off as fast as he could to some safe retreat. He was fearful of going to any settlement, either of Indians or white men" (II:17). So though Pleydel is dressed like an Indian, and enough like one to fool his wife and aunt, he is still afraid of them. Even in a book where the Indians are generally treated favorably, they are seen as a threat to civilized people. Pleydel is constantly grateful to have found his Indian traveling companions, but just as afraid they will turn on him. His identity has become lost somewhere between savagery and civility. While the Indians are aware of his Englishness, and essential difference from themselves, his own aunt is just as certain of his savagery.

The idea of Americans as animalistic appears in many novels, most hilariously in *The Adventures of Jonathan Corncob* (1787), an anonymous novel narrated from the viewpoint of an American loyalist during the American Revolution. Jonathan's experiences regularly reinforce the notions of Americans as a semi-savage people, whose origins owe as much to Indian influences as to English ones. His father is

---

35 *The School for Fathers; or, the Victim of a Curse* (3 vols, London, 1788), vol. 1, p. 227. Further references cited parenthetically.

"a rigid Presbyterian; he considered any man who played at cards as irrevocably d—n'd, as well as any one who walked out on a Sunday."[36] This man's religious enthusiasm and strong Protestantism of the Scottish variety are of course in keeping with the description of the type of British emigrant who makes up the newly emerging American character. Habakkuk Corncob's enthusiasm consists of long, violent bouts of Bible reading, specifically the Old Testament. "He employed every part of that day, that was not spent at the meeting-house," Jonathan says, "in reading the book of Leviticus, for the instruction of his family, and thought himself peculiarly indulgent, when, by way of amusement, he favoured us with the history of Shadrach, Meshach, and Abednego, or a few pages of the Pilgrim's Progress" (6).

While Jonathan absorbs a degree of primitivism from his father, he gets the savage side of his nature from his mother. "My honourable mother, Mrs. Charity Corncob," he tells us, "was an excellent woman: she bred like a rabbit; scolded all day like a cat in love; and snored at night as loud as the foreman of a jury on a tedious trial. During her pregnancy, she dreamed that she was brought to bed of a screech owl, and went to consult an old woman in the neighbourhood who passed for a witch" who told her the baby would die young or violently (5). Jonathan does neither. But his mother's multiple totemic alliances are indicative of a view of the American as susceptible to entering a natural state marked more by ethnographic writings and racial categorization than by that states of nature theorized by Locke, Hobbes, or Rousseau.

In Search of a Land Without History

In a sense, our discussion of a vision of Americans as developed and developing out of a dialectic between savagery and civility now shifts, but the new dichotomy is analogous to the one it replaces. Wordsworth and several other writers of the Romantic period—particularly Coleridge, Byron, and Keats—considered the state of nature more organically than their seventeenth- and eighteenth-century predecessors. Nature for Locke, Hobbes, and Rousseau, and those influenced by them, almost always refers to an anthropocentric formulation, and is mainly concerned with human relations, either with each other, or with their landscape. While Coleridge, as I argued in Chapter Two, sought to build a new society with his Pantisocracy, and in doing so to begin a new history purged of the excesses and bloodiness of Europe's past, Wordsworth and Byron looked to America as an ahistorical space, where no new history needed to be created. They sought empty space as an escape from history altogether.

The Romantics discussed here rewrite the savage-civil dialectic as a natural-artificial one, with people in rural and country settings more apt to approach the idealized condition of natural man than their urban counterparts because they felt their organic integration into the universe in ways that those in artificial society could not. None should be thought of as putting forth this distinction absolutely or

---

36 *Adventures of Jonathan Corncob, Loyal American Refugee, Written by Himself* (London, 1787. Reprint, Boston, 1976), p. 6. Further references cited parenthetically.

uncomplicatedly—even Wordsworth. But all saw the civilization of England during and after the Napoleonic wars as corrupt, and history as the record of unnatural, bloody, and selfish acts. America offered the example of a society organized along principles with which most of these writers sympathized, in a natural environment where urban corruption seemed absent. Unsurprisingly, several writers looked for natural man—the literate counterpart of the savage man feared by earlier writers—in the United States.

William Faux traveled to the United States in 1818–20, to gather information for a book intended for the use of English people considering emigrating to America. His *Memorable Days in America* (1832) begins optimistically and proceeds through a great deal of ambivalence, before concluding that the Americans were servile imitators of European culture. "It was by mere accident that they ever had a constitution," he wrote.

> (I)t came not from wise choice or preference. In England only, exists such a preference and real love of liberty. She must continue to be the Great Nation in spite of all her enemies, foreign or domestic, while America, you see, is retrograding and quite unable of herself to achieve any thing grand. If A, B, C, be taught her, she cannot teach herself D; yet she possesses the boasting, vain-glorious egotism of all-knowing Europe, although of and in herself, knowing nothing.[37]

Faux was not the first Englishman to travel to America expecting to find a republican simplicity and cultural originality that suited a desire to leave behind a Europe that seemed to be collapsing under the weight of its own current history. Nor was he the first to discover that the simplicity and originality he hoped to find failed to present themselves. Faux's Americans, in not being able to progress beyond what is taught them, are incapable of acting historically, despite the fact they occupy an historical condition. Neither nature nor ahistoricity can be found. In their place are an egotism and insistence that they belong among civilized nations, along with a tendency to move backwards rather than to progress.

Most English observers of North America in the late eighteenth and early nineteenth centuries, as we have seen, considered humanity in a state of nature prone to savagery. But others, most particularly Wordsworth, promoted the belief that natural surroundings elevated man, and that too active a participation in civilization—at least concentrated, urban civilization—impoverished him. Considering Wordsworth's version of Romantic ideology, it should be no surprise that his only extended poetic treatment of the United States should begin with a traveler's quest for a sublime land, whose history must be shaped by its abundance of natural wonders.

But while this Romantic quest is understandable enough, at the heart of it, I would like to suggest, is an attempt to replace the presence of European events with their absence, not with American events. In one sense, it is a quest for an anthropology to replace a history that has become overwhelming. America becomes a place where things do not just happen, but life simply *is*. The problem with such a quest is that it neither stops things from happening, in Europe or America, nor creates a state of

---

37 William Faux, *Memorable Days in America: Being a Journal of a Tour in the United States* (London, 1832), p. 126.

being that can satisfy the preconceived notions of disillusioned writers. It instead brings about an awkward epistemological shift that denies America and Americans status as historical entities, and turns them largely into anthropological constructs. In replacing the apperception of history, understood as a succession of momentous events, with culture, Wordsworth, and to a degree Byron, did not understand that America failed them by not answering the quest for an absence—a search for a place that had seceded not just from Europe, but from history. Byron comes closest to satisfying his needs by referring both to the overt actions of George Washington and to the mode of life embodied for him by Daniel Boone, thereby combining these ways of understanding America. But by idealizing the former and romanticizing the latter, he removes America from any history that can be understood as coeval with European history, yet fails to create an ahistorical space.

"We use a large number of dates to code some periods of history; and fewer for others," Lévi-Strauss writes in *The Savage Mind*. "This variable quantity of dates applied to periods of equal duration are a gauge of what might be called the pressure of history: there are 'hot' chronologies," he argues, "which are those of periods where in the eyes of the historian numerous events appear as differential elements; others, on the contrary, where for him (although not of course for the men who lived through them) very little or nothing took place."[38] English writers of the late eighteenth and early nineteenth centuries lived in a remarkably hot chronology, according to this argument. The dates are emblematic of the events: 1776—the American Revolution, 1789—the fall of the Bastille, 1793—the Terror, 1798—the Irish Rebellion, 1812—War with America, 1815—Waterloo, 1819—the Peterloo massacre, to name just a few.

We can easily understand why Wordsworth and his contemporaries would want to escape such a history. The Enlightenment discourse leading back to Hobbes, Locke, and Rousseau concerning the state of nature, and the metaphorical placement of that state in North America, offer an apparent way to leave history for a philosophical space, which actually existed in nature. Fernand Braudel argued for a view of history different from "traditional narrative history," which concerns itself with "the individual and the event."[39] He called the "short time span ... the most capricious and the most delusive of all."[40] Along with other members of the Annales school in mid twentieth-century France, he formulated a way of looking at history termed the *longue durée*, which argued for "an alteration in traditional historical time. A day, a year once seemed useful gauges. Time, after all, was made up of an accumulation of days."[41] Braudel's situation, as a European historian working in the years after World War II, is in some ways analogous to that of Romantic writers trying to manage history in the wake of the French Revolution. I do not wish to suggest that the Holocaust and

---

38 Claude Lévi-Strauss, *The Savage Mind* (Chicago, 1966), p. 259. For a thorough discussion of Lévi-Strauss's view of history, and the question of chronologies and dates in the Romantic period, see James Chandler's *England in 1819: The Politics of Literary Culture and the Case of Romantic Historicism* (Chicago, 1998), especially pp. 53–71.

39 Fernand Braudel, *On History*, trans. Sarah Matthews (Chicago, 1980), p. 27.

40 Ibid., p. 28.

41 Ibid., p. 29.

the Terror are typologically the same. But the reactions of those who saw history as an exchange between perpetrators and victims bears some resemblance. History as it had been practiced meant chaos, violence, and repression. It was time for a history of centuries and epochs, institutions and civilizations. Braudel argued that it was "in relation to these expanses of slow-moving history that the whole of history is to be rethought, as if on the basis of an infrastructure. All the stages, all the thousands of stages, all the thousand explosions of historical time can be understood on the basis of these depths, this semistillness."[42]

The Romantic poets' attempt to turn from history is an earlier, less systematic version of this move by twentieth-century historiography. The intellectual legacy that first argued for a philosophical state of nature that alternately included religious and secular versions of paradise, or visions of political perfection without violent upheaval, created the territory for such a retreat. The metaphorical placement of this territory in North America made this philosophical territory specific. Wordsworth and Byron can both be seen as moving from their histories to what they tried to conceive as a philosophical ideal, geographically realized.

The Excursion (1814), the second part of Wordsworth's never to be finished philosophical poem, *The Recluse*, brings English readers to the United States through the travels of the Solitary. The Solitary has spent time in France, hoping the Revolution there presaged a birth of freedom that would spread and elevate the condition of persecuted peoples everywhere. When this hope turns to bitter disappointment, the Solitary sails for America:

> Long wished-for sight, the Western World appeared;
> And, when the ship was moored, I leaped ashore
> Indignantly—resolved to be a man,
> Who, having o'er the past no power, would live
> No longer in subjection to the past ... (III:870–74)[43]

The Solitary's defiant rejection of European history almost hides the fact that, new and original as America is for him, it already occupies a place in his personal history, that of his longings. This "Western World," as a "Long wished-for sight," is at the end of a telos, the pertinence of whose beginning the Solitary unconvincingly denies. When did this wishing for the sight of the "Western World" begin? Was it before his failure to control the past became apparent? And what expectations does he have for America and its people?

Newness and originality seem the most likely answers. The Solitary longs for a people who, unlike the English, tired in body and soul from two decades of war with France, which emptied the national treasury and saw repeated diminution of civil liberties, were fresh and free. This posited originality and freedom are ahistorical, or nearly so, existing as they do in a nation controlled by nature rather than human events. America is a place one senses physically rather than reads about. "Respiring

---

42 Ibid., p. 33.

43 William Wordsworth, "The Excursion." *Poetical Works*, ed. Thomas Hutchinson, rev. Ernest De Selincourt (Oxford, 1969).

I looked round," the Solitary exclaims. Before him he sees the harmony of man and nature he expected:

> How bright the sun,
> The breeze how soft! Can any thing produced
> In the old World compare, thought I, for power
> And majesty with this gigantic stream,
> Sprung from the desert? And behold a city
> Fresh, youthful, and aspiring! (III:880–85)

The Hudson River, rather than an artificially chosen, mentally decaying king, provides the "majesty" in this world. Its natural force feeds a city which, in its "youthful" potential, can become a new, or "Fresh" example of a polity, free from the history that oppresses the "old World" and its productions. Like this new people and its sublime surroundings, the Solitary pronounces himself free, but his freedom is of a dispiriting kind. His echoes of Hamlet's reactions to witnessing a player's tears over Hecuba's loss link him to an inability to feel as well as act:

> What are these
> To me, or I to them? As much, at least
> As he desired that they should be, whom winds
> And waves have wafted to this distant shore,
> In the condition of a damaged seed,
> Whose fibres cannot, if they would, take root.
> Here may I roam at large;—my business is,
> Roaming at large, to observe, and not to feel
> And, therefore, not to act—convinced that all
> Which bears the name of action, howsoe'er
> Beginning, ends in servitude—still painful,
> And mostly profitless (III:885–96)

The identification with nature that the Solitary accords the people of the United States attaches to him as well, but just as the old world's productions are tired and damaged, his naturalness is feeble and infertile. "Winds and waves" have brought him to America, rather than any power of his own. This "damaged seed's" inability to "take root" turns him into a passive observer. In this condition he is ostensibly better able to deny history. But his desire "not to feel" and his conviction that all action "ends in servitude" are products of his active participation in recent French history, and as such are historical products rather than successful retreats. And soon he finds that even these supposedly natural people have a connection with the history he has left behind. The Americans, rather than "Fresh" and "free," are merely "aspiring," and aspiring towards attaining Europe's basest achievements. "On nearer view," he discovers,

> a motley spectacle
> Appeared, of high pretensions—unreproved
> But by the obstreperous voice of higher still;
> Big passions strutting on a petty stage (III:897–900).

The Solitary's disappointment is remarkably similar to Wordsworth's own in Book VI of *The Prelude* when he realizes he has crossed the Alps unknowingly. I would like to turn now to Alan Liu's historicizing of this passage to point out some parallels, and also hopefully to show that while Wordsworth was able to combat history by turning his disappointment into imagination's triumph over contemporary events, the nature of the Solitary's quest does not permit such a rewriting. History, when brought back to America and the state of nature, is at its metaphorical beginning. If it fails in such a location, it fails everywhere.

Liu opens his reading by quoting from James Bruce's *Travels to Discover the Source of the Nile* (1790). Bruce's emotions when at the summit of achievement are remarkably similar to Wordsworth's in the Simplon Pass. "I was, at that very moment," Bruce writes,

> in possession of what had, for many years, been the principal object of my ambition and wishes: indifference, which from the usual infirmity of human nature follows, at least for a time, complete enjoyment, had taken place of it. The marsh, and the fountains, upon comparison with the rise of many of our rivers, became now a trifling object in my sight. I remembered that magnificent scene in my own native country, where the Tweed, Clyde, and Annan rise in one hill; three rivers, as I now thought, not inferior to the Nile in beauty ...[44]

The comparison between this passage from Bruce and Book VI of *The Prelude*, as Liu notes, fills the "reader of Wordsworth with déjà vu."[45] And although *The Excursion* has had fewer readers, and the episode of the Solitary in America has inspired far fewer readings, the sense of déjà vu is just as acute, if not more so. Bruce and the Solitary both set off on specific quests. Bruce's search for the source of the Nile is perhaps more specific than the Solitary's yearning for a natural place that produced a fresh, free people, but the status of each as the object of quests is no less palpable to their seekers. Both also turn to England to repair the damages their expectations have suffered. Bruce's immediate remembrance of the sight of the "Tweed, Clyde, and Annan" in "my own native country" represents a nationalistic substitution of a nature more legitimately within the author's inheritance than the distant source of the Nile. The Solitary, after giving up on America, also returns to England, to live as a virtual hermit in a natural setting more conducive to his peace.

Liu compares the Simplon Pass section of *The Prelude* to Bruce's passage to point out that disappointment "inheres in any tour aimed toward a goal."[46] He goes on to argue that suppressed in Wordsworth's description of the Alps is the history of Napoleon's military victories over the Swiss republics, and that Napoleon himself is represented by Mont Blanc.[47] But while Wordsworth was able to submerge a history he sought to deny in an unpopulated mountain range, the Solitary could not be expected to succeed at submerging Americans within their own sublime surroundings, since it was those very surroundings that were supposed to have produced their freedom

---

44 Alan Liu, *Wordsworth: The Sense of History* (Stanford, 1989), p. 3.
45 Ibid., p. 3.
46 Ibid., p. 4.
47 Ibid., p. 24.

from history. The Americans as a people of nature are inseparable from nature itself. Napoleon's armies traveled through the Alps to achieve victory, thereby becoming associated with the landscape in Liu's reading. But in the Solitary's reading, the American people, like the Hudson, have "sprung from the desert," and when they disappoint, history can no longer be denied.

This is not to say that he makes no effort to salvage his quest. Once the Solitary finds that the Americans are no better than a poor imitation of the English, he seeks a purer example of a natural people:

> Let us, then, I said,
> Leave this unknit Republic to the scourge
> Of her own passions, and to regions haste,
> Whose shades have never felt the encroaching axe,
> Or soil endured a transfer in the mart
> Of dire rapacity. There, Man abides,
> Primeval Nature's child (III:913–19).

While by this point it is becoming clear that the Solitary is unlikely to find pleasure among any people, the nature of a quest is that it must either find its object or fail. The terms with which he condemns the United States—"this unknit Republic"— demonstrate an internal conflict between his quest for naturalness and a longing for order. It should not be surprising, then, when he finds "Primeval Nature's child"— the only ahistorical people he can imagine—that they are even more defeated by history than himself. He expects to find the American Indian

> A creature weak
> In combination, (wherefore else driven back
> So far, and of his old inheritance
> So easily deprived?) but, for that cause,
> More dignified, and stronger in himself;
> Whether to act, judge, suffer, or enjoy (III:919–24).

But just here, where the Wordsworthian self seems about to appear and to surmount the oppression of events, just as Wordsworth's own self does in the Simplon Pass, the Solitary runs out of history. Having traveled back to humanity's metaphorical source—as Bruce traced the Nile back to its actual source—he fails in his quest. "(T)hat pure archetype of human greatness," he laments,

> I found him not. There, in his stead, appeared
> A creature, squalid, vengeful, and impure;
> Remorseless, and submissive to no law
> But superstitious fear, and abject sloth (III:951–5).

The Solitary's final hope for mankind is no better than one of Rousseau's savages, wandering "in the forests without industry, without speech, without settled abode" with "only the sentiments and the enlightenment suited to this state."[48]

---

48 Rousseau, "Discourse on the Origin and Foundations of Inequality Among Men," p. 157.

The Solitary seeks a virtue he had found lacking in England, and a political commitment he found perverted in France. While his turn toward America is characteristic of many during the age, the fact that he fails to find a quality that transcends the littleness common to an industrial, commercial society in a nation that had developed into just that, is not surprising. He seeks a people who exist outside of history—and, according to his need to find a transcendent quality—in a place that is superior to history. But Americans have a history, and their sublime wilderness is reduced to a landscape. While the Solitary would appreciate the absence a wilderness implies, and the accompanying sublimity, he cannot recreate his impression of Americans by removing history the way Wordsworth can replace his disappointment in the Simplon Pass with exultation in the poetic process. Landscapes can be rewritten, as can military histories made up of discrete events, but a people, with a history made up of a matrix of relationships to each other, to other peoples, and to their physical surroundings, cannot. He has entered a consciousness of history as *longue durée*, of duration rather than events, and such a history is undeniable.

In *The Prelude*, the failure is in the perceiver; once Imagination can be summoned, the scenery is off the hook. But for the Solitary, the perceived are guilty. His idea of America is one shaped both by sublime nature and a progressive, republican society. His Americans are imagined solitaries—why would they be there except for the reasons he wants to be—to escape history? In that sense, they are, before the Solitary's trip, tourists like him, seeking to enjoy passing through (or living) the wilderness of scenery. And, as Liu puts it, "(a) tourist in Wordsworth's mold is a historical man who, as soon as he spots scenery, thinks himself primitive and original."[49] Being primitive—natural or "simple," in the way pioneer republicans were supposed to be "simple"—and original, are important in the constitution of the Wordsworthian self, which has defeated history, or can convince itself it has. But Wordsworth denies the Solitary the capacity to deny history the way he himself is able to. Perhaps this is a mark of his failure, by 1814, to deny it any longer himself. In the Introduction to *The Excursion*, Wordsworth comes across like the chairman of the Save Grasmere Lake Committee, with his class-based, dismissive complaints about a nouveau-riche newly-minted gentleman's building project, which introduces the present history of social mobility into the semi-pristine Lake District. Just as the Solitary has staked out republican simplicity as his province, and is disappointed at finding the striving tradespeople invade this ideal, Wordsworth has chosen a particular natural landscape for his domain, and is being similarly invaded.

American Heroes

As unsurprising as Wordsworth's sending the Solitary to America in search of a way to love mankind through a love of nature, is Byron's location of the heroic in representative Americans. A gesture towards the age's intermittent preoccupation with America appears near the end of the Preface to Cantos I and II of *Don Juan*. Byron labels Robert Southey, who is attacked hilariously in the work's ironic dedication,

---

49 Liu, *Wordsworth*, p. 12.

"this Pantisocratic apostle of apostasy," linking the poet laureate's political crimes to a betrayal of his plans with Coleridge to set up a poets' utopia in Pennsylvania (V:40).[50] In a way, then, the poem opens as a contest over the idea of America, or rather of the qualifications required to participate in that idea. For Byron, America still represents political freedom. Southey, who has gone from ardent republican to Tory, has forfeited his claim to Pantisocracy.

Byron's quest for a hero progresses poorly in Don Juan's travels across Europe. But when he looks to America, he offers some hope that its people may be keeping the spirit of freedom alive despite its retreat at home in England, and across Europe. The uncertainty of the times has made heroism an ephemeral quality, Byron suggests in the opening to *Don Juan*:

> I want a hero, an uncommon want,
> When every year and month sends forth a new one,
> Till after cloying the gazettes with cant,
> The age discovers he is not the true one (I:1, 1–4).

He quickly dismisses a host of would-be heroes, including "Vernon, the butcher Cumberland, Wolfe, Hawke, Prince Ferdinand, Granby, Burgoyne, Keppel, Howe, Buonaparté, Dumourier, Barnave, Brissot, Condorcet, Mirabeau, Petion, Clootz, Danton, Marat, La Fayette, Joubert, Hoche, Marceau, Lannes, Dessaix, Moreau, Nelson, Duncan, Howe and Jervis" (I:2, I:3, I:4). Some have turned from their principles. Others have gone out of fashion. Several have proved "Exceedingly remarkable at times, / But not at all adapted to my rhymes" (I:37–8).

America's first mention is hardly heroic, in the conventional sense, at least. While discussing the benefits and drawbacks of recent science, Byron mentions that "the smallpox has gone out of late; / Perhaps it may be followed by the great" (I:130, 7–8). This "great" pox is rumored to have come "from America," where perhaps it may return:

> The population there so spreads, they say
> 'Tis grown high time to thin it in its turn
> With war or plague or famine, any way,
> So that civilization they may learn (I:131, 2–5).

But while Byron's sarcastic suggestion that "war," "plague," and "famine" teach "civilization" is clearly a critique of the state of affairs in Europe after the Napoleonic wars, his implication that the United States is not a civilized nation should not be taken as wholly satirical. While Byron does not associate Americans with savagery, he does suggest a longing for a natural man, uncorrupted by the effects of an excess of civilization. The United States's population had grown dramatically from approximately three million at the beginning of the War of Independence to twelve million forty years later, when Byron composed *Don Juan*. This growth owed much to emigration, and many of the newcomers were English. Many went seeking an

---

50 All citations to Byron's poetry refer to Byron, Lord (George Gordon), *The Complete Poetical Works*, ed. Jerome McGann, 7 vols (Oxford, 1986).

escape from what they saw as the degeneration of their society. Morris Birkbeck, who traveled to the United States in 1817 looking for land to create a utopian society, wrote that he left England "to secure a timely retreat from the approaching crisis— either of anarchy or despotism" which he sees coming because of the economic hard times that resulted from the Napoleonic wars.[51] Birkbeck, like other adventurous emigrants in the years leading up to Peterloo and afterwards, sought a place where he could

> find an exemption from that wearisome solicitude about pecuniary affairs, from which, even the affluent find no refuge in England; and for my children, a career of enterprize, and wholesome family connections, in a society whose institutions are favourable to virtue; and at last the consolation of leaving them efficient members of a flourishing, public-spirited, energetic community, where the insolence of wealth, and the servility of pauperism, between which, in England, there is scarcely an interval remaining, are alike unknown.[52]

The likelihood that Birkbeck's ideal could be found in America was fiercely debated by William Cobbett among others.[53] John Keats's brother George was convinced, and followed Birkbeck to his Albion in Indiana, but very soon left. But while this is not the place for a discussion of that debate, it is important to note that the fear of savagery so common to English settlers in America for centuries seems to have receded after the War of 1812, to be replaced by a longing, or distaste, for the prospects of what was increasingly seen as a more natural existence.

Savagery has a place in *Don Juan*, but it is not associated with Native Americans. It is shown as the underside of civility rather than its temporal predecessor, when Juan's ship sinks, and the castaways in the lifeboat run out of food. They feel "The longings of the cannibal arise / (Although they spoke not) in their wolfish eyes" (II:72, 7–8). And though the horror of the situation "Lulled even the savage hunger which demanded, / Like the Promethean vulture, this pollution," when the lot falls on "Juan's luckless tutor," this savage quality must be served (II:75, 3–4, 8). But naturalness is set off from savagery in *Don Juan*, as it is for most of the Romantics. On the Greek island, after Juan's shipwreck, in Haidée we see a primeval character idolized:

> She was all which pure ignorance allows
> And flew to her young mate like a young bird,
> And never having dreamt of falsehood, she
> Had not one word to say of constancy (II:190, 5–8).

Her naturalness helps Juan find his own, and together they echo primeval nature. "They were / So loving and so lovely; till then never, Excepting our first parents, such a pair / Had run the risk of being damned forever" (II:193, 1–4). Haidée is

---

51 Morris Birkbeck, *Notes on a journey in America, from the coast of Virginia to the territory of Illinois* (London, 1818), p. 8.

52 Ibid., pp. 9–10.

53 See Cobbett's *Journal of a Year's Residence in the United States of America* (London, 1819).

"Nature's bride" and "Passion's child ... She had nought to fear, / Hope, care, nor love beyond; her heart beat here" (II:202, 1, 2, 7–8). Byron, then, locates paradise not in America, as had many English writers, but in the ancient world, along with that primeval innocence Wordsworth's Solitary had hoped to find in the Amerian Indians.

A likely reason for this is that, while Byron's luscious description of Haidée's island and Juan's time there are tempting, this world comes from plunder, the piracy of European goods from merchant ships in the Mediterranean, all linked to a decadent culture of luxury. The quality Byron ranks highest is not innocence, but heroism, and a couple of lovers surrounded by jewels, furs, silks, and slaves are hardly fit objects of a quest for heroes. The figure who stands out most heroically in *Don Juan* is George Washington, whose greatness Byron specifically ties to a scorn for wealth, position, and enervating luxury. Byron's natural man is Daniel Boone, a figure integrated into nature and uncorrupted by history.

Washington personifies republican simplicity and manly heroism for Byron. Remarks on war at the beginning of Canto VIII criticize the warriors of the age for overrunning weaker people. Byron characterizes modern warfare as "mere conquest to advance" (VIII:3, 6), and the conduct of its recent "heroes" as calculated to win "pensions from a nation ... A higher title or a loftier station" (VIII:4, 3, 5). But he makes an exception for the American Revolution and other fights he considers just. As he puts it, bloody acts "in the end except in freedom's battles / Are nothing but a child of Murder's rattles" (VIII:4, 7–8). And he leaves no doubt that Washington's fight for American independence ranks as one of "freedom's battles":

> And such they are, and such they will be found.
> Not so Leonidas[54] and Washington,
> Whose every battlefield is holy ground,
> Which breathes of nations saved, not worlds undone.
> How sweetly on the ear such echoes sound.
> While the mere victor's may appal or stun
> The servile and the vain, such names will be
> A watchword till the future shall be free (VIII:5, 1–8).

Ambitions appear to have shrunk here. While earlier writers, such as Blake and Coleridge, had turned to the American Revolution as the beginning of a worldwide shift from monarchy and despotism to republicanism and freedom, Byron confines Washington's effects as he exalts them. Washington has saved a nation, not the world. Violent history seems a more potent source, in that it is able to undo worlds.

But limited as Washington's power is to change history in its broadest sense, it at least provides an example for future greatness. Byron sets him as a type of Romantic hero, personifying virtue and heroism:

> Great men have always scorned great recompenses.
> Epaminondas saved his Thebes and died,
> Not leaving even his funeral expenses.

---

54 Leonidas was a king of Sparta and the hero of the defense of Thermopylae against the Persians in 480 B.C. (*Don Juan*, n. 663).

George Washington had thanks and nought beside,
Except the all-cloudless glory (which few men's is)
To free his country. Pitt too had his pride
And as a high-souled minister of state is
Renowned for ruining Great Britain gratis (IX:8, 1–8).

The distinction between Washington and Pitt is clear enough.

Byron had earlier referred to Washington in the concluding stanza of his "Ode to Napoleon Buonaparte" (1814), where, again, the representative American stands alone:

Where may the wearied eye repose,
When gazing on the Great;
Where neither guilty glory glows,
Nor despicable state?
Yes—one—the first—the last—the best—
The Cincinnatus of the West,
Whom envy dared not hate,
Bequeath'd the name of Washington,
To make man blush there was but one! (4–14)

This separation of Washington from Napoleon also seems to be a separation of him from any conception of Americans as a great people. In remarks to an American in Italy several years later, Byron edges closer to the sense of Americans acting historically as a people. He calls Washington "the chief man among a people who did a great thing."[55] But despite asserting that American independence was "a great thing" achieved by its people, the conversation goes on to show an insistent focus on individual acts in history. This conversation, like the poem of 1814, contrasts Washington favorably with Napoleon, who, according to Byron "did great things himself; the nation goes for nothing in his history; it is a passive instrument in his hands. Napoleon's history and greatness must be regarded as a personal affair."[56] It is Napoleon's history being contrasted with Washington's history here, a possessable and personalizable force. The Americans did "a great thing" because Washington either allowed them to be active "in his hands," or made them active.

Byron's earlier works had shown a belief in history, specifically the Whig version of history, with its emphasis on a "cult of opposition, the rhetoric of resistance," as Malcolm Kelsall has argued.[57] *Childe Harold* (1813), "politically considered, is an attempt to formulate, within a well-established poetic tradition, an overall historical philosophy of recent events in which frustrations of Whig idealism are placed as part of a larger pattern."[58] *Don Juan*, in Kelsall's view, is governed by the idea that "i(n) spite of all changes, all the multifarious miscellaneity of things, nothing has

55 D.A., "Conversations of an American with Lord Byron," *New Monthly Magazine and Literary Journal*, 45 (October, November 1835): 193–203, 291–302; 295.

56 Ibid., p. 295.

57 Malcolm Kelsall, *Byron's Politics* (Sussex, 1987), p. 7.

58 Ibid., p. 56.

changed."[59] His brief references to Washington, with their offer of a brief and distant hope, followed by the unescapable present reality of Pitt's ruinous stewardship of Britain, would seem to confirm this. Flashes of disconnected heroism can be found, but a steady pattern of virtuous behavior is absent from this atomized view of history as a series of events.

But like Wordsworth, Byron turns to a different view of history that offers much more promise, and is also focused on America. Washington, worthy of praise as he is, represents a man in action rather than a people over the course of time. Daniel Boone makes an appearance in Canto VIII in a way that updates the concept of the natural man and associates it with the American. This section of *Don Juan*, and fragments scattered throughout the accounts of Americans who met Byron in Italy, show an interest and perhaps even a belief in a process that, while historical, transcended the sort of events Byron understood as history.

His interest in the western settlements of North America has been documented, usually in connection with the reception of his own works there. Speaking of *Childe Harold* in 1813, after being brought news that his work was popular in America, he wrote: "These are the first tidings that have ever sounded like Fame to my ears—to be redde on the banks of the Ohio! ... To be popular in a rising and far country has a kind of *posthumous* feel, very different from the ephemeral *éclat* and *fête-ing*, buzzing and party-ing compliments of the well-dressed multitude."[60] He would later say that he was

> extremely partial ... to the Americans; and if I enjoy any reputation among them, I can rely upon it as arising from an unbiased judgment. They can have, of course, no original predilections for a titled personage, and the praise they bestow upon me must be sincere. I remember reading in the biography of George Frederic Cooke an extract from his journal, wherein he mentioned having seen the 'English Bards and Scotch Reviewers' lying on the table of a public-house somewhere in the interior of the United States. This was the first thing that sounded in my ears like real fame.[61]

This sense of "posthumous" fame brings us closer to Byron articulating a sense of history as a process, and America as belonging to a different age than England. The age is difficult to specify. The sense of the United States as a "rising" country places it at the vanguard of history. The "posthumous" fame Byron mentions even places it in the future. Yet the idea of America as new also places it in a period prior to the one in which England exists. So America is both past and future, but never contemporary with Europe, when seen as a society in a process of development.

Byron gets closest to conceiving of America as an ahistorical natural state in Canto VIII of *Don Juan*, when discussing Daniel Boone, right after the siege of Ismail. "The town was entered," Byron writes, and then quotes Cowper: "'God made the country, and man made the town'" (VIII:60,1–2). He depicts the war and the fall of Ismail as examples of vain human attempts to create things that endure. "(W)hen

---

59 Ibid., p. 146.

60 Byron, *Letters and Journals*, ed. J.E. Prothero (3 vols, London, 1922–24), vol. 2, p. 360; Dec. 3, 1813.

61 "Conversations," 195.

I see cast down / Rome, Babylon, Tyre, Carthage, Nineveh ... And pondering on the present and the past," the narrator says he begins to believe "the woods shall be our home at last" (VIII:60,4–5, 6–8). Then he takes us there, and introduces us to Boone, "backwoodsman of Kentucky," who "Was happiest amongst mortals anywhere" (VIII:61, 4–5). His happiness is founded explicitly on his rejection of civilization:

> Crime came not near him; she is not the child
> Of solitude. Health shrank not from him, for
> Her home is in the rarely-trodden wild,
> Where if men seek her not, and death be more
> Their choice than life, forgive them, as beguiled
> By habit to what their own hearts abhor
> In cities caged. The present case in point I
> Cite is that Boon lived hunting up to ninety (VIII:62, 1–8).

Boone's efforts to escape civilization are arduous. He "moved some hundred miles off for a station" when settlers came too near him. His attempt is to remain the Romantic individual, in Byron's version. "The inconvenience of civilization," he writes, "Is that you neither can be pleased nor please; / But where he met the individual man / He showed himself as kind as mortal can" (VIII:64, 3, 5–8). But this individualism is subsumed in a fellowship of children of nature who gather around Boone. As Byron writes, "around him grew / A sylvan tribe of children of the chase, / Whose young, unwakened world was ever new." This newness is conditioned on the absence of historical forces understood as political and military events. "Nor sword nor sorrow yet had left a trace" on this natural scene (VIII:65, 1–4). And as I have argued above, this state is natural, not savage.

> The green woods were their portions.
> No sinking spirits told them they grew grey.
> No Fashion made them apes of her distortions.
> Simple they were, not savage ... (VIII:66, 4–7).

But this escape from history is brief, dismissed as an unrealistic alternative to a world that is too much with the poet and his subjects. "So much for Nature, by way of variety," he writes:

> Now back to the great joys, civilization,
> And the sweet consequence of large society:
> War, pestilence, the despot's desolation,
> The kingly scourge, the lust of notoriety,
> The millions slain by soldiers for their ration,
> The scenes like Catherine's boudoir at three-score,
> With Ismail's storm to soften it the more (VIII:68, 1–8).

And Byron's brief speculations in letters about exiling himself to America are dismissed in language that shows he understands his fantasy of a natural state of existence is just that. In October of 1817 he writes that "in Italy I have no debts, and I could leave it when I choose. The Anglo-Americans are a little too coarse for me, and their climate too cold, and I should prefer the others."[62] Washington may have been a heroic individual, and he and Daniel Boone may have been able to inspire greatness, or at least felicity, among Americans. But in the end, Byron must admit that the state of nature remains a philosophical place, and the Americans are just as historical a people as the Europeans.

---

62 Byron, *Letters*, pp. 355–7.

Chapter Four

A Breed Apart:
The Traveler as Ethnographer

Captain Basil Hall experienced America as if he were traveling through the history of civilization. The retired British naval officer visited the United States with his wife and child in 1827–28 with the intent, he claimed, to see the progress of the new nation with unbiased eyes. What he saw was a nation in every imaginable state of development. "In the course of 50 miles' travelling," in upstate New York, "we came repeatedly in sight of almost every successive period of agricultural advancement through which America has run, or is actually running ..." The towns he sees have a "dreary aspect ... much heightened by the black sort of gigantic wall formed of the abrupt edge of the forest, choked up with underwood, now for the first time exposed to the light of the sun."[1] He notes that the area has progressed from barbarism to a decent level of civilization in a rapid period of time. "The village of Utica stands a step higher in this progressive scale of civilisation" because it has churches and a college. But "what with towns and cities, Indians, forests, cleared log-houses, painted churches, villas, canals, and manufactories, and hundreds of thousands of human beings, starting into life, all within the ken of one day's rapid journey, there was plenty of stuff for the imagination to work on."[2]

Plenty of stuff indeed. Through the early decades of the nineteenth century many English observers would come to America to exercise their imaginations. The result is a comparative ethnology that created the American as Other more firmly than previous works had done. They were slovenly, sullen, intemperate, ill-educated, and insensible to artistic as well as natural beauty. They spoke an English so corrupted that it was hardly recognizable in certain regions. They were greedy and inhospitable. Most of all, they were a "they," an unmistakably separate breed from the English particularly, and Europeans more generally. The emerging methods of anthropology, and more specifically, ethnography, were used in numerous works by travelers who set out to explain an egalitarian people to an England trying to come to terms with decades of repression, and approaching the reformation of its own political system along more democratic lines. Defining the Other in the first three decades of the nineteenth century resulted in an ethnographic distancing that did more to establish who the Americans were for the English than any of the works written from the 1770s through the end of the eighteenth century, when it became apparent that such distancing and definition was necessary.

---

   1   Basil Hall, *Travels in North America in the years 1827 and 1828* (2 vols, Edinburgh, 1829), vol. 1, p. 128.

   2   Ibid., vol. 1, p. 131.

Hall's depiction of upstate New York in the 1820s offers a tableau of humanity in its various stages according to economic and cultural development as theorized by French and Scottish Enlightenment thinkers from the middle of the eighteenth century through the early years of the nineteenth century. His depiction of the area places the Indians—who, as I have argued in the previous chapter, typified the first age of humanity in seventeenth- and eighteenth-century writings—in a landscape that included every successive stage of development. This chapter will briefly examine the theories developed by French philosophes and Scottish thinkers to explain the progressive evolution all human societies were thought to travel. Figures such as Adam Ferguson, Adam Smith, and William Robertson identified four successive stages—hunting and gathering, the pastoral, the agricultural, and the commercial—which they considered an unvarying pattern in the course of human societies. I will then go on to explore the possibility of an untheorized but discursively rich fifth stage, which amateur ethnography posited beyond these four. This fifth stage—not an economically determined one, but a socially developmental one I have identified in the works of this period—emerges clearly in Frances Trollope's *Domestic Manners of the Americans* (1832). Trollope suggests that beyond these theories that focus entirely on the mode of a society's subsistence and its effect on its culture, lies the stage of refined manners which the Americans, because of their simultaneous involvement in all of the stages that precede it, have not entered. Because of this persistent, uneven economic development, the American is seen in Trollope's work, and works after it, most notably Dickens's *American Notes* (1842), as a hybrid, neither savage nor completely civil. This conclusion leads to a composite view of Americans as a breed apart from the English, living in a mongrelized time, with various supposedly successive stages existing all at once.

I have used the words "ethnography" and "ethnology" to describe the generic type and the kind of meaning the works discussed in this chapter produced. While these words do not appear to have entered the language until shortly after this time, the practices to which they refer had long been common. The first recorded usages of these terms appear in the decade following Trollope's *Domestic Manners*. Going on the assumption that most words are invented to refer to things, ideas, and practices common enough to require naming, it seems fair to treat these first appearances of "ethnography" and "ethnology" as expressions of the examples this chapter discusses. The *Penny Cyclopaedia of the Society for the Diffusion of Useful Knowledge* described ethnography in 1834 as "a series of anthropographies," or studies of the particularities of a humanity still considered as belonging to a universal category.[3] This first recorded usage of the term, according to the *Oxford English Dictionary*, describes it in terms very much in line with the temporal argument I have been advancing here. This "series of anthropographies, of different epochs," the *Penny Cyclopaedia* continues, forms "the true basis of ethnography."[4] The first recorded use of the term "ethnology" listed in the *Oxford English Dictionary* comes from James Cowles Prichard's *Natural History of Man* (1842), and explicitly refers

3   *Penny Cyclopaedia of the Society for the Diffusion of Useful Knowledge* (London, 1833–43).

4   Ibid., vol. 2, p. 97.

to the "history of nations."[5] This focus on "history" again reinforces the idea that authors of the period saw national differences as the production of experience over time. Prichard's use of the term "nations" rather than "races" makes it clear that at least a decade after the period with which this study is concerned, an ethnology of white people by white people was considered a feasible project.

Uneven Development and the Four Stages Theory

By the end of the eighteenth century, several French and Scottish Enlightenment philosophers had come up with theories of cultural evolution that saw human development as a universal process traveling through four distinct stages. Each stage was based on a society's mode of subsistence. The first stage, similar to the state of nature discussed in the previous chapter, was that of hunters, gatherers, and fishermen. Population growth causes the move to a system of pasturage, then agriculture, to make greater use of less land for more people. Agriculture and commercial society are seen by many of the proponents of the four stages theory as simultaneous, interdependent modes of subsistence.

Jean Francois Lafitau is cited by both Anthony Pagden and Ronald Meek as an influential precursor to later works of comparative ethnology. Lafitau's *Moeurs des Sauvages Ameriquains, comparées aux moeurs des premiers temps* (1724), "was very widely quoted by the social scientists in the second half of the century," and a forerunner of the four stages theory.[6] Many of these eighteenth-century social scientists seemed convinced that Lafitau had developed "a convincing demonstration of the fact that contemporary American society could be regarded as a kind of living model—conveniently laid out for study, as if in a laboratory—of human society in the 'first' or 'earliest' stage of its development."[7]

After Lafitau, Turgot, in his *On Political Geography* (1751), and *On Universal History* (1752), delivers fairly clear statements of the four stages theory. Turgot discusses "'hunters', 'shepherds', and 'husbandmen'" and assigns them "to different types of society *clearly conceived as succeeding one another over time*" (italics in original).[8] Adam Smith and Adam Ferguson developed economic arguments along similar lines, and by the end of the century, the idea that all human progress went through these four stages was widely accepted. As Pagden writes, the

> new historical account of the origin and growth of human societies ... was most fully developed in Adam Smith's celebrated 'four-stages theory', which although it was intended to explain the origins of the market society could be mapped by others, such as William Robertson, onto the progressive evolution of man's moral—as well as intellectual— being. By the middle of the eighteenth century, then, the claim that differences in cultural

---

5   *Oxford English Dictionary* (Oxford, 1989).

6   Ronald Meek, *Social Science and the Ignoble Savage* (Cambridge, 1976), p. 57. Anthony Pagden, *The Fall of Natural Man: The American Indian and the Origins of Comparative Ethnology* (Cambridge, 1986).

7   Meek, *Social Science and the Ignoble Savage*, p. 57.

8   Ibid., p. 72.

behaviour could be accounted for as differences in rates of historical growth, had become a commonplace.[9]

Pagden correctly links the acceptance of this theory to the European "discovery of American man." The history he sketches "ends with a simple proposition: that for the cultural historian—who had inherited from the theologians that project which in the nineteenth century came to be 'anthropology'—differences in place may be identical to differences in time."[10]

As we have seen, Basil Hall in his *Travels in North America in the Years 1827 and 1828* presents a version of these four stages spread out over a space of just fifty miles. Hall's work, and that of Frances Trollope, sees European emigrants living in the sort of "laboratory" in which the thinkers who conceptualized the four stages theory placed Native Americans. This suggests a number of problems that English travelers to America would seek to resolve, with varied success. If mankind progressed through four stages towards an ever more advanced state of society, how was one to explain the uncouth manners of the Americans, who were clearly living in a society that mixed the agricultural and commercial stages just as the English did? Had some Americans, by settling far to the west of the more advanced cities of the east coast, regressed? If so, what did such a possibility imply for the English themselves? As I have suggested, one solution to these questions was the unofficial and unscientific creation of a fifth stage, dependent upon manners rather than the mode of subsistence. Another was the creation of an intermediate category, or categories, for Americans, either between the hunter/gatherer and agricultural stages, or combining several stages at once. Crèvecoeur's comments on the backwoodsmen of America, "living on the flesh of wild animals when they can catch them, and when they are not able, ... on grain," places the frontiersman in the first stage of development.[11] As I have argued in Chapter Three, in Crèvecoeur's reading the farmer replaced the frontiersman in about a decade. He did not develop himself into a higher being. This would seem to leave a perpetually westward-moving primitive American in regular contact with the westward-moving farmer, creating a uniquely American version of an uneven pattern of economic development.

Hall and Trollope consolidated an ethnographic discourse about Americans that began to emerge in the early years of the nineteenth century. While most of the accounts we have from travelers from the early decades of the nineteenth century claim a sympathy with the United States' republican government and social egalitarianism, many of the qualities Hall and Trollope would establish as American traits in their widely read works—for English readers primarily, but for Europeans at large, as well as for Americans who recognized a lack of refinement in their own society—began to emerge at least a decade before Hall's *Travels* were published in 1829.

Henry Bradshaw Fearon's *Sketches of America: A Narrative of a Journey of Five Thousand Miles Through the Eastern and Western States of America* (1818)

---

9 Pagden, *Fall of Natural Man*, p. 2.
10 Ibid., p. 2.
11 Crèvecoeur, *Letters from an American Farmer*, p. 72

was widely read and discussed.[12] It presented a view of an enviable landscape, occasionally admirable social equality, and unacceptable manners and mores. His method is a conspicuous part of his narrative, a feature common to Hall's and Trollope's accounts. He founds the authenticity of his representations on a claim of objectivity, which, while not substantiated, is presented often and vociferously enough to carry rhetorical weight if nothing else. And in works like these, rhetorical weight should not be discounted. Fearon insists on "the *faithfulness* and *sincerity* of my statements ... I have," he claims, "had every motive to speak what I thought the truth, and none to conceal or pervert it."[13]

Such a claim affords Fearon room for statements that seem to emerge from differing, often contradictory ideological predilections. Sometimes he presents himself as an ardent convert to republicanism. At other times he is so fastidious in manners and appearance that he seems the guardian of an older English probity Americans have recklessly abandoned. On board the *Washington* from the Isle of Wight to New York, in the summer 1817, he serves as liberty's champion. Fearon professes himself in favor of a worldwide conversion to "liberty," and claims that he and George Washington Adams—John Quincy Adams's eldest son—are the only ones on board who are "warm friends of political liberty ... we stood alone in wishing its extension to England, to unfortunate Ireland, to France, to the European Continent generally, and to the brave South Americans."[14] Since John Quincy Adams himself was a fellow passenger, Fearon presents his commitment to what American ideals *should* be as even greater than that of a high official of the American government.[15]

But Fearon's attachment to political liberty does not prevent him from noticing the faults social equality engenders among the Americans. New York—a city most visitors of the time, including Hall and Trollope, depict as immensely more civilized than other parts of the Union—causes him to qualify his view of true liberty, at least as it is displayed there. "A walk through New York," he writes, "will disappoint an Englishman: there is, on the surface of society, a carelessness, a laziness, an unsocial indifference, which freezes the blood and disgusts the judgment ..."[16] Fearon knows that his comments place him at odds with the republican feeling so warmly embraced on his passage from England, and he tries to justify his claim that he understands liberty better than those he is observing. Shopkeepers' "cold indifference, may, by themselves, be mistaken for independence," he writes. "(B)ut

---

12 Henry Bradshaw Fearon, *Sketches of America; a narrative of a journey of five thousand miles through the eastern and western states of America; contained in eight reports addressed to the thirty-nine English families by whom the author was deputed, in June 1817, to ascertain whether any, and what part of the United States would be suitable for their residence. With remarks on Mr. Birkbeck's "Notes" and "Letters"*. (London, 1818). For a discussion of the influence of Fearon's work among the London literati, especially among those in Thomas Moore's circle in 1819, see James Chandler's *England in 1819* (Chicago, 1998), pp. 278–9.

13 Fearon, *Sketches*, pp. x–xi.

14 Ibid., p. 2.

15 At the time, J.Q. Adams was on his way home from England following his ambassadorship to the Court of St. James in the Madison administration, to become Secretary of State under James Monroe.

16 Fearon, *Sketches*, p. 11.

no person of thought and observation will ever concede to them that they have selected a wise mode of exhibiting that dignified feeling."[17] Aware that his criticisms might betray hypocrisy, or at least inconsistency, Fearon immediately justifies his judgment. "I disapprove most decidedly of the obsequious servility of many London shopkeepers," he writes, "but I am not prepared to go the length of those in New York, who stand with their hats on, or sit or lie along their counters, smoking segars, and spitting in every direction, to a degree offensive to any man of decent feelings."[18] In the end, the fact that he represents his objections not as hostility to liberty, but rather as disgust with the abuse of "decent feelings" saves the ideals of progressive politics for civilization while indicting the social advancement of a particular people who can be identified in their specificity and segregated.

Fearon's earlier abstract praise of liberty thus moves towards an ethnographic account—mostly negative—of the Americans as a people. He sets out to correct what he deems the uncritically positive views of earlier writers, most particularly Morris Birkbeck and George Flower, who had founded a utopian colony in Albion, Indiana.[19] "I might fill many pages" with praise of America," he writes. "(W)hen I survey this city (New York), and remember that but two centuries since, the spot on which it stands was a wilderness, I cannot but be struck with its comparative extent and opulence ... but (the U.S.) is not, as some would represent it, a paradise, any more than the city of New York is as yet a rival either in population, riches, or extent to that of London."[20] Bostonians are worse than New Yorkers, Fearon claims, because they have a sense of class incompatible with liberty. "*Distinctions* exist to an extent rather ludicrous under a free and popular government: there are the first class, second class, third class, and the 'old families.'"[21] He observes that "what I fear pervades this new world, (is) an affectation of splendour, or what may be called *style*, in those things which are intended to meet the public eye; with a lamentable want even of cleanliness in such matters as are removed *from* that ordeal."[22] He contrasts this striving to solid, middle-class domestic virtue. "To this" pretentiousness "may be added," he writes, "an appearance of uncomfortable extravagance, and an ignorance of that kind of order and neatness which constitute ... the principal charm of domestic life."[23]

In the end, Fearon abandons his earlier praise of an American government based on equality for a lament that, in forming a new national character, the Americans have thrown away all the benefits they could have gained by maintaining English manners and learning. "National, like individual character," he writes, "must be in a great measure formed or controlled by the circumstances in which men are situated," echoing Blumenbach's environmental determinants of race. "For the creation of a

---

17 Ibid., p. 11.

18 Ibid., pp. 11–12.

19 George and Georgiana Keats, brother and sister-in-law of the poet, were some of the early followers of Birkbeck and Flower. But they did not last long. After a few months, they had moved to western Pennsylvania, in search of a healthier climate for George's consumption.

20 Fearon, *Sketches*, pp. 20–22.

21 Ibid., p. 107.

22 Ibid., p. 136.

23 Ibid.

valuable standard of character," Fearon continues, "Americans are disadvantageously placed: they are far removed from that mass of floating intelligence which pervades Europe, but more especially England."[24] This failure is compounded by the fact that, as Fearon sees it, the Americans have won their liberty too cheaply. "(T)hey have nothing to contend for—nothing to call forth their energies, and but little of external excitement beyond the pursuits of gain, and merely animal gratification."[25] Apparently the Revolution, creation of a federal government out of fractious states, and moral crises over slavery and the displacement and genocide of the native peoples escaped Fearon's observation. "In their civil condition," he writes, "all obtain a living with ease ... To become intellectual, energetic, and virtuous, in the present state of our existence, seems to require that we should first know sorrow, and have been acquainted with grief."[26] Here, as throughout Fearon's *Sketches*, only white Americans are considered in the contemplation or identification of national character. The author claims that he does not "wish to see transplanted into this free and hitherto unoppressed country, enormous taxation—iniquity in high places—civil disabilities—religious exclusions—standing armies—and hired spies and informers."[27] His equation of oppression with English oppression, here and elsewhere, is clear, as is his inability to see the real, unique problems Americans faced. Fearon is insistent that if the Americans are ever to deserve "their unparalleled natural and political advantages" then "a something *must* occur" to rouse "this people ... from their present lethargy."[28]

A year after Fearon's *Sketches* appeared, William Cobbett's *A Year's Residence in America* (1819) described the English radical's exile on Long Island. His account is generally more favorable than Fearon's. But the political ethnography Fearon sketches out is present throughout Cobbett's book, as are several of the tropes that would pervade later writers' observations on the Americans. Even a political radical who was generally well disposed to the Americans as was Cobbett at this point in his career tends to treat Americanness almost as an ethnographic category. Like Fearon before him, and Trollope and Hall after, Cobbett's authority to write comes from his claim that he has based his account on "actual *experience*. I will say what I *know* and what I have *seen* and what I have *done*."[29]

While Cobbett claims that in America "Governors, Legislators, Presidents, all are farmers," and that an American farmer "is not the poor dependent wretch" that he is in England but a prospering, respected, and free member of society, he also claims that American farmers lack the order and diligence that English farmers display. This disorder, he claims, "is hereditary from the first settlers."[30] In other words, it is a distinguishing feature of the American breed. On the other hand, Cobbett describes the manners, customs, and characters of the Americans as, "generally speaking, the

---

24 Ibid., p. 352.
25 Ibid.
26 Ibid.
27 Ibid., p. 353.
28 Ibid.
29 William Cobbett, *A Year's Residence in America* (London, 1818–19), p. xvii.
30 Ibid., p. 3.

same as those of the people of England." He further claims, contradicting virtually every other English writer on Americans of this period, that "this is a country of *universal civility.*"[31] But despite these generally positive assessments, Cobbett still participates in a discourse that sees Americans as subjects of observation much more than as the neighbors and acquaintances they were; as such, he contributes to the project of comparative ethnology in which other, less positively inclined observers participated.

The 1820s and '30s

As travelers came to the United States in increasing numbers during the 1820s and 1830s, their concerns expanded to include not just how the Americans subsisted, or how republicanism progressed, but in what state of society and comfort they lived, and how much education and taste they displayed. Basil Hall's *Travels* are filled with comments on what seemed to him antiquated conditions for travelers. During a trip to Massachusetts in June, 1827, he finds American manners and the level of physical improvements confusing in their failure to conform to a set period or place. As he writes:

> Many things occurred during this trip into Massachusetts to revive those ideas, in which probably most people have indulged their fancy at some time of their lives, as to what might possibly have been the state of travelling, and other things, in Europe a century ago. At other moments there came across our view little circumstances which irresistibly linked our thoughts to the present date and place; and anon others started up, which were so exactly English in appearance, that we almost forgot how far we were off, till suddenly recalled to the spot by some touch of foreign idiom, or manners, or scenery.[32]

This constant feeling of familiarity, suddenly disturbed by a foreignness of speech, manners, or landscape, is what continually brings the English traveler back to attempts to place the American in an earlier time, in Hall's case here, to the England of the early eighteenth century.

Differences in tastes and manners are less easy to explain away. One feature of American life in the 1820s that invariably bewilders, and often disheartens and disgusts, English observers is the silent mode of dining common to rooming houses and hotels. Hall writes that his "main object" upon arriving in the United States, at New York, "was to get acquainted with some of the natives, and this, we imagined, would be the easiest thing in the world."[33] After all, he reasons, the streets "recalled the seaports of England... The signs over the shop doors were written in English." While he is a little put off by the fact that "the language we heard spoken was different in tone from what we had been accustomed to," he reconciles himself to the fact that, "(s)till it was English ... The whole seemed at times, more like a dream

---

31   Ibid., pp. 153–4.
32   Hall, *Travels*, vol. 1, pp. 105–6.
33   Ibid., I:10.

than a sober reality. For there was so much about it that looked like England, that we half fancied ourselves back again."[34]

This illusion is disturbed at mealtime. His description of dinner at The Plate House in New York is typical of travelers' accounts. "The sole object of the company," Hall writes, "was evidently to get through a certain quantum of victuals with as much dispatch as possible; and as all the world knows that talking interferes with eating, every art was used in this said most excellent Plate House, to utter as few words as might be, and only those absolutely essential to the ceremony."[35] The deception produced by the seeming omnipresence of the most significant mark of Englishness—the use of a common language so insistent that it causes Hall to doubt the foreignness of his surroundings—is dispelled by a silencing physicality. The very Englishness of America, heard in its language, is silenced by an American mode of eating both particular to the United States—the unsociable practice of chowing down is almost always discussed in the context of the conversational nature of English common meals—and bordering on the animalistic.

Frances Trollope also finds fault with this persistent silence of the Americans at table. She sees in it a bestial quality she found everywhere in America. "They ate in perfect silence," Trollope writes of her first meal in a Memphis hotel, "and with such astonishing rapidity that their dinner was over literally before ours was began … The only sounds heard were those produced by the knives and forks, with the unceasing chorus of coughing, &c."[36] This ravenous hunger is treated as a national trait, and extended beyond the dinner table to modes of subsistence and enrichment. Trollope later complains that in Cincinnati, "a city of extraordinary size and importance, when it is remembered that thirty years ago the aboriginal forest occupied the ground where it stands," this ravenousness is equivalent to greed. Comparing Americans to bees in a hive, she reports that she never saw either "a beggar, nor a man of sufficient fortune to permit his ceasing his efforts to increase it; thus every bee in the hive is actively employed in search of that honey of Hybla, vulgarly called money; neither art, science, learning, nor pleasure can seduce them from its pursuit." She condemns this "unity of purpose, backed by the spirit of enterprise, and joined with an acuteness and *total* absence of probity."[37]

Frances Trollope, somewhat like Cobbett, traveled to America to find refuge from troubles from home. Cobbett had gone abroad to escape almost certain imprisonment for his seditious writings. Trollope went in the hopes of reversing her family's fortunes, which had been ruined by her husband Thomas's failed attempts at gentleman farming, and inattention to his legal practice. She went as the companion of Frances Wright, a radical reformer whose Nashoba settlement in Tennessee was an attempt to bring white and black Americans together in a demonstration of racial equality that was somehow intended to end slavery in the United States, possibly by force of example. Wright had attempted to entice Mary Shelley to join her in Tennessee. Shelley, possibly tired from a lifetime of reforming society as a Godwin

34 Ibid., vol. 1, p. 6.
35 Ibid., vol. 1, p. 32.
36 Trollope, *Domestic Manners*, p. 25.
37 Ibid., p. 38.

and as Percy Shelley's wife, politely refused. Trollope decided America might be the place to revive her fortunes, and find employment for her son Henry. So in November 1827, Trollope, two daughters, and Henry, along with a French artist and two servants, sailed for America.[38] She stopped first in New Orleans. From there she made her way towards Wright's settlement, staying in Memphis along the way.

Her initial desire upon arriving in Memphis—where she had her first silent American meal—after a trip up the Mississippi from New Orleans, is to eat her "dinner of hard venison and peach-sauce in a private room," but she discovers this would not only be considered rude, but "would be assuredly refused." Trollope then describes eating at a "table ... laid for fifty persons." The distinction of sitting near "'the lady,'" is quickly placed into context. "(T)he proud feelings to which such distinction might give birth" are checked by the fact that Trollope's servant is placed across from her.[39]

Trollope's objections to such forced intimacy with people she considers her social inferiors could be passed off as simple snobbery, if it did not appear in the accounts of virtually all travelers to the United States during the period, middle class and wealthy alike. Trollope herself could hardly have been considered a member of the elite, having traveled to the United States to attempt to repair her ruined finances, with hopes of placing Henry in some sort of business.[40] She was also, in her own way, a liberal. Her plan to join Wright's settlement may have been hastily considered, and was almost immediately abandoned. But she considered herself a progressive, adventurous bohemian. This, however, was not to survive her nearly four years in America. As she put it: "I had a little leaning towards sedition myself when I set out, but before I had half completed my tour I was quite cured."[41] The ultimate curative is linked directly to the manners she found at mealtimes. Trollope is highly critical of the equality that she believes mars society, and keeps it from improving. Part of this is seen in the lack of distinction at table.

Political Reform—The Example of the United States

One reason American equality—social as well as political—is a matter of such urgent concern in Trollope's book especially, but in Hall's as well, is the agitation for reform that was gaining powerful momentum by the time their travels took place. As Helen Heineman quite rightly points out in her biography of Trollope, *Domestic Manners* "fueled the then-current controversy over the extension of the suffrage (the Reform Bill of 1832) and was cited by both liberals and conservatives, who saw in the newly created American republic the clear results of democratic principles."[42] Such results

---

38 Helen Heineman, *Frances Trollope* (Boston, 1984), p. 6.

39 Trollope, *American Manners*, p. 32.

40 Trollope's main commodity was her English culture. Her major financial venture in America was "Trollope's Bazaar," a "representation in wax scenes from Dante's Inferno." See Heineman, *Frances Trollope*, pp. 7–9.

41 Trollope, *Domestic Manners*, p. 39.

42 Heineman, *Frances Trollope*, p. 25. Heineman writes that *Domestic Manners* "follows Frances Trollope's gradual transformation from daring adventurer, to beleaguered resident, to

were apparent even to a liberal like Fearon, and a radical like Cobbett. Trollope helped make America and the Americans symbolic of the worst excesses of equality.

The lack of "probity" to which Trollope refers suggests that accounts like Hall's and Trollope's imply—without explicitly arguing for—a stage in human development, beyond those dedicated to the material subsistence of either body, through a disgusting greed at the common dinner table, or fortune. The equality Trollope condemns prevents Americans from pursuing "art, science, learning (or) pleasure," and thus attaining the level of politeness that the middle and upper classes in England can afford because of the relegation of the actual work that goes into the third and fourth stages of development—farming and trading—to a class not to be seen in English dining-rooms or parlors. Election reform, and the inevitable social leveling Trollope saw resulting from it, threatened to take away the leisure to learn and continue developing in terms of politeness and culture that those not obligated to perform manual labor enjoyed.

In Trollope's *The Refugee in America* (1832), the story of a nobleman forced to flee England after fearing he has murdered a man in self-defense and the noble family who has brought him away to shield him from the legal consequences, American table manners are a constant source of disgust, and sometimes amusement, to the cultured English travelers. "It was hardly possible," Trollope remarks, "for the easy graceful manners of Miss Gordon, or the polite vivacity of her father, to overcome the cold silence of an American dinner-table."[43] Miss Gordon is a vivacious young woman who sees much to laugh at in the American character, but the meals have a depressing effect even on her. "She talked ... yet, still Mr. Warner replied by three words at a time, and his sons continued to feed with ravenous rapidity, and imperturbable gravity of countenance ... the Warner family seemed to have no other object in sitting down to dinner than to swallow their food."[44]

As a result, meals are fast. Breakfast at the Warner house in Rochester, a more civilized place than most in this novel, does not "last long; though, as it occupied twenty minutes, it was at least double its ordinary duration in any American family; which waste of time was not indeed to be avoided, from the 'national slowness' of the English at table."[45] At Washington, where the traveling English party goes near the end of its ordeals in the new republic, the members of Congress dine like pigs at a trough. Congress breaks for the day at about four p.m.: "(I)t therefore often happens that half an hour afterwards five hundred of the most eloquent mouths in the Union are open to receive the restoratives of sturgeon and shad, roast beef and turkey, canvass-backs and custards."[46]

---

observant, note-taking tourist and author" (26). While all these stages of Trollope's American experience appear in the book, the author makes a concerted effort to present herself as the distant, unbiased reporter from the beginning of her trip in 1828, through the book's publication in 1832, effacing much of her participation in the commerce and social life of the United States along the way.

43 Frances Trollope, *The Refugee in America: A Novel* (4 vols, London, 1832), vol. 1, p. 142.

44 Ibid., vol. 1, p. 142.

45 Ibid., vol. 1, p. 174.

46 Ibid., vol. 3, pp. 59–60.

The linkage of poor American table manners to poor American governance is clear. Trollope includes many scenes of the business of the nation being conducted with a surprising lack of ability. Hall also refers to the failure of American republicanism, in terms that conflate national greatness with domestic politeness. "These gentlemen," Hall writes of the members of the New York legislature, "were described to me as being chiefly farmers, shopkeepers, and country lawyers, and other persons quite unaccustomed to abstract reasoning ..." Many of the legislators, "not having made public business a regular profession or study, were ignorant of what had been done before—and had come to the legislature, straight from the plough—or from behind the counter—from chopping down trees—or from the bar, under the impression that they were at once to be converted into statesmen."[47] Social class tends to lead to social behavior, as is clear by Hall's last remark. The "bar" he refers to is that of a saloon, not the legal profession.

The silent American table was one place where a lack of manners was in evidence. Two other habits remarked upon by most English travelers during this period were more dramatically offensive. Both Hall and Trollope, as well as William Cobbett, find the Americans indistinguishable from those previously considered the native, namely the Indians, in their intemperance. Hall writes that

> a deeper curse never afflicted any nation. The evil is manifested in almost every walk of life, contaminates all it touches, and at last finds its consummation in the alms-house, the penitentiary, or the insane institution; so that, while it threatens to sap the foundation of every thing good in America—political and domestic—it may truly be said to be worse than the yellow fever, or the negro slavery, because apparently more irremediable.[48]

Like Trollope, Hall ascribes the evils of widespread drinking to the leveling effects of the equality that pervades social as well as political society in America. "(I)n a country where all effective power is placed," he writes, "not indirectly and for a time, but directly, universally, and permanently—in the hands of the lowest and most numerous class of the community, the characteristic habits of that class must of necessity predominate, in spite of every conceivable device recommended and adopted by the wise and the good men of the nation."[49] Hall complains that bars are everywhere—in museums, theaters, and at natural sights. "(A)t the Cauterskill Falls we saw two; one on each side of the cataract, to the utter ruin of the unhappy sublime and beautiful."[50]

As is seen in Hall's reference to Burke and the ruinous effect of the signs of this "national evil" on the landscape, one of the main problems with such a habit is its destruction of the sensibilities of the more refined classes to see and appreciate natural beauty. It is linked directly to Trollope's complaint that higher pursuits could make no progress in America because social equality tended to prevent anyone from becoming susceptible to polite virtues and aesthetic accomplishments, such as viewing waterfalls as an example of the sublime in nature. In Hall's view, the result

47 Hall, *Travels*, vol. 2, pp. 35–6.
48 Ibid., vol. 2, p. 84.
49 Ibid., vol. 2, p. 85.
50 Ibid., vol. 1, p. 126.

of this alcohol-induced dullness—and throughout his work and Trollope's drinking is depicted as just as unsociable a pastime as eating—is that Americans are "nearly as insensible to the beauties of nature as we had reason to fear, from their public exhibitions, they were to the graces of art."[51]

Tobacco chewing and spitting are the third much-lamented American pastime. Trollope asserts that this habit alters the physiognomy of the Americans. The lips of American males "are almost uniformly thin and compressed," and Trollope can arrive at no explanation other than the "universal" practice of "expressing the juices of this loathsome herb," which she claims "enforces exactly that position of the lips, which gives this remarkable peculiarity to the American countenance."[52] An American farmer in upstate New York is similarly disfigured by tobacco in Trollope's *Refugee in America*. She describes Silas Burns as "a tall stout man, about forty, (who) would have been handsome, had not his mouth been rendered unseemly by the hue of tobacco, and his eyes sunk, as if out of health."[53] In her travel book she describes a scene at a theater in Washington, where those in the first rows sit with their legs across the seats in front of them, spitting "incessantly."[54] The theme of spitting flows throughout *Domestic Manners*, Cobbett's *Year's Residence* and Hall's *Travels*. It amounts to a significant trope in the English definition of Americanness in the early nineteenth century.

Old Time Religion

American religion and religious enthusiasm are depicted as particularly grotesque and primitive examples of the national character by both Hall and Trollope. Hall's description of a meeting of Shakers in Lebanon, Massachusetts, is particularly telling in respect to what he views as peculiarly American institutions. He writes that the Shakers he saw "appear to be a very orderly, industrious, and harmless set of persons." But he cannot help finding their rites and practices absolutely alien. He remarks that "though I have witnessed some strange forms of worship in former travels, I cannot say that I ever beheld any thing, even in Hindoostan, to match these Shakers." Hall attempts to back away from condemning them by declaring that "there is always something so objectionable in treating any religious observance with levity, however ridiculous it may appear to persons of a different persuasion, that I think it right to sacrifice altogether what amusement a description of the proceedings at Lebanon might afford."[55] But Hall's forbearance is entirely owing to the foreignness of the ceremonies he witnesses, and his conviction that "these absurdities" were not "likely to spread in the world."[56]

Trollope has no qualms about exposing the "absurdities" of American religious practices. Her first experience of American religion that she relates in *Domestic*

---

51 Ibid., vol. 1, p. 124.
52 Trollope, *Domestic Manners*, p. 177.
53 Trollope, *The Refugee in America*, vol. 1, p. 60.
54 Trollope, *Domestic Manners*, p. 321.
55 Hall, *Travels*, vol. 1, p. 111.
56 Ibid., vol. 1, pp. 111–12.

Manners occurs at a revival at Cincinnati, when several of the churches are opened up to itinerant preachers. She is offended constantly by what can be interpreted as sexual domination of young ignorant women by preachers terrifying their audiences "with the immediacy of fire and brimstone."[57] The religious gatherings Trollope depicts are all characterized by overwhelmingly young, female congregations being brought to indecent, almost orgasmic shuddering and insensibility by older, male preachers. She writes that "the coarsest comedy ever written would be a less detestable exhibition for the eyes of youth and innocence than such a scene."[58] In a subsequent scene, her fears would extend beyond the "eyes" to the body.

Her most memorable experience is of a camp meeting "in a wild district on the confines of Indiana."[59] She anticipates the meeting in terms that transcend Americanness, or anything as mundane as nationality of any variety. "I had heard it said," she writes, "that being at a camp-meeting was like finding yourself at the gate of heaven, and seeing it opening before you; I had heard it said, that being at a camp-meeting was like finding yourself within the gates of hell." She then brings the experience down to its proper sphere: "in either case," she writes, "there must be something to gratify curiosity, and compensate one for the fatigue of a long rumbling ride and sleepless night."[60]

What she finds is a frightening mix of English entertainment and primitive enthusiasm, served up to a mass audience which behaves with indecent, sexually suggestive raptures:

> The first glance reminded me of Vauxhall, from the effect of the lights among the trees, and the moving crowd below them; the second shewed a scene totally unlike any thing I had ever witnessed. Four high frames, constructed in the form of altars, were placed at the four corners of the enclosure; on these were supported layers of earth and sod, on which burned immense fires of blazing pine-wood. On one side a rude platform was erected to accommodate the preachers, fifteen of whom attended this meeting, and with very short intervals for necessary refreshment and private devotion, preached in rotation, day and night, from Tuesday to Saturday.[61]

In one tent, Trollope witnesses a group of about thirty people being moved by the spirit. The lurid sexuality of the scene appalls and frightens her and her English companions. She describes a young man and girl, embracing on the straw on the ground inside the tent. The girl's "features" work "with the most violent agitation," as if in the throes of sexual passion; "soon after they both fell forward on the straw, as if unable to endure in any other attitude the burning eloquence of a tall grim figure in black, who, standing erect in the centre, was uttering with incredible vehemence an oration that seemed to hover between praying and preaching."[62]

---

57 Johanna Johnston, *The Life, Manners and Travels of Fanny Trollope* (New York, 1978), p. 87.

58 Trollope, *Domestic Manners*, p. 91.

59 Ibid., p. 126.

60 Ibid.

61 Ibid., p. 127.

62 Ibid., p. 128.

The primitiveness she sees in this scene is unmistakable, as is her view that those at the meeting are moving closer towards animal nature than a spiritual state. One of the preachers herds the people taking part in the meeting into a place called "the pen," where the people fall on their knees, and throw about "their limbs with such incessant motion," uttering "convulsive groans, shrieks and screams the most appalling."[63] The actions of the ministers towards the young women in "the pen," in the midst of this animalistic and sexualized primitivistic scene, anger her to the point where she claims that had she "been a man, I am sure I should have been guilty of some rash act of interference."[64]

Fearon depicts a similar revulsion at the sexual aspect of American religious practices. He reports visiting a church where worshippers groaned, shrieked, and shouted. "Feeling disposed to get a nearer sight of the beings who sent forth such terrifying yells," he writes, "I endeavoured to approach them, but was stopped by several of the brethren, who would not allow of a near approach towards the holy sisterhood."[65] He reports that his "feelings soon gave way to an emotion of melancholy horror, when I considered the gloomy picture it represented of human nature …"[66] He, like Trollope, takes refuge in the role of reporter of strange customs, and claims he cannot explain what he has seen. "In Ireland I have also witnessed occasional (religious) violence," he writes, but there "we make some allowance for national character: they are all fire—all feeling; but with Americans, whatever may be their excellences or their defects, they are certainly not chargeable with possessing a superabundance of warm blood: they are, on the contrary, most remarkable for complete and general coldness of characters and disposition."[67] The conflation of coldness in feeling with primitive enthusiasm is another example of this collective view of the American as a racial hybrid. The race they represent is unspecifiable for writers like Trollope and Fearon, but the conviction that it is separate from that to which the English belong is consistently communicated.

Trollope's description of the Indiana camp meeting, in linking American religion directly to a bestial behavior incommensurate with anything to be found in England, implies that the effect of an egalitarian communion in "the depths of their eternal forests" is to move Americans closer to a primitive state.[68] Those who enter this state are members of a society that has successfully, if amazingly swiftly, passed through the four stages described by Ferguson, Smith, and Turgot. Yet they still retain natures radically at odds with peoples of other nations who have progressed to the same material condition. The explanation Trollope, Hall, and contemporary English travelers in America give to explain such a distinct national character in a people who share a culture and a language with the English is that this progress has occurred too quickly, in a natural setting that remains as yet untamed.

---

63 Ibid., p. 130.
64 Ibid., p. 131.
65 Fearon, *Sketches*, p. 164.
66 Ibid., p. 165.
67 Ibid., p. 166.
68 Trollope, *Domestic Manners*, p. 130.

The Traveler as Ethnographer

A persistent feature of these works is the authors' insistence that their observations are unbiased accounts given by one who has actually been to America and seen it. The rise of positivism in the period is evident in every traveler's account, with its evidentiary claims, and just as importantly, the consciousness that such claims are important to establish authenticity. An obvious tension resides in the requirement that observers be unbiased, despite having been in the midst of what they describe. But that tension is especially necessary for English observers of a people who, but for a war and an ocean, could be seen as very much like themselves. In order to present a believable account of the Americans, Hall and Trollope must emphasize their long residence in the United States. But, as in Trollope's description of the Indiana camp meeting, it is just as important for these authors to maintain a distance, an Englishness apart from the Americanness they are witnessing, in order to invent the Americans as a separate breed of people.

Trollope and Hall use several anthropological techniques to establish their authority. First of all, they both claim that their assessment of American culture is based on extensive experience and long familiarity. In short, they claim to have done their field work. Hall claims not even to have read the works of travelers who have preceded him, just as a few years later, Trollope would claim not to have read Hall. "The chief object I had in view in visiting America," Hall claims, "was to see things with my own eyes ... To avoid all undue influence," he writes,

> I considered it best to defer reading the works of preceding travelers, until I should have formed my own opinions on the subject; but I found so much pleasure during the journey, from the freshness of original and unbiassed observation, that on my return I resolved to persevere in this self-denial somewhat longer, that my narrative also might be derived, as far as possible, from those local sources of information which had fallen within the reach of my own enquiries.[69]

Simply put, the traveler's account of a place like America can be a work of truly original scholarship, or inquiry. Hall begins his account with this claim, which makes it seem as if the United States were an unknown, exotic country, and he himself an ethnographer.

Hall presents his work as an obligation to the English public. He has seen something new, in his interpretation of his travels, and since this new thing must be of value to his compatriots, he is obligated to report what he has seen. As he puts it, one of the "duties of the traveller" is to describe his adventures. "For how is he to furnish his pictures of society without going into company, and by reporting what he sees there, acting more or less the ungenerous part of a spy?"[70]

Hall's duty is not only to English readers, but to the American themselves. While Hall disclaims that he wants "to bring others to my way of thinking," he feels obligated to explain not just his opinions, but his methods, and why those methods result in a more accurate depiction of Americanness than other accounts might. His opinions, he

---

69 Hall, *Travels*, vol. 1, pp. i–ii.

70 Ibid., vol. 1, p. 13.

claims, "were formed, not by fostering prejudices, or by predetermining to see things in certain lights, but by the gradual progress of a pretty extensive observation, varied and checked in a thousand ways, and under circumstances probably as favourable as a traveller could expect to meet with, and perhaps better than most natives could hope to find, even if their own country were the object of research."[71]

Consistently acting the part of the ethnographer performing field work, Hall founds the accuracy of his observation on his notes. His own journal text is his most important witness. "It is often useful in travelling," Hall writes, "to record at the instant those trivial but peculiar circumstances, which first strike the eye of a stranger, since, in a short time, they become so familiar as entirely to escape attention."[72] These first impressions, he argues, have often stood the test of time. Their endurance through months, even years of experiences, "often surprises me when I look over my early notes. One of the greatest difficulties of travelling, indeed, is to distinguish fairly between those circumstances which are permanently characteristic, and those which are contingent upon transient causes."[73] By claiming that his first impressions have stood up so well, he both claims astuteness as an observer, and a careful methodology based on long observation.

Trollope's claims to authenticity are just as insistent, and also based on the traveler's journal of things of which she has had direct experience. She claims her observations on American religion are accurate, as her "early notes" which "contain many observations on the subject" attest. She also labels the religious customs of Americans universal, "as nearly the same scenes recurred in every part of the country."[74] When she recounts a conversation between two "Yankees" overheard on a canal boat on the Erie Canal, in order to give a sample of American dialect, she fears she will "spoil it" by reducing it to text, but vouches for its accuracy by claiming she "wrote it down immediately."[75] In this case, the traveler's journal both testifies to the accuracy of description, and the even greater knowledge of the observer, who, having heard the actual sounds in the actual place, has unchallenged authority to represent the American. The reader gets the sense that Trollope's main occupation was examining American behavior, despite the fact that she went to the States to take part in commerce for personal gain. "Our mornings were spent," she writes about a several months' stay in Philadelphia, "as all travellers' mornings must be, in asking questions, and in seeing all that the answers told us it was necessary to see."[76]

Trollope and Hall, both having "been there," also claim that their accounts—both of which are largely condemnations of American boorishness—are unbiased. Both strive to excuse their writings from any taint of non-objective reporting, in a gesture that reinforces their separateness from their subject, and their authority to represent it. Trollope claims to have gone through soul searching before publishing her views, which take the form of a dialogue, not between the English traveler

71 Ibid., vol. 1, pp. 108–9.
72 Ibid., vol. 1, p. 17.
73 Ibid., vol. 1, p. 105.
74 Trollope, *Domestic Manners*, p. 84.
75 Ibid., pp. 287–8.
76 Ibid., p. 205.

and the American subject, but between the amateur ethnographer and her journal. "While reading and transcribing my notes," she writes, near the end of *Domestic Manners*, where she is concerned with making her methods transparent to the reader, "I underwent a strict self-examination. I passed in review all I had seen, all I had felt, and scrupulously challenged every expression of disapprobation; the result was, that I omitted in transcription much that I had written, as containing unnecessary details of things which had displeased me; yet, as I did so, I felt strongly that there was no exaggeration in them."[77]

Trollope's claim to objectivity, then, even extends to suppressing information she knows her readers will consider too negative. What these could be is hard to imagine, since the book is packed with entertaining malice towards her subject. But the claim continues to set her apart, and to stake her place as the ethnographer pursuing rational methods to deliver an accurate depiction of the culture she represents. Armed with this authority, she feels free to make general pronouncements on the American character, usually backed up by repeated claims about the untainted nature of the source of this authority. In a discussion of American greed, she asserts that, "after four years of attentive and earnest observation and enquiry, my honest conviction is, that the standard of moral character in the United States is very greatly lower than in Europe." In the end, this leads to her presentation of a comparative ethnology, where American manners are judged against European ones. Her assertion "that both Protestant England and Catholic France shew an infinitely superior religious and moral aspect to mortal observation, both as to reverend decency of external observance, and as to the inward fruit of honest dealing between man and man," is just one of many examples where a condemnation of an American trait leads to the elevation of a comparative European one.[78] While it seems clear that the acts of comparison and judgment probably precede, or accompany the judgment against American manners, Trollope's insistence on her objectivity and method make them appear as scientific conclusions deduced from the evidence she has just presented.

Hall's proclamations of objectivity are generally mixed with protestations that he has been an honest guest among the Americans, and should not be accused of malice in his judgments. "I have not held one language in this country, and another in my own," he claims. "(F)or every word I now publish to the world, I have repeatedly and openly spoken in company in all parts of the United States."[79] This claim, like Trollope's remarks on French and English religion, not only establishes his authority to speak on the subject of the Americans, but exalts the writer as an honest Englishman, which will continually distance him from Americans, whom he regularly accuses of underhanded treatment in financial matters throughout the three volumes of his travels.

Trollope's and Hall's claims to be delivering unbiased, quasi-scientific accounts of a people's manners, modes of subsistence, and worship, while setting them up as participants in an anthropological discourse, inevitably turn the Americans they observe into subjects of inquiry who speak, but not in response to the ethnographic

---

77 Ibid., p. 229.
78 Ibid., p. 235.
79 Hall, *Travels*, vol. 1, p. 15.

text they constitute. This reinforces the distance English writers sought to establish between themselves and those they no longer wished to see as Anglo-Americans. It also tends to generalize Americans, and turn them into a universal construct, which can seemingly be understood in broad terms. The English, as represented by Hall, Trollope, and other travelers during the first decades of the nineteenth century, such as Fearon, William Faux, and John Melish, have moved from the sympathetic identification with American suffering we found in the works discussed in the first chapter, such as Samuel Jackson Pratt's *Emma Corbett*, Helen Maria Williams's *Julia*, and Robert Bage's *Mt. Henneth*, where Americans are depicted as a wounded part of the English family, to objectifying and totalizing Americans, to marking them as unmistakably Other through the use of ethnographic observation.[80]

Hall reinforces his claims to proper English breeding while making a claim to be able to capture an American representativeness. "I think it best, in order to avoid all cause of offence," he writes, "to say nothing, direct or indirect, which can implicate personally any one with whom I have made acquaintance in America. My observations, therefore, whether laudatory or otherwise, I have confined as much as possible to those broad features which characterize the country generally."[81] Hall regularly refers back to this intent in places where he wants to offer broad generalizations about American character based on the behavior of individual people he refuses to name, in what often seem like particularized circumstances.

Trollope is much freer with her generalizing tendencies concerning American character and manners. We get observations concerning Kentucky flat-boat men, "a most disorderly set of persons, constantly gambling and wrangling, very seldom sober, and never suffering a night to pass without giving practical proof of the respect in which they hold the doctrines of equality, and community of property," and her favorite subject, spitting: "I hardly know any annoyance so deeply repugnant to English feelings," she writes, "as the incessant, remorseless spitting of Americans." She goes on to claim that this habit *might* not be universal in terms that make it clear she is convinced it is:

> I feel that I owe my readers an apology for the repeated use of this, and several other odious words; but I cannot avoid them, without suffering the fidelity of description to escape me. It is possible that in the phrase, 'Americans,' I may be too general. The United States form a continent of almost distinct nations, and I must now, and always, be understood to speak only of that portion of them which I have seen. In conversing with Americans I have constantly found that if I alluded to any thing which they thought I considered as uncouth, they would assure me it was local, and not national; the accidental peculiarity of a very small part, and by no means a specimen of the whole. 'That is because you know so little of America,' is a phrase I have listened to a thousand times, and in nearly as many different places. *It may be so*—and having made this concession, I protest against the charge of injustice in relating what I have seen.[82]

---

80 See John Melish, *Travels in the United States of America, in the years 1806 & 1807, and 1809, 1810, & 1811* (Philadelphia, 1815); William Faux, *Memorable Days in America* (London, 1823).

81 Hall, *Travels*, vol. 1, p. 13.

82 Trollope, *Domestic Manners*, pp. 18–19.

The constant reference back to insisting on "relating what I have seen" and the claim this act of looking has made her an authority, just as it has made the Americans a universalizable subject, observed "a thousand times … in nearly as many different places," makes this comment typical of Trollope's way of generalizing while seeming to particularize.

By the end of *Domestic Manners*, Trollope becomes freer with her expressions of opinion. Her final verdict on the Americans makes no pretense to objectivity. Of "the population generally" she decides, "I do not like them. I do not like their principles, I do not like their manners, I do not like their opinions."[83] But even this statement of personal distaste, coming as it does at the end of a book that sets itself up as an unbiased account of ethnography based on extensive observation, carries a certain authority. Even her opinions are scientific, in a sense, because of the distancing of herself from her subject throughout the text, and the transparency of methodology she strives to project. Heineman writes that Trollope relies on a "technique of direct reporting, an almost documentary approach to scene and character, with passage after passage in which the author lets people speak for themselves, with little or no background comment."[84] This technique conveys the sense that she has viewed America as an anthropologist, much the way Margaret Mead would later view and reproduce Samoans, E.E. Evans-Pritchard would represent the Azande, or Malinowski would describe the people of New Guinea. But the "little" background comment that Trollope provides is invariably pointed. Her reportage presents itself as unmediated, presented as evidence not just of who and how the Americans are, but that she has been there herself and has the authority to represent this newly constructed Other. But her remarks continually instruct the reader in a word or a sentence how to read the Americans.

A Breed Apart

Trollope, in *The Refugee in America*, introduces one tolerable American character in the boorish cast who makes it possible to argue that while the people as a whole, conditioned as they are by their economic, natural, and moral climate, are irretrievably Other, individuals may be reclaimed for civility. The crucial factor in this project of reclamation is that the American in question must not be "bred" to Americanness, despite being born to it. An exposure to European, specifically English, culture, and a sympathetic identification with it, places even Americans reared in unfavorable surroundings in a redeemable state. But this redemption of individuals makes the characterization of the general population as a breed apart an even more firmly embedded part of the English discourse on Americans by the early 1830s. If there can be exceptions, there must be a rule.

Trollope's exception in *The Refugee* is Emily Williams of Rochester, the daughter of a former secretary of state. The noble Lord Darcy, still fearing he has murdered a man in England, comes to Rochester under the care of Edward Gordon. Gordon's

---

83   Ibid., p. 314.
84   Heineman, *Frances Trollope*, p. 26.

daughter Caroline is also with them. They take a house in Rochester to await news from England that will either determine a time for the House of Lords to try Lord Darcy for murder, or for evidence proving the man he supposedly murdered is still alive. They keep the reason for their travels secret, inspiring gossip that accuses them of much more serious offenses, including multiple murders and sexual depravity involving Caroline and the two men. Emily Williams is the only one in Rochester not convinced that the Gordons and Darcy are depraved criminals, with some terrible secret they refuse to reveal.

Emily's mother, the widow of a former secretary of state, has the highest claim in the book to anything approaching social status, or rank. But Trollope only elevates her position to denigrate her worthiness of it, along with the notion of any form of nobility or merit existing in a country whose republican manners and government bring everything down to the lowest common denominator. Mrs. Williams is described as "well dressed," with "nothing that deserved the epithet of vulgar in (her) appearance or manner."[85] But despite this tepid praise, Caroline Gordon can find nothing impressive about her, as might be expected in the widow of a secretary of state. She reflects that "there existed a something sufficiently unlike the air, look, manner, and tone of persons in a similar station in Europe, to set Caroline's mind to work to define in what it consisted. Had she been obliged to characterise it by one word, she would have used *homeliness* ... She felt that it could not be the effect of that republican simplicity so often vaunted."[86] Subsequent experiences in Washington make it clear that this young English girl feels completely competent to judge affairs of state as well as manners and taste, and America fails each of her tests. She finds Mrs. Williams's grace a manner which "made one feel more inclined to yawn than to bow before it."[87]

Emily, being young and untutored, becomes Caroline's reclamation project. Her humility is a significant qualification for her eventual ascent to an English version of civility. Caroline's first task is to fix Emily's speech, and Emily is an abjectly willing pupil. When Emily asks Caroline to "learn" her to speak English as she does, Caroline replies, "'I will teach you, Emily; and it is you must learn. Try to remember that, dear. Do you not see that it is nonsense to talk of my learning, where it is I who am to teach?'"[88] Emily does not see this at first, but eventually will. What she knows at this early point is that those among whom she has grown up speak incorrectly, and that Caroline's speech is a measure of her civility. When Caroline asks her why she wants to speak like her, Emily explains by asking if Caroline had ever heard a book using "the same words and expressions that you hear us use?"[89] Part of Emily's preparation to become civil has come from "listening" to the English authors she has read. Caroline and her father speak, in her view, the language of the books she

85 Trollope, *The Refugee in America*, vol. 1, p. 149.
86 Ibid., vol. 1, p. 149.
87 Ibid., vol. 1, p. 150.
88 Ibid., vol. 1, p. 179.
89 Ibid.

has read. "(A)nd you look exactly like the beings I have read of in them," she says. Those books are "Cecilia, and Belinda, and Tremaine, and Granby ..."[90] Her literary listening has been largely in popular, but respectable novels, such as Frances Burney's *Evelina*, Maria Edgeworth's *Belinda*, and Samuel Richardson's *Sir Charles Grandison*. Emily has also read Shakespeare, but would not dream of speaking like the characters there, "'because my thoughts would not be great enough for such words. I expect it would be like serving up corn cakes in golden dishes.'"[91] Caroline, who is repeating all these words of humble wisdom from Emily concerning her deficiencies in her journal, leaves them stand with no contradiction, despite her affection for this one sensible friend among the barbarians. The result of this is that Emily joins Caroline, her father, and Lord Darcy in a sort of drawing room culture the English refugees set up in Rochester. She learns to speak proper English, to carry on conversations during meals, and to recognize the bad manners of her mother and other family members and friends.

Caroline views her tutelage of Emily as a community service for all of Rochester, if not for the republic as a whole. "I will confer an inestimable blessing on the Rochester community, by adopting little Emily Williams as my particular friend," she claims, "developing all her talents, and teaching her to speak English; and then, you know, when we depart, we shall leave them a glass by which to dress themselves."[92] But she recognizes that Emily's society might not appreciate the change Caroline seeks to bring about. This makes her decide not just to appropriate Emily's education, but Emily herself. If the Americans don't approve of her product, "if they do not all fall down and worship her, I will pack her up and carry her" back home like a possession and specimen in the tradition of explorers who brought impressive Indians such as Pocahantas back to England to place on display.[93] Later when Emily is singing at the Gordon's house and the refugees are impressed with the loveliness of her voice, Caroline asks her father: "'Are we not fortunate to have found such a singing bird in the wilderness?'"[94]

The insistence that even an American city like Rochester is still a wilderness, and that Emily is a specimen which can be appropriated and repatriated into an English yew—a singing bird in the wilderness—brings the language and activity of the ethnographic text into Trollope's novel. Later, when Lord Darcy falls in love with Emily, it is remarked that "(l)ovely as she was," her true qualities wouldn't have been noticed "had she only appeared to him surrounded by her kinsfolk and acquaintance." Environment is everything. "But in Caroline's little drawing-room, she seemed like a delicate flower that they had found in the forest, transplanted and cherished, till it had become fairer than any the garden could offer."[95] English agency

---

90 Ibid., vol. 1, p. 180. Emily is most likely referring to Frances Burney's *Cecilia* (1782), Maria Edgeworth's *Belinda* (1801), and the Silver Fork novels *Tremaine* (1825) by Robert Plumer Ward, and *Granby* (1826) by Thomas Henry.

91 Ibid.

92 Ibid., vol. 1, pp. 200–201.

93 Ibid., vol. 1, p. 201.

94 Ibid., vol. 2, p. 100.

95 Ibid., vol. 2, p. 293.

is indispensable in the creation of the superiority of the only American character worth noticing, whether she be flora or fauna.

In the end, Lord Darcy's supposed victim is found to be alive, partially through the heroic agency of Emily, who brings the supposedly dead man's wife to testify at the last minute in front of the House of Lords. Emily then becomes Lady Darcy. By this point her un-Americanness has become complete. Her daringness in crossing the ocean in defiance of her family is a declaration of independence of her own, from the stultifying manners and society of Rochester society in favor of the greater breeding of the English. Her natural nobility shows in her willingness to face hardships to rescue the man she loves. In the end, the one worthwhile American in Trollope's novel becomes so only by leaving her Americanness behind and embracing Englishness. Throughout the novel, Americans are derided for adhering to a rigid social code that keeps women sequestered and chaperoned. Emily's adventure is much more in the spirit of Caroline's trek through America, or akin to the action of characters like Fielding's Sophia Western, than the performance of a respectable American woman according to Trollope's representations. Before the refugees' departure for England and Emily's heroic journey, there are thoughts of bringing Lord Darcy's mother to him in America. But Caroline absolutely rejects this idea. "'The Countess would die," she says, "if she were to sojourn in this land of whiskey, and equal rights. With such a mind as my father and Edward describe, she would weep at what makes me laugh. No, it must not be here that we restore her Edward to her.'"[96] So, in order to become a part of the Darcy family, Emily must cease being an American altogether. This, it seems, is no great sacrifice, at least for Caroline, who assures Emily she does not belong in America.

After one of many scenes of American rudeness and crassness, Caroline tells Emily that "you must not live and die where such things be!" Emily, resignedly, protests that "'I am born to it, Miss Gordon.'" Caroline counters by telling her that, while "born" to Americanness, she is "hardly bred to it; we caught you young, and we have spoiled you for ever as an American lady." Her lessons in civility, it seems, have been lessons against Americanness. "Emily," she tells her pupil, "you are no more fit to sit at the head of a table with a dozen lengthy republicans round it, drawling out the praises of your canvass-back ducks, and carving every dish within your reach, with the same spoon, and perhaps the aid of your own knife, than— than I am, Emily.'"[97] Finally, the most proper education a young American lady can receive, is to be taught to be a young English lady, like Caroline Gordon.

Evolutionary Mongrels

My suggestion that an unofficial, untheorized fifth stage of development emerges as a temporal period in works like Hall's and Trollope's, in dialectical opposition to the United States, is not a claim that English social science developed in this direction. This stage of politeness and culture is largely a discursive invention used to distance

---

96 Ibid., vol. 2, p. 186.
97 Ibid., vol. 3, p. 90.

the Americans from the English as much as possible. Trollope's political aims for doing so are unmistakable. She wrote and published *Domestic Manners* as the debate over the 1832 Reform Bill intensified, with the hopes of showing English readers the negative effects of a more extensive franchise and political representation. While she failed to head off reform at home, she succeeded in making a country full of enemies across the Atlantic. She also succeeded in establishing the discourse that would dominate English representations of Americans for decades, and that still persists in reduced and fragmented form today. When a United States president refers to Iraq, Iran, and North Korea as an "axis of evil," it does not surprise the more civilized world. Trollope had long ago cemented the perception that though America is a fully civilized nation in economic terms, it is unevenly so, and insufficiently so, in terms of decorum, manners, and public policy. When Florida's vote in the 2000 election became an international scandal, English academics—and American ones—took great pleasure in a slightly malicious email that circulated widely, declaring that Queen Elizabeth II had revoked American independence for a host of cultural and political reasons, all related to the very absence of decorum and manners that Trollope so effectively discussed in 1832.[98]

---

98 The text of the e-mail follows: "**NOTICE OF REVOCATION OF INDEPENDENCE.** To the residents of the United States of America, In view of your abject failure to elect a President and thus to govern yourselves, We give hereby Notice of the Revocation of your Independence, effective today at Five O'clock Greenwich Mean Time. Her Britannic Majesty Queen Elizabeth II will resume sovereign duties forthwith over all states, commonwealths, and other territories. Except Florida, which Shall be returned to His Illustrious Catholic Majesty, King Juan Carlos of Spain. Your new Prime Minister (The Rt Hon Tony Blair, for the 97.85% of you who have until now been unaware that there is a world outside your borders) will suggest to Her Majesty a Governor-General for America without the need for further elections. Congress and the Senate will be disbanded. A questionnaire will be circulated next year to determine whether any of you noticed. To aid in the transition to a British Crown Dependency, the following rules are introduced with immediate effect: 1. You should look up "revocation" in the Oxford English Dictionary. Then look up "aluminum". Check the pronunciation guide. You will be amazed at just how wrongly you have been pronouncing it. Generally, you should raise your vocabulary to acceptable levels. Look up "vocabulary." Using the same twenty-seven words interspersed with filler noises such as "like" and "you know" is an unacceptable and inefficient form of communication. Look up "interspersed." 2. There is no such thing as "US English." We will let Microsoft know on your behalf. 3. You should learn to distinguish the English and Australian accents. It really isn't that difficult. 4. Hollywood will be required occasionally to cast British actors as the good guys. 5. You should relearn your original national anthem, "God Save The Queen," but only after fully carrying out Task 1. We would not want you to get confused and give up half way through. 6. You should stop playing American "football." There is only one kind of football. What you refer to as American "football" is not a very good game. The 2.15% of you who are aware that there is a world outside your borders may have noticed that no one else plays "American" football. You will no longer be allowed to play it, and should instead play proper football. Initially, it would be best if you played with the girls. It is a difficult game. Those of you brave enough will, in time, be allowed to play rugby (which is similar to American "football," but does not involve stopping for a rest every twenty seconds or wearing full kevlar body armour). We are hoping to get together at least an American rugby sevens side by 2005. 7. You should

While the email was satirical, and taken as such by most of its readers on both sides of the Atlantic, the Pacific, and elsewhere, Trollope's travel book, though satirical in tone, claimed to be a true representation of the American character. It was widely read both in England and in the United States, loved by the British and lambasted by a sensitive American audience which possibly felt the truth of many of her judgments. Trollope's preface is a blatant attack on the Reform Bill of 1832, an intentional alignment of the book with the Tory cause, and more importantly, a calculated polemic that placed *Domestic Manners* in the heated debate in an effort to increase sales. It worked. *Domestic Manners* went through four editions within a year.[99] Wordsworth and Southey both read the book, and were reportedly "delighted" with it.[100] American readers read the book just as avidly, though with much less delight. Insulting Americans in a witty way became known as "Trollopizing." A critical travel account of the United States became known as a "Trollopiad." Words like these, and similar ones, became part of fashionable English discourse for a time.

As I have tried to make clear, gross table manners, religious primitivism, a degraded speech, an inclination to spit on the carpet, and constant drinking all defined the American as a civilized barbarian in works like Trollope's and Hall's. The fifth stage of development at which Trollope's and Hall's English people had arrived was owing mostly to responses to the inequalities in economic roles wrought by the Industrial Revolution, which made class distinctions more dramatic, and politeness more necessary as a defense mechanism against the growing impoliteness of the physical world. The one access to this fifth stage, as we have seen in Trollope's *The Refugee in America*, was through an adoption of Englishness, most markedly written as an appropriation of English speech and learning. The Americans Trollope and Hall encountered, however, are unable to see that they are a stage behind—or more properly, are caught between the primitive hunting stage in the growing western states and territories, and the agricultural and commercial stages, and thus are in a confused temporal no man's land. This is partly because they believe they are as civilized as the English.

Americans were, for Trollope, clearly a new, anthropological subject of study. As she writes when her son Anthony, soon to be a well-known author himself, has joined her and her younger son in Cincinnati: "The young men, fresh from a public school, found America so totally unlike all the nations with which their reading had made them acquainted." Greece, Rome, France, and Italy are all countries with histories studied in school, or talked about in polite society. "(B)ut at our public schools

---

declare war on Quebec and France, using nuclear weapons if they give you any "merde." The 97.85% of you who were not aware that there is a world outside your borders should count yourselves lucky. The Russians have never been the bad guys. 8. July 4th is no longer a public holiday. November 8th will be a new national holiday, but only in the British Empire. It will be called "Indecisive Day." 9. All American cars are hereby banned. They are crap and it is for your own good. When we show you German cars, you will understand what we mean. 10. Please tell us who killed JFK. It's been driving us crazy."

99 Pamela Neville-Sington, *Fanny Trollope: The Life and Adventures of a Clever Woman* (New York, 1998), p. 171.

100 Ibid., p. 172.

America (except perhaps as to her geographical position) is hardly better known than Fairy Land; and the American character has not been much more deeply studied than that of the Anthropophagi: all, therefore, was new, and every thing amusing."[101] Whether America is "Fairy Land"—a place outside time, and all other categorical imperatives—or is a savage place, where cannibals like the "Anthropophagi" roam, is always an open question. But by Trollope's time, the verdict was that time in America was unplaceable on the normal continuum from savage to civil society.

Fearon's summation of what makes the Americans an inferior breed is perhaps the best example of the thinking that appears in English accounts of the time. It combines a mongrelized racial foundation with a failure to improve upon the advantages that should have resulted from English beginnings. "The emigrant to a wilderness," he writes, will "rarely be a man ... possessed of regular habits, or a cultivated mind ... Such then were the seeds of American society ... They left Europe at a dark period, not themselves the finest specimens of the national picture ... There was besides no history attached to their country; they lived *indeed* in a new world."[102] Upheavals in Europe—the French Revolution, the Irish rebellion of 1798—brought in more immigrants, "certainly very diseased members of the body politic; while the accession of multitudes of the most ignorant classes of society from Holland and Germany, together with the vast increase of black population, rapidly added to the numerical population, extending the range and increasing the produce of manual labour without adding any thing that was valuable to, if I may so express myself, the stock of national mind."[103]

Greed and the constant move westward make Americans a commercial people, an agricultural people, but hardly a civil people. The time they occupy is unplottable on the English trajectory. Their primitiveness combined with their commercial advances makes their time a mongrelized one, and their race distinct from the English. *Domestic Manners* represents the emergence of a people culturally and linguistically independent of the English, with elements both of the savage and the mercenary and concludes that republicanism is a dangerous system that has leveled the entire society. The Americans are now a separate race, in a unique evolutionary trajectory distinct both from the Native American one, which is a slower version of a universal progress shared by the English; and from the European, which is at the forefront of the progress of civilization.

---

101 Trollope, *Domestic Manners*, p. 78.
102 Fearon, *Sketches*, pp. 354–5.
103 Ibid., p. 361.

Conclusion

While Frances Trollope and Basil Hall did more than any other English writers of their time to fix an idea of what the Americans were like for English readers, neither put forth clearly considered philosophical positions about where their subjects belonged in the history of civilization. Hall's talent was for presenting American practices and rituals in measured tones, and in doing so delivering a broad picture of the American national character, something that had only appeared in bits and pieces before his *Travels* were published in 1828. Trollope's gift was more novelistic. She describes individuals and groups of individuals so vividly that she conveys the sense not only that the author was really there, but that, vicariously, the reader is too. The speech patterns, vocabulary, eating habits, manners, morals, and preoccupations of the Americans come alive in *Domestic Manners of the Americans* much more than they do in Hall's *Travels*. Both works represent their subjects as an independent, alien, and strange people, but neither seeks to place them chronologically in the history of civilization, or explain their historical relevance and relationship to the English in any systematic way. While England is the constant point of comparison for both Hall and Trollope, and the cumulative effect of their work is the creation of a comparative ethnology that stresses difference, neither comments at any length on America as an historical place or Americans as an historical people.

America's place among nations and its inhabitants' collective character were summed up more clearly by writers who never crossed the Atlantic. Perhaps this is not surprising. Hall and Trollope, while not averse to broad generalizations about the Americans, saw and experienced too much of the United States to theorize grandly. John Keats and William Hazlitt wrote briefly but tellingly about Americans in ways that suggest that the questions with which this study has been preoccupied—America as an historical place, Americans as historical or anthropological subjects—had become the questions commonly asked by those trying to understand the new nation. Keats's brother George and sister-in-law Georgiana emigrated in 1818, following Morris Birkbeck to his prairie utopia in Indiana, and the letters he sent them betray his culture's thoughts and prejudices about their adopted land and new compatriots.

In Keats's view, the Americans could never be a great people specifically because they were unhistorical, and, more importantly, not sublime. Having listened to Charles Wentworth Dilke claim that "America will be the country to take up the human intellect where england leaves off," he declares such an idea unacceptable:

> A country like the united states whose greatest Men are Franklins and Washingtons will never do that—They are great Men doubtless but how are they to be compared to those our countreymen Milton and the two Sidneys—The one is a philosophical Quaker full of mean and thrifty maxims the other sold the very Charger who had taken him through all

his Battles. Those Americans are great but they are not sublime Man—the humanity of the United States can never reach the sublime.[1]

In focusing on America's two most representative men—for the people of the United States as well as for those in Europe—Keats makes his point both sweepingly and economically. Byron may have considered Washington an historical agent in a country otherwise devoid of history, but Keats, focusing on Washington's *sense* of history more than his actions, indicts the national imagination. Franklin's "mean and thrifty maxims" are even less likely to induce an historical sense in a people interested more in present gain than in artistic expression.

In another letter, Keats is even more explicit about the meanness—figured as greed—of the Americans. He urges his brother to come back to England when he can find the funds because of his fears that the Americans will cheat him if he remains among them. "[B]e careful of those Americans," he urges. "I could almost advise you to come whenever you have the sum of 500£ to England—Those Americans will I am afraid still fleece you."[2] "Those Americans" had become, by the time Keats wrote these letters in 1818 and 1819, removed enough from their English beginnings to be considered as a separate people. Keats's concern is with their artistic abilities and imaginative capacity as factors of their historical richness as a people. His verdict, clearly, is that they lack the first, and therefore are of negligible importance in the second. Keats, like Wollstonecraft and Coleridge before him, can see America rising only by reconnecting to its English cultural beginnings. In Keats's case, this infusion was more personally connected. He complains that "Birkbeck's mind is too much in the American Style"—too practical, not poetic enough. The poet was unaware at this time that George and Georgiana had left Birkbeck's settlement after just a few weeks, and were looking to settle in Pennsylvania. "[Y]ou must endeavour to infuse a little Spirit of another sort into the Settlement," he wrote, "always with great caution, for thereby you may do your descendents more good than you may imagine." Presumably, even a poet's brother had a better chance of introducing sublimity than one of "those Americans" Keats mistrusted. "If I had a prayer to make for any great good," he wrote, "it should be that one of your Children should be the first American Poet."[3]

Hazlitt also found the Americans unhistorical. But this judgment did not cause him to develop as negative an assessment of the American people's prospects for the future as it did Keats. Hazlitt asserted that the Americans had "no *natural imagination*," but considered this lack a strength. His comments come in a digression about Brockden Brown's novels and their "banquet of [Gothic] horrors" that interrupts a review of Ellery Channing's sermons. He finds Brown's evocation of the supernatural "forced, violent, and shocking." This is because America, for Hazlitt, is without the sort of history that makes the Gothic plausible. The reason "no ghost, we will venture to say, was ever seen in North America" is that ghosts "do not walk in broad day; and

---

1   John Keats, *The Letters of John Keats*, ed. Maurice Buxton Forman (London, 1952), p. 234.

2   Ibid., p. 423.

3   Ibid., p. 234.

the night of ignorance and superstition which favours their appearance, was long past before the United States lifted up their head beyond the Atlantic wave."[4]

England's problem, for Hazlitt—for Keats it was clearly its strength—was the burden of past history. "[T]here is here an old and solid ground in previous manners and opinion for imagination to rest upon," Hazlitt writes. "The air of this bleak northern clime is filled with legendary lore: not a castle without the stain of blood upon its floor or winding steps: not a glen without its ambush or its feat of arms: not a lake without its Lady!"[5] The situation in American couldn't be more different. Its map "is not historical; and, therefore, works of fiction do not take root in it; for the fiction, to be good for any thing, must not be in the author's mind, but belong to the age or country in which he lives. The genius of America is essentially mechanical and modern."[6] This mechanical advancement and unvitiated modernity are evidence of a state moving beyond the failings of England. Americans, Hazlitt writes, "hoot the *Beggar's Opera* from the stage: with them, poverty and crime, pickpockets and highwaymen, the lock-up house and the gallows, are things incredible to sense."[7] The perfection Godwin theorized about, and Wollstonecraft and Imlay hoped for, are in Hazlitt's view realized in America's freedom from European history.

While the belief that America had no history, and was not in the process of creating any, was widespread, the transformation of its people into proper ethnographic subjects was less easily accomplished. The main challenge to the view put forth by Hall, Trollope, Charles Dickens, and other travelers to America throughout the early nineteenth century, came from the Americans themselves, who presented the inconvenience of Others capable of self-representation. Some well-known examples were in England's collective understanding from the revolutionary years and earlier. Benjamin West, the leading painter, favorite of George III, and president of the Royal Academy, submerged his Americanness in Englishness almost completely, disputing by example the notion that humanity had regressed to the savage in the Americas, and that once it had done so, was unlikely to recover its former level of civility. Others—John Adams and Benjamin Franklin in the 1770s and 1780s, Gilbert Imlay later—performed Americanness in ways that could satisfy champions of the new nation as well as critics, combining erudition and cosmopolitanism with rusticity and republican simplicity. Joel Barlow was set up by many as the New World's bard, with his well-known (but probably little-read) epic *The Columbiad* offering a self-consciously national literature recognizable to English readers, who expected significant nations to be represented by significant literary works.

Washington Irving might have been the first American writer known to English readers to point out the nature of the project of identification emerging in English texts about Americans, and to offer an overview of American dissatisfaction with it. Irving's *Sketchbook of Geoffrey Crayon, Gent.* (1819–20) views America and England through the temporal and historical paradigm I have been discussing

---

4 William Hazlitt, *The Complete Works of William Hazlitt, Literary and Political Criticism* (New York, AMS Press, 1967), vol. 19, p. 318.

5 Ibid., pp. 319–20.

6 Ibid., p. 320.

7 Ibid.

throughout this study. The *Sketchbook* is a collection of occasional pieces, knit together by its narrator's persona, and by his perspective as an American visiting England for the first time. "My native country was full of youthful promise," writes Irving. "Europe was rich in the accumulated treasures of age. Her very ruins told the history of times gone by, and every mouldering stone was a chronicle. I longed … to escape … from the commonplace realities of the present, and lose myself among the shadowy grandeurs of the past."[8] His first view of England reinforces this conception of the Old World as an historical place, vastly different from the "trackless forests" and "tremendous cataracts, thundering in their solitudes" he left behind.[9] On board ship, approaching England, he surveys the shores of the Mersey through a telescope. "My eye dwelt with delight on neat cottages, with their trim shrubberies and green grass plots," he writes. "I saw the mouldering ruin of an abbey overrun with ivy, and the taper spire of a village church rising from the brow of a neighboring hill,—all were characteristic of England."[10] The landscape, with much mouldering, is an ancient volume for the American traveler, with chapters on rural life, the religions of its past and present all in view. It bears remarkable similarity to the landscape Hazlitt has in mind when faulting the inescapable historical saturation that surrounded the English.

But while Irving seems to accept the temporal gap between his country and England, he is not so ready to admit that such a gap extends to his people, or, if it does, that they are necessarily inferior to their English cousins. With characteristic irony, Irving takes up the natural history of writers like Buffon and Blumenbach, making clear his awareness of the debate in which his country has suffered, along with his unwillingness to accept the verdict:

> I had read in the works of various philosophers, that all animals degenerated in America, and man among the number. A great man of Europe, thought I, must therefore be as superior to a great man of America, as a peak of the Alps to a highland of the Hudson, and in this idea I was confirmed, by observing the comparative importance and swelling magnitude of many English travelers among us, who, I was assured, were very little people in their own country. I will visit this land of wonders, thought I, and see the gigantic race from which I am degenerated.[11]

Thomas Jefferson had sent stuffed buffalo and other large specimens to Buffon to prove to him the superiority, or at least the impressiveness, of American animals in this early "size matters" debate. Irving's gentler approach in pointing out the prejudices of European accounts was better suited to winning over his English readers.

This ability to address an English audience in terms and tones it understood might have made some readers at least consider Irving's appeal for a more polite discourse about Americans. In one of his more serious sketches, Irving laments the fact that though "the London press has teemed with volumes of travels through the Republic," these accounts "seem intended to diffuse error rather than knowledge; and

---

8   Washington Irving, *The Sketchbook of Geoffrey Crayon, Gent.* (New York, 1939), p. 4.
9   Ibid., p. 4.
10   Ibid., p. 13.
11   Ibid., p. 5.

so successful have they been, that, notwithstanding the constant intercourse between the nations, there is no people concerning whom the great mass of the British public have less pure information, or entertain more numerous prejudices."[12] Irving may have had recent books by Henry Bradshaw Fearon and William Faux in mind. He complains that America has been

> visited by the worst kind of English travelers. While men of philosophical spirit and cultivated minds have been sent from England to ransack the poles, to penetrate the deserts, and to study the manners and customs of barbarous nations with which she can have no permanent intercourse of profit or pleasure; it has been left to the broken-down tradesman, the scheming adventurer, the wandering mechanic, the Manchester and Birmingham agent, to be her oracles respecting America.[13]

There is a great deal of truth in this complaint. Fearon was the agent of prospective emigrants from the Midlands. It would not be a stretch to label Faux a "wandering mechanic." And within little more than a decade Trollope, a sort of "scheming adventurer" with her Cincinnati wax show depicting scenes from Dante, would deliver the most damning denunciation of the Americans.

Despite the positive reception of Irving's work, the growing impression in the minds of English readers concerning Americans was of a rude people living in a savage wilderness. James Fenimore Cooper's *Leatherstocking Tales* were widely read in England—though not nearly as widely read as Irving's *Sketchbook*. And though they might have been expected to counter this view by representing the frontiersman as a man with civilized feelings despite traveling among savages, one who jealously guards his identity—recall Hawkeye's regular declarations that he respects the Mohicans, but that his gifts are those of a white man, while the Indians are those of red men—they only seem to have reinforced them. Trollope's description of her experience of reading Cooper's novels while living in Cincinnati place the question firmly in the debate concerning the proximity of Americanness to savagery. "I now first read the whole of Mr. Cooper's novels," she writes. "By the time these American studies were completed, I never closed my eyes without seeing myriads of bloody scalps floating round me; long slender figures of Red Indians crept through my dreams with noiseless tread; panthers glared; forests blazed; and whichever way I fled, a light foot, a keen eye, and a long rifle were sure to be on my trail."[14] Cooper's representation of cultural struggles and accommodations are lost on Trollope, who sees "bloody scalps" and Hawkeye's "long rifle" as part not just of the same discourse, but as constituting the same people. Her cure begins with "a course of fashionable novels," and is only fully completed by a reading of all of Scott's Waverley novels.[15] The American savage—white or red—and its bloody anthropological strife, is only defeated by English and Scottish history.

Given these vigorous attempts to write the American out of European history—or in Trollope's case, to read him out of it—it is not surprising that Irving's impression

---

12 Ibid., p. 53.
13 Ibid., p. 54.
14 Trollope, *Domestic Manners of the Americans*, p. 135.
15 Ibid., p. 135.

upon arriving in England, "the land of my forefathers," is that he "was a stranger in the land."[16] More than fifty years later, Henry James was still grappling with the same problem. The American had been so effectively depicted as a separate, inferior breed, that even the wealthy, polished Christopher Newman, the title character of James's *The American* (1877), is seen as unacceptable. His French acquaintances find it impossible that he can be polished and civilized, as much because of his Americanness as anything. James would eventually solve Newman's problem for himself by becoming as English as the English themselves, eventually becoming a British citizen, ironically, just about the time that this discourse that distances Americans temporally began to fall apart with the advent of a truly cosmopolitan artistic class of expatriates in Europe during and after World War I.

I have tried to show that the image of the vulgar American long prominent in English writing was the product of numerous texts published during the half century following the American Revolution. Just as those in America were working to explain their own national identity, the English were seeking to answer for themselves Crèvecoeur's question, "What is an American?" I have also tried to show that underlying the identification of vulgarity is a more significant project of comparative ethnology that removes Americans from history by trading on the idea that North America was temporally behind Europe, often in complicated ways. Americans may have challenged this project by writing back, but the simple fact is that they were rarely heard across the ocean. Trollope, Hall, and Dickens had much more influence on the English assessment of Americanness than Irving, Barlow or Emerson did. By the time *Domestic Manners of the Americans* appeared in 1832, a generation of travel writing, periodical pieces, and novels had depicted the American as a breed apart for the English. This collective understanding would prove resilient enough to last, in diminished form, at least until the end of World War I, and exists in bits and pieces to this day.

---

16 Irving, *The Sketchbook*, p. 14.

Bibliography

Printed Primary Sources

Adventures of Jonathan Corncob, Loyal American Refugee, Written by Himself (London, 1787).

Bage, Robert, *Mount Henneth; A Novel, in a Series of Letters* (London, 1788).

Blake, William, *Blake's Illuminated Books. Vol. 4. The Continental Prophecies*, ed. D.W. Dörrbecker, gen. ed. David Bindman (Princeton, 1995).

——, *Blake's Illuminated Books. Vol. 1. Jerusalem: The Emanation of the Great Albion*, ed. Morton D. Paley, gen ed. David Bindman (Princeton, 1991).

Blumenbach, Johann Friedrich, *The Anthropological Treatises of Johann Friedrich Blumenbach* (London: Longman, 1865).

Brackenridge, H.M., *Views of Louisiana* (London, 1814).

Burke, William, *An Account of the European Settlements in America* (Dublin, 1762).

Burney, Frances, *Evelina, or, The History of Young Lady's Entrance into the World*, ed. Stewart J. Cooke (New York, 1998).

Byron, George Gordon, Lord, *Don Juan*, in Jerome McGann (ed.), *The Complete Poetical Works* (Oxford, 1986).

——, *The Complete Miscellaneous Prose*, ed. Andrew Nicholson (Oxford, 1991).

Cobbett, William, *A Year's Residence in America* (London, 1819).

Colden, Cadwallader, *The history of the Five Indian nations of Canada, which are dependent on the province of New-York in America* (London, 1747).

Coleridge, S.T., *Biographia Literaria*. ed. James Engell and W. Jackson Bate, in *The Collected Words of Samuel Taylor Coleridge* (2 vols, Princeton, 1983).

——, *Collected Letters of Samuel Taylor Coleridge*, ed. Earl Leslie Griggs (Oxford, 1956).

——, *The Complete Poetical Works of Samuel Taylor Coleridge*, ed. E.H. Coleridge (Oxford, 1912).

——, *Essays on his Times*, ed. David V. Erdman, in *The Collected Works of Samuel Taylor Coleridge* (3 vols, London, 1978).

——, *The Friend*, ed. Barbara Rooke, in *The Collected Works of Samuel Taylor Coleridge* (2 vols, Princeton, 1969).

——, *Lectures 1795 On Politics and Religion*, ed. Lewis Patton and Peter Mann, in *The Collected Works of Samuel Taylor Coleridge* (Princeton, 1971).

——, *On the Constitution of the Church and State*, ed. John Barrell (London, 1972).

——, *Osorio: The Sketch of a Tragedy*. Rough draft in The Huntington Library, San Marino, California. HM 361.

——, *Poetical Works: Part 2. Poems (Variorum Text)*. ed. J.C.C. Mays, in *The Collected Works of Samuel Taylor Coleridge* (Princeton, 2001).

——, *Table Talk*, ed. Carl Woodring, in *The Collected Works of Samuel Taylor Coleridge* (London, 1990).

——, *The Watchman*, ed. Lewis Patton, in *The Collected Works of Samuel Taylor Coleridge* (Princeton, 1970).

Considerations on the Present State of Affair Between England and America (London, 1778).

Cooper, Thomas, *Some Information Respecting America* (London, 1794).

Crèvecoeur, J. Hector St. John de, *Letters from an American Farmer*, ed. Albert E. Stone (New York, 1981).

D.A., "Conversations of an American with Lord Byron," *New Monthly Magazine and Literary Journal*, 45 (1835): 193–203, 291–302.

Day, Thomas, *The Desolation of America* (London, 1777).

Defoe, Daniel, *Robinson Crusoe*, ed. Michael Shinagel (New York, 1994).

Dickens, Charles, *American Notes and Pictures from Italy* (Oxford, 1957).

Disobedience (London, 1797).

Dryden, John, *The Conquest of Granada*, in Montague Summers (ed.), *The Dramatic Works* (6 vols, London, 1931).

——, *The Indian Queen*, in Montague Summers (ed.), *The Dramatic Works* (6 vols, London, 1931).

Erdman, David, ed., *The Complete Poetry & Prose of William Blake*, commentary by Harold Bloom (New York, 1988).

Faux, W., *Memorable Days in America: Being a Journal of a Tour in the United States* (London, 1823).

Fearon, Henry Bradshaw, *Sketches of America: A Narrative of a Journey of Five Thousand Miles through the Eastern and Western States of America* (London, 1818).

Ferguson, Adam, *An Essay on the History of Civil Society*, ed. Fania Oz-Salzberger (Cambridge, 1995).

Filmer, Sir Robert, *Patriarcha and Other Writings*, ed. Johann P. Sommerville (Cambridge, 1991).

Hall, Basil, *Travels in North America in the years 1827 and 1828* (Edinburgh, 1829).

——, *Forty Etchings from Sketches Made with the Camera Lucida in North America in 1827 and 1828* (Edinburgh, 1829).

Hall, Francis, *Travels in Canada, and the United States, in 1816 and 1817* (London, 1818).

The History of the British Empire in North America (London, 1773).

Hobbes, Thomas, *Leviathan*, ed. Richard Tuck (Cambridge, 1996).

——, *De Corpore Politico*, ed. J.C.A. Gaskin (Oxford, 1994).

Humboldt, Wilhelm von, *Linguistic Variability & Intellectual Development*, trans. George C. Buck and Frithjof A. Raven (Coral Gables, 1971).

Imlay, Gilbert, *A Topographical Description of the Western Territory of North America* (London, 1792).

Irving, Washington, *The Sketchbook of Geoffrey Crayon, Gent* (New York, 1939).

Jefferson, Thomas, *Writings* (New York, 1984).

Johnson, Samuel, "Taxation No Tyranny", in Donald J. Greene (ed.), *The Yale Edition of The Works of Samuel Johnson: Vol. 10, Political Writings* (New Haven, 1977).

Lafitau, Joseph François, *Mœurs des sauvages ameriquains—Customs of the American Indians compared with the customs of primitive times*, ed. and trans. William N. Fenton and Elizabeth L. Moore (2 vols, Toronto, 1974–1977).

Lennox, Charlotte, *Euphemia* (London, 1992).

The Liberal American: A Novel, In a Series of Letters, By a Lady (London, 1785).

Locke, John, *The Second Discourse on Government*, in Peter Laslett (ed.), *Two Treatises of Government* (Cambridge: Cambridge University Press, 1988).

Louisa Wharton. A Story Founded on Facts (London, 1780?).

Mackenzie, Henry, *The Man of Feeling*, in *The Works of Henry Mackenzie, Esq.* (8 vols, Edinburgh, 1808).

——, *Man of the World*, in *The Works of Henry Mackenzie, Esq.* (8 vols, Edinburgh, 1808).

Melish, John, *Travels in the United States of America, in the years 1806 & 1807, and 1809, 1810, & 1811* (Philadelphia, 1815).

Oldmixon, John, *The British Empire in America: Containing The History of the Discovery, Settlement, Progress and State of the British Colonies on the Continent and Islands of America* (London, 1710, 1741).

Parsons, Eliza, *The Voluntary Exile* (London, 1795).

Penny Cyclopaedia of the Society for the Diffusion of Useful Knowledge (London, 1834).

Pope, Alexander, "The Rape of the Lock," in John Butt (ed.), *The Poems of Alexander Pope* (New Haven, 1963).

Pratt, Samuel Jackson, *Emma Corbett; or the Miseries of Civil War* (Bath and London, 1780).

Prichard, James Cowles, *The Natural History of Man* (London, 1842).

Richardson, Samuel, *Clarissa: Or the History of a Young Lady*, ed. Angus Ross (New York, 1985).

Robertson, William, *The History of the Discovery and Settlement of America* (New York, 1855).

——, *The History of Scotland* (New York, 1787).

Rousseau, Jean Jacques, *The Discourses and other Early Political Writings*, ed. Victor Gourevitch (Cambridge, 1997).

The School for Fathers; or, the Victim of a Curse (London, 1788).

Seward, Anna, "Monody on Major André," in Walter Scott (ed.), *The Poetical Works of Anna Seward* (3 vols, Edinburgh and London, 1810).

Shakespeare, William, *Romeo and Juliet* (New York: Bedford, 1996).

Smith, Adam, *Wealth of Nations* (Amherst, N.Y., 1991).

Smith, Charlotte, *The Old Manor House* (London, 1987).

——, *The Young Philosopher*, ed. Elizabeth Kraft (Lexington, 1999).

Smollett, Tobias, *The Expedition of Humphry Clinker*, ed. Thomas R. Preston (Athens, Georgia, 1990).

——, *The Miscellaneous Works*, ed. Robert Anderson (5 vols, Edinburgh, 1809).

Sterne, Laurence, *A Sentimental Journey through France and Italy by Mr. Yorick* (Berkeley: University of California Press, 1967).

Trollope, Frances, *Domestic Manners of the Americans*, ed. Pamela Neville-Sington (New York, 1997).

——, *The Refugee in America* (4 vols, London, 1832).
Willard, Susannah, *Francis the Philanthropist: An Unfashionable Tale* (3 vols, London, 1786).
Williams, Helen Maria, *Julia, a Novel; Interspersed with Some Poetical Pieces* (Dublin, 1790).
Wollstonecraft, Mary and Gilbert Imlay, *The Emigrants*, ed. Robert R. Hare (Gainesville, 1964).
——, *A Vindication of the Rights of Men* (London, 1790).
——, *A Vindication of the Rights of Women* (London, 1793).
Wordsworth, William, "The Excursion," in Thomas Hutchinson (ed.), Ernest De Selincourt (rev.), *Poetical Works* (Oxford, 1969).

Secondary Sources

Abrams, M.H., *Natural Supernaturalism: Traditional and Revolution in Romantic Literature* (New York: Norton, 1971).
Anderson, Benedict, *Imagined Communities: Reflections on the Origin and Spread of Nationalism* (London: Verso, 1991).
Aristotle, *Poetics*, trans. Richard Janko (Indianapolis: Hackett, 1987).
Armitage, David, "The New World and British Historical Thought: From Richard Hakluyt to William Robertson," in Karen Ordahl Kupperman (ed.), *America in European Consciousness, 1493–1750* (Chapel Hill: University of North Carolina Press, 1995).
Axtell, James, *The European and the Indian: Essays in the Ethnohistory of Colonial North America* (Oxford: Oxford University Press, 1981).
Bakhtin, Mikhail, *The Dialogic Imagination: Four Essays*, ed. Michael Holquest, trans. Caryl Emerson and Michael Holquist (Austin: University of Texas Press, 1981).
Barrell, John, *Imagining the King's Death: Figurative Treason, Fantasies of Regicide, 1793–1796* (Oxford: Oxford University Press, 2000).
Beasley, Jerry C., "Robert Bage," in Martin Battestin (ed.), *Dictionary of Literary Biography. Vol. 39. British Novelists, 1660–1800* (Detroit: Gale, 1985).
Benjamin, Walter, *Illuminations*, ed. Hannah Arendt, trans. Harry Zohn (New York: Shocken, 1968).
Berg, Temma F., "Getting the Mother's Story Right: Charlotte Lennox and the New World," *Papers on Language and Literature: A Journal for Scholars and Critics of Language and Literature*, 32 (1996): 369–98.
Bloom, Harold, "The Internalization of Quest-Romance," in Harold Bloom (ed.), *Romanticism and Consciousness: Essays in Criticism* (New York: Norton, 1970).
Boas, Frederick S., *American Scenes, Tudor to Georgian, in the English Literary Mirror* (Oxford: The English Association, 1944).
Braudel, Fernand, *On History*, trans. Sarah Matthews (Chicago: University of Chicago Press, 1980).
Chandler, James, *England in 1819: The Politics of Literary Culture and the Case of Romantic Historicism* (Chicago: University of Chicago Press, 1998).

——, *Wordsworth's Second Nature: A Study of the Poetry and Politics* (Chicago: University of Chicago Press, 1984).

Christensen, Jerome, *Coleridge's Blessed Machine of Language* (Ithaca: Cornell University Press, 1981).

Clubbe, John, *Byron's Natural Man: Daniel Boone & Kentucky* (Lexington: King Library Press, 1980).

Coburn, Kathleen (ed.), *Inquiring Spirit: A New Presentation of Coleridge from his Published and Unpublished Prose Writings* (London: Routledge & Kegan Paul, 1951).

Cook, Elizabeth Heckendorn, *Epistolary Bodies: Gender and Genre in the Eighteenth-Century Republic of Letters* (Stanford: Stanford University Press, 1996).

De Baecque, Antoine, *Body Politic: Corporeal Metaphor in Revolutionary France, 1770–1800*, trans. Charlotte Mandell (Stanford: Stanford University Press, 1997).

Dumbaugh, Winnifred, *William Blake's Vision of America* (Pacific Grove, CA: Boxwood Press, 1971).

Ellingson, Ter, *The Myth of the Noble Savage* (Berkeley: University of California Press, 2001).

Erdman, David, "*America*: New Expanses", in David Erdman and John E. Grant (eds), *Blake's Visionary Forms Dramatic* (Princeton: Princeton University Press, 1970).

——, *Blake: Prophet Against Empire* (Princeton: Princeton University Press, 1954).

Fabian, Johannes, *Time and the Other: How Anthropology Makes its Object* (New York: Columbia University Press, 1983).

——, *Time and the Work of Anthropology: Critical Essays 1971–1991* (Philadelphia: Harwood, 1991).

Fliegelman, Jay, *Prodigals and Pilgrims: The American Revolution against Patriarchal Authority 1750–1800* (Cambridge: Cambridge University Press, 1982).

Foucault, Michel, *The Archaeology of Knowledge & The Discourse on Language*, trans. A.M. Sheridan Smith (New York: Pantheon, 1972).

Friedman, Geraldine. *The Insistence of History: Revolution in Burke, Wordsworth, Keats, and Baudelaire* (Stanford: Stanford University Press, 1996).

Frye, Northrop, *Anatomy of Criticism: Four Essays* (Princeton: Princeton University Press, 1957).

Geertz, Clifford, *The Interpretation of Cultures* (New York: Basic Books, 1973; 2000).

——, *Works and Lives: The Anthropologist as Author* (Stanford: Stanford University Press, 1988).

Gilroy, Amanda, "Espousing the Cause of Oppressed Women: Cultural Captivities in Gilbert Imlay's *The Emigrants*," in W.M. Verhoeven and Beth Dolan Kautz (ed.), *Revolutions & Watersheds: Transatlantic Dialogues 1775–1815* (Amsterdam-Atlanta: Rodopi, 1999).

Glausser, Wayne. *Locke and Blake: A Conversation across the Eighteenth Century* (Tallahasee: University Press of Florida, 1998).

Gravil, Richard. *Romantic Dialogues: Anglo-American Continuities 1776–1862* (New York: St. Martin's, 2000).

Guest, Harriet. *Small Change: Women, Learning, Patriotism, 1750–1810* (Chicago: University of Chicago Press, 2000).

Hegel, G.W.F., *Phenomenology of Spirit*, trans. A.V. Miller (Oxford: Oxford University Press, 1977).

Heilman, Robert B., *America in English Fiction: 1760–1800* (Baton Rouge: Louisiana State University Press, 1937).

Heineman, Helen K., *Frances Trollope* (Boston: Twayne, 1984).

——, *Three Victorians in the New World* (New York: Peter Lang, 1992).

Hobsbawm, E.J., *Nations and Nationalism Since 1780: Programme, Myth, Reality* (Cambridge: Cambridge University Press, 1990).

Holmes, Richard, *Coleridge: Early Visions* (New York: Viking, 1989).

Hudson, Nicholas, "From Nation to 'Race': The Origin of Racial Classification in Eighteenth-Century Thought," *Eighteenth-Century Studies*, 29 (1996): 247–64.

Jackson, Richard, "The Romantic Metaphysics of Time," *Studies in Romanticism*, 19 (1980): 19–30.

Johnston, Johanna, *The Life, Manners, and Travels of Fanny Trollope: A Biography* (New York: Hawthorn Books, 1978).

Johnston, Kenneth, *Wordsworth and "The Recluse"* (New Haven: Yale University Press, 1984).

Jones, Joseph Jay, "Lord Byron on America," *Texas University Studies in English*, 21 (1941): 121–37.

Kelsall, Malcolm, *Byron's Politics* (Sussex: The Harvester Press, 1987).

Kermode, Frank, *The Sense of an Ending: Studies in the Theory of Fiction* (Oxford: Oxford University Press, 1966; 2000).

Leonard, William E., *Byron and Byronism in America* (New York: Haskell House, 1964).

Lévi-Strauss, Claude, *The Savage Mind* (Chicago: University of Chicago Press, 1966).

——, *Totemism*, trans. Rodney Needham (Boston: Beacon Press, 1963).

Lincoln, Andrew, "Blake and the 'Reasoning Historian,'" in Steve Clark and David Worrall (ed.), *Historicizing Blake* (London: Macmillan, 1994).

Liu, Alan, *Wordsworth: The Sense of History* (Stanford: Stanford University Press, 1989).

London, April, "Samuel Jackson Pratt," in Martin C. Battestin (ed.), *Dictionary of Literary Biography. Vol. 39. British Novelists, 1660–1800* (Detroit: Gale, 1985).

Looby, Christopher, *Voicing America: Language, Literary Form, and the Origins of the United States* (Chicago: University of Chicago Press, 1996).

Lovett, Robert William, *The Use of America for Setting and as Image in Eighteenth Century Fiction from the Restoration to the American Revolution* (Ann Arbor: UMI, 1969).

Lukács, Georg, *The Historical Novel*, trans. Hannah and Stanley Mitchell (Lincoln: University of Nebraska Press, 1983).

Makdisi, Saree, *Romantic Imperialism: Universal Empire and the Culture of Modernity* (Cambridge: Cambridge University Press, 1998).

McCord, James, "West of Atlantis: William Blake's Unromantic View of the American War," *The Centennial Review*, 30 (1986): 383–99.

McKusick, James C., *Coleridge's Philosophy of Language* (New Haven: Yale University Press, 1986).

——, "'Wisely forgetful': Coleridge and the Politics of Pantisocracy", in Tim Fulford and Peter Kitson (eds), *Romanticism and Colonialism: Writing and Empire, 1780–1830* (Cambridge: Cambridge University Press, 1998).

Meek, Ronald L., *Social Science and the Ignoble Savage* (Cambridge: Cambridge University Press, 1976).

Mellor, Anne, *Romanticism & Gender* (London: Routledge, 1993).

——, "*Frankenstein*, Racial Science, and the Yellow Peril," *Nineteenth-Century Contexts*, 23 (2001): 1–28.

Mesick, Jane Louise, *The English Traveller in America, 1785–1835* (New York: Columbia University Press, 1922).

Miles, Peter, "Smollett, Rowlandson, and a Problem of Identity: Decoding Names, Bodies, and Gender in *Humphry Clinker*," *Eighteenth Century Life* 20 (1996): 1–23.

Mumford, Lewis, *The Story of Utopias* (New York: Viking, 1962).

Neville-Sington, Pamela, *Fanny Trollope: The Life and Adventures of a Clever Woman* (New York: Viking, 1998).

Nevins, Allan, *America Through British Eyes* (New York: Oxford University Press, 1948).

Pagden, Anthony, *The Fall of Natural Man: The American Indian and the Origins of Comparative Ethnology* (Cambridge: Cambridge University Press, 1986).

Pratt, Mary Louise, *Imperial Eyes: Travel Writing and Transculturation* (London: Routledge, 1992).

Ricoeur, Paul, *Lectures on Ideology and Utopia*, ed. George H. Taylor (New York: Columbia University Press, 1986).

——, *Oneself as Another*, trans. Kathleen Blamey (Chicago: University of Chicago Press, 1988).

——, *Time and Narrative*, trans. Kathleen McLaughlin and David Pellauer (3 vols, Chicago: University of Chicago Press, 1984).

Robinson, Daniel, "'Work Without Hope': Anxiety and Embarrassment in Coleridge's Sonnets," *Studies in Romanticism*, 39 (2000): 82–110.

Roe, Nicholas, *Wordsworth and Coleridge: The Radical Years* (Oxford: Clarendon, 1988).

Rosenblum, Michael, "Smollett's *Humphry Clinker*," in John Richetti (ed.), *The Cambridge Companion to the Eighteenth Century Novel* (Cambridge: Cambridge University Press, 1996).

Sheehan, Bernard, *Savagism & Civility: Indians and Englishmen in Colonial Virginia* (Cambridge: Cambridge University Press, 1980).

Sherman, Stuart, *Telling Time: Clocks, Diaries, and English Diurnal Form, 1660–1785* (Chicago: University of Chicago Press, 1996).

Shy, John, "The American Colonies in War and Revolution, 1748–1783," in P.J. Marshall (ed.), *The Oxford History of the British Empire*, Vol. II. *The Eighteenth Century* (Oxford: Oxford University Press, 1998).

Simpson, David, *Romanticism, Nationalism, and the Revolt against Theory* (Chicago: University of Chicago Press, 1993).

———, *Wordsworth's Historical Imagination: The Poetry of Displacement* (New York: Methuen, 1987).

Sorensen, Janet, *The Grammar of Empire in Eighteenth-Century British Writing* (Cambridge: Cambridge University Press, 2000).

Spiller, Robert E., *The American in England During the First Half Century of Independence* (New York: Henry Holt, 1926).

Stern, Julia, *The Plight of Feeling: Sympathy and Dissent in the Early American Novel* (Chicago: University of Chicago Press, 1997).

Sussman, Charlotte, "Lismahago's Captivity: Transculturation in *Humphry Clinker*," *English Literary History*, 61 (1994): 597–618.

Todd, Janet, *Mary Wollstonecraft: A Revolutionary Life* (New York: Columbia University Press, 2000).

Todorov, Tzvetan, *The Conquest of America: The Question of the Other* (Norman: University of Oklahoma Press, 1999).

———, *On Human Diversity: Nationalism, Racism, and Exoticism in French Thought* (Cambridge: Harvard University Press, 1993).

Verhoeven, W.M. and Amanda Gilroy, "Introduction," in *The Emigrants* by Gilbert Imlay (New York: Penguin, 1998).

Watson, Nicola J., *Revolution and the Form of the English Novel, 1790–1825: Intercepted Letters, Interrupted Seductions* (Oxford: Clarendon, 1994).

Watt, Ian, *The Rise of the Novel: Studies in Defoe, Richardson and Fielding* (Berkeley: University of California Press, 1957).

White, Hayden, *The Content of the Form: Narrative Discourse and Historical Representation* (Baltimore: Johns Hopkins University Press, 1987).

Williams, Nicholas M., *Ideology and Utopia in the Poetry of William Blake* (Cambridge: Cambridge University Press, 1998).

Woodring, Carl, *Politics in the Poetry of Coleridge* (Madison: University of Wisconsin Press, 1961).

Zammito, John H., *Kant, Herder, and the Birth of Anthropology* (Chicago: University of Chicago Press, 2002).

Index